The Management of Interpersonal Skills Training

Keri Phillips and Tony Fraser

Gower

Published by
Gower Publishing Company Limited,
Aldershot, Hants, England

Reprinted 1984, 1985

British Library Cataloguing in Publication Data

Phillips, Keri
   The management of interpersonal skills training.
   1. Interpersonal communication
   I. Title   II. Fraser, Tony
   158.2   BF637.C45

   ISBN 0 566 02286 9

Typeset by Inforum Ltd, Portsmouth
Printed and bound in Great Britain by
Biddles Ltd, Guildford and King's Lynn

The Management of Interpersonal Skills Training

Contents

The thinking method – The doing method – The feeling method

Formulating a contract – The training proposal – Group size – Group mix – Location and facilities – Timing of training – Time-table – Duration – Course design – Course design: further choices and considerations – Summary

The early stages – Self awareness – Involvement and detachment – Confrontation – Constructive and destructive discomfort – Individual and group focus – Relationships with colleagues – Manipulation – Conflict – Training and therapy Catharsis – Saying goodbye – Conclusion

Preface

The last ten years have seen a rapid growth in interpersonal skills training (IST) for managers accompanied by a considerable increase in the number of techniques and approaches involved. At the same time the role of the manager in managing his relationships has become even more important:

1 Rapid technical and organisational change has meant that managers require greater skills in handling people. The very presence of change can have a dramatic impact, positively or negatively, on motivation. Change can also make jobs much more or much less demanding, help or hinder promotion prospects and require the use of technical specialists whose expertise can become an alternative and sometimes rival source of authority. Under these circumstances the manager requires particular interpersonal skills in dealing with staff, colleagues, clients and bosses. If these skills are not present then technical and organisational changes, however necessary they may be, are unlikely to reach fruition.
2 The higher mobility of labour has made it vital for individuals to be integrated rapidly into teams and organisations. This has been accompanied by a greater reliance on the team approach as a means of introducing flexibility into the organisation in the face of a fast changing environment. This in turn has led to particular attention being given to the skills and styles of leadership.
3 Cultural and educational changes have led people to be more willing to express their own individual needs and expectations. This has put a greater onus on managers to treat their staff as individuals, recognising that individual needs vary widely, and have the skills to do this.

4   Employment legislation now emphasises the demands on all
    levels of management to deal fairly with the problems of people
    at work. These demands lead to the need for high standards in
    recruitment, appraisal counselling, coaching, staff development,
    negotiating and safety – all of which require a wide range of
    interpersonal skills.

It is against this background of the growth of IST and its importance that we believe there is a need for a closer examination of these
types of training from the point of view of the provider (trainer both
internal and external), the recipient (manager and management
development manager) and those, such as training advisers, whose
responsibilities can give them a wide mixture of roles.

Trainers, training advisers and those managers who are directly or
indirectly responsible for the development of interpersonal skills in
others will be particularly interested in the methods available, how
they relate to each other, their particular strengths and limitations
and the evaluation of IST (i.e. Chapters 1 and 7 and Appendix 1
which gives a more detailed description of a number of approaches
together with references and contact points). The chapters on programme design (2), ethical and professional issues (3), group management (5) and feedback (6) have been written with the trainer in
mind, but our intention has been to do it in such a way that others
involved or interested in IST will enjoy reading them. The chapter on
body-language (4) has been written for both the training specialist
and the general reader. The final chapter, IST in perspective (8) is a
summary which also points the way forward to future developments.

In IST it is possible to identify four broad and sequential aims; that
is for people to:

1   Increase *awareness*, i.e. to learn more about themselves, their
    impact on others, and others' impact on them.
2   Develop more *choices* in handling relationships.
3   *Experiment* in trying out some of these new choices.
4   Make *decisions* about what 'works' and makes sense.

These aims are reflected in the book. We hope that managers,
trainers and training advisers will develop greater awareness of their
values and attitudes to IST; that they will develop more choices
either in terms of the training they carry out, or recommend for
themselves or others; that they will experiment to make decisions
about what works for them and fits in with their own values and
organisational culture.

The book has been written largely from the perspective of short
training courses, measured in weeks, with limited numbers ranging
from about six to twenty people, and usually residential. There are a
number of reasons for concentrating on this type of training.

Firstly this is where our own expertise lies. Roffey Park Management College concentrates on running short courses for managers who are concerned to learn about human relations at work and who want to acquire some skills and knowledge which are of immediate practical value. Sometimes the course groups are made up of managers from the same organisation, at other times many different organisations are represented. Our experience in designing and running IST courses leads us to believe for reasons outlined in Chapter 2 that residential courses are an especially valuable means for acquiring interpersonal skills. Secondly, a great deal of IST is carried out in this way, the amount of time generally ranging from one or two days to three weeks, sometimes being broken into modules. The short course is still well favoured whether for internal or external training.

Thirdly, some of the alternative forms of training do have a short course component. For example, a number of Organisational Development (OD) interventions require the group to go away together, normally residentially, for a few days. Also, some of these alternatives are based on the assumption of a short term training course in the first place. For example, on-the-job counselling is a valuable way of training, yet the counsellors themselves are often trained through going away on a counselling course. We fully recognise the importance of the alternatives to short training courses – coaching, appraisal, projects, job rotation, self-development programmes, action learning, counselling as well as OD and longer term training activities which are to be measured in months or possibly years.

A number of important beliefs and assumptions which we hold are explicitly or implicitly expressed in this book. Almost by definition there is a strong emphasis on the importance of the human factor in management. Technical skills and competence are of markedly less value unless supported by skills in handling people. Another belief is in people's potential for growth and development. Generally managers have more ability to change and to increase their effectiveness than they give themselves credit for. Many of the limits they see as external constraints are really self-imposed. It is important for managers to be proactive and take the initiative in solving problems and generally making their lives more satisfying. A third belief is a recognition of the need for a flexibility of approach in IST. It is not our intention to suggest that one approach or technique is by definition better than another. What is important is a conscious and informed decision, particularly in times of economic difficulty, not blind adherence to an established pattern. Ultimately it is a matter of making choices and being willing and able to learn from the consequences.

A final point concerns style. Throughout the text, for the sake of convenience, we have used the masculine pronoun; however, in the vast majority of instances 'he' and 'she' can be regarded as interchangeable.

Keri Phillips
Tony Fraser

Acknowledgements

We wish to record our appreciation for the support, encouragement and facilities that have been provided by others during the writing of this book.

The atmosphere at Roffey Park Management College creates an ideal setting in which to embark on a writing project and all those who work there have made an important contribution to this book. In particular John Giles has offered continuing interest and advice in a most helpful way, whilst Robin Evenden has planned useful breathing spaces which allowed the work of writing to continue. Special thanks go to the office staff at Roffey for their patience and diligence in producing and amending the manuscript and to Claire Richardson for her additional work in its production.

We are grateful to Ben Bennett, Neil Clark and Jim Richardson for their material help and enthusiastic support.

Perhaps most important is the thanks to our families who have helped in so many different ways to make the task easier and more enjoyable.

KP
TF

List of tables

Introduction

Interpersonal skills training (IST) is any form of training that is designed to help people understand themselves more, learn about how others see them and make choices as a means of developing skills in their behaviour. In the area of management training it covers a wide variety of activities and subject matter: the activities can include lectures on human behaviour and attitudes, role-play interviews, group problem-solving exercises and the exploration of 'here and now' relationships in the training group; the subject matter includes the following areas of training — interviewing (e.g. selection, appraisal, counselling, disciplinary, problem solving), group leadership and membership skills, management styles, team-building, industrial relations, negotiating skills, customer contact and the management of change.

Associated with this, the training needs can vary widely ranging in examples from a manager with strong technical background who has recently been given staff to manage and needs to be sensitive to the people-dimension at work; to a manager who is in a 'life-crisis' and needs to do some fundamental stocktaking of his values and purpose in life; to a manager needing new skills in handling people because organisational changes have generated a requirement for different management styles and ways of working.

Comparison with technical training

Another way of defining IST is to compare it with technical training, from which it differs in some fundamental ways.

1   Technical training puts a strong emphasis on right answers simply because there are right and wrong ways of doing things, the wrong ways sometimes causing danger or physical harm.

In IST it simply is not possible to emphasise right answers because so few exist. In a number of instances, for example in interviewing, it is possible to provide guidelines but even there, in the final analysis everybody has to make their own decisions, particularly because there is no way of guaranteeing a response: asking open questions does not necessarily lead somebody to talk more.

2   In most organisations it is generally accepted that there is a need for technical training because it is so clearly job related, and it is sometimes required before somebody can even start to do a job.

The attitude to IST is frequently very different, even for those jobs that require a high degree of face to face skills. Managers are expected to manage naturally and IST can be seen as something of a luxury. The manager himself may not be too keen, possibly regarding it as an insult that he should be selected for training and may even be thinking that some important aspects of his personality are being questioned.

3   In technical training it is expected that everybody reaches the same identifiable level of skills; if they do not, then remedial training may well be required.

In IST it is far less clear cut. Sometimes, for better or worse, the aims of the training cannot be formulated in identifiable behavioural terms. An example would be the aim of greater self-confidence which may be apparent in implicit ways rather than anything which the manager specifically says or does. Allied to this, it may well be difficult to identify progress because so often the learning outcomes will vary. One person may learn to be more participative in their management style; his course colleague may learn to be more directive. On top of all this it is quite possible for somebody's learning needs to change as the training progresses. For example, he may come on a course believing he needs to listen more carefully and then discover that his 'real problem' or underlying problem is to do with a lack of assertiveness.

4   It should be clear by now that IST is much more difficult to evaluate than technical training. This in turn can lead to greater resistance in organisations to IST.

5   IST involves a wide range of ethical and moral issues as compared to technical training. There are several reasons for this. Firstly, IST can have domestic implications where people are explicitly or implicitly encouraged to consider the whole range of relationships, not just those at work. The very decision about whether or not to bring in home relationships has, by its very nature, to be made on an ethical basis. Secondly, the way in which the trainer acts in front of

the group ('modelling') is of crucial importance in IST because he is actually using his interpersonal skills and any difference between theory and practice will be glaringly apparent. In technical training, how the trainer is as a person is much less important than the quality or relevance of what he is saying, or the particular skills he is demonstrating. This is not to say that the technical trainer does not need interpersonal skills.

The aims of IST

These were briefly mentioned in the Preface and are now examined in more detail.

1   Greater awareness of self and one's impact on others. Awareness of self in general terms means being sensitive to one's own feelings, thoughts, words and non-verbal communication and one's reactions to others. This usually means attention to detail, for example, a glimmering of fear or confusion, or a 'difficult' moment. IST approaches vary in the particular aspects they emphasise. There may be more attention paid to the words used than the feelings behind the words. The same applies with regard to awareness of one's impact on others. Some approaches emphasise attention to the non-verbal signals coming from the other person, rather than their words.

This aim of awareness can, in the training context, be achieved in a number of ways: feedback, closed circuit television, the checking of self against theory, questioning and/or confrontation, thinking and /or reflecting back on experiences and the observation of others.

2   Increasing the range of choices. This means increasing one's repertoire of ways of handling relationships; in particular breaking out of stereotyped patterns. Where there are rigid patterns they frequently represent extreme ends of a spectrum; the person who sees the world in terms of dominance or submission is denying himself a whole range of choices in between. The additional choices can come in the same ways as awareness.

3   Experimentation. This means trying out some of the new choices and seeing whether they are effective. Often this experimentation will take place during the training programme, for example through role plays or trying out new behaviour in the group. Additionally, or alternatively, it may be carried out back at work and would be a sign that the person had learned how to learn.

4   Decisions. These conclude the experimentation and may involve 'big' or 'small' decisions, for example, 'I'm going to stop putting myself down', or 'I'm going to ask a greater number of open-ended questions at appraisal interviews'.

The decisions may not ultimately lead to any definite change, but may rather be a confirmation of existing values or behaviours. 'I have experimented with expressing my feelings and I have discovered that, for me, it generally gets in the way of my effectiveness as a manager, so I'm going back to my old ways'.

Thus the ultimate aim of interpersonal skills training is an increase of confidence so that the manager is willing and able, on the job, to learn from awkward and unsatisfying relationships and to take the initiative in helping himself and others to increase effectiveness. This is one of the pre-requisites for a healthy and developing organisation.

1 A framework for interpersonal skills training

As a result of the growth of IST it has become increasingly important for the trainer, training adviser and manager to be aware of the variety of methods that are available and to be sensitive to the moral issues and dilemmas which seem to occur so readily when one person is seeking to help another to become more effective in his/her relationships. Our intention in this chapter, therefore, is to provide an overview of the main approaches to carrying out IST for managers and to explore their implications. Also, the way ahead is pointed at in terms of raising issues and then indicating where in the subsequent chapters they are dealt with in more depth.

Firstly, one can identify the differing emphases of the ways in which IST is carried out: some approaches emphasise conceptual (thinking) learning, others are based on a large amount of practical activity (learning through doing), while others value learning through the exploration of feelings. Each of these approaches is now examined in more depth.

The thinking method

Trainers sometimes put considerable emphasis on conceptual learning and participants are encouraged to think (nothing more) about how effective they are in relating to others and achieving satisfactory work relationships. Typical training methods would be lectures, 'structured' discussions (i.e. discussions run to illustrate the trainer's points) films and case studies.[1]

1

An illustration of this is the way in which the topic of managing conflict could be dealt with on a basic introduction to management course. The design of the session might include a tutor-led seminar on the causes and nature of conflict in organisations (differing objectives, tribal warfare etc.), a sharing of participants' ideas about conflict at work, and then a further discussion of the ways in which conflict could be dealt with. Clearly this approach has a number of advantages. Firstly, it is probably a 'safe' introduction to the topic (in this case managing conflict). 'Safe' meaning here that the participants are unlikely to feel that their credibility is at stake and they can keep the discussions at a fairly academic level. Within this safe environment participants can then move on and start sharing experiences. Also it is likely that this approach matches the learning to which the managers have been accustomed, i.e. their educational background from school onwards probably involved an 'expert' who was the major source of knowledge. Finally, the theory introduced by the trainer may well make sense and provide a number of 'right answers' for the managers.

Equally, however, this approach has disadvantages. Firstly it provides little scope for the participants to develop and practise skills in managing conflict. There is a danger of the participants seeing conflict as something external which happens to them, rather than an element of human relations in which they have a share of responsibility. Allied to this there can be too great a reliance on the trainer – a reliance on him to do all the thinking and provide all the answers and all the learning – (after all, that is what he is being paid to do!). If the participants have this expectation then there can be the added frustration of a lack of right answers. This has already been referred to in contrasting interpersonal with technical skills training. Also the advantage of safety can become a disadvantage where everybody is very comfortably 'talking about' but not really moving towards problem-solving. (The notion of safety is crucial in IST and frequent reference is made to it, particularly in Chapter 2.) At worst, this 'talking about' can degenerate into a game of 'Ain't it Awful', where responsibility for problems is pushed onto others, e.g. management, the unions, government, etc.

A key element in all training is modelling, i.e. practising what is preached. In the 'thinking' approach examples of failures to do this, which we have either experienced or heard about, are a lecture on the value of two-way communication and a session on time-management which over-runs! Such events can be amusing and cause a considerable loss of credibility.

The doing method

Sometimes the emphasis is on learning at the 'doing' level. Here practical tasks are heavily favoured, such as a team making a tower from toy bricks. This is a well-tried exercise whereby competing teams are required to build towers made from toy bricks using a limited number of bricks and within a time limit. While the task itself is unimportant, the social processes that evolve are the main source of learning. This method can be used to examine and practise such skills as leadership, working as a member of a team, job allocation, the management of resources and inter-group relations. The exercises are not always 'unreal' and many management games are designed clearly to simulate a job environment.[2]

The general design for the 'doing' type of training, pursuing the example of managing conflict, would quite possibly be the following:

1 Introductory theory session, (e.g. the nature of conflict and its causes: win/lose orientations, rigid definitions of role, escalation from minor grievances etc.).
2 Practical activity, (e.g. a team is established to build a toy brick tower of certain specifications with limited resources, particularly time. Those course participants who are not in the team will probably be given a check-list based on the theory session, so that they can assess the effectiveness of the group).
3 Analysis of the activity, including feedback from the trainer and the observers to the task group in terms of the conflicts they saw and how these were handled. (Feedback and ways of handling it are covered in detail in Chapter 6.)
4 Summarising and a further elaboration of theory in preparation for the next practical activity – probably with the observers and task group switching roles.

The advantage of the 'doing' approach is that the participants have the opportunity to practise various ways of handling themselves and others. Frequently the importance of experimenting with behaviour is stressed. (E.g. 'Experiment with being more directive next time and see how it goes'.) Also participants are able to try out their own ideas and see whether they work or not. Additionally this form of training can be accompanied by some form of interaction analysis (i.e. analysis of behaviour using specific categories, e.g. Rackham,[3] Bales,[4] and Honey[5]). During this process alternative forms of behaviour and choices for the participants can be clearly identified and detailed feedback offered. This is a rich learning opportunity if it is accompanied by trust. (This point is elaborated in Chapter 5.) Finally, the 'doing' approach can be quite challenging and involve a high degree of satisfaction when a task has been successfully accomplished.

On the other hand, the approach has disadvantages. The participants may have difficulty in relating the ability to manage a group of strangers in the building of a toy brick tower to managing a group at work. Also the feelings behind the behaviour might well be ignored. As a result the person may, for example, leave the course aware of how his behaviour means that he does not fit in well as a member of a team, but uncertain about the underlying process which leads to this behaviour. We believe that without some information about why he behaves as he does the motivation to experiment may well be short lived. Also it is possible, with this type of training, for a trainee to go through the motions of putting on a 'good performance' and engage in the 'right behaviours' but fail to internalise any learning, i.e. fails to decide what really makes sense for him. These last two points with their emphasis on feelings and internalisation indicate some of the distinctions between humanism and behaviourism (see Chapter 8).

Finally, this training approach can be too challenging where some of the participants believe that they 'failed' and lost credibility because, for example, a task deadline was not achieved. This sense of failure can lead to the total rejection of the training programme. The trainer clearly needs to be sensitive to this reaction and be aware of his choices in handling it (Chapters 2 and 3). Trainers need to take care of the extent to which they stress success and failure – an over-emphasis will lead participants to take fewer risks and hence probably learn less.

The feeling method

Some interpersonal skills trainers encourage participants to learn at the level of feelings. Here the design is usually 'unstructured' and emphasis is put on the expression of feelings and needs. 'Unstructured' means that the trainer does not take responsibility for providing a structure and there is no set programme for the training. (In many ways the word 'unstructured' is a misnomer since these groups can become quite rigid in the pattern they develop during the period of their existence). The 'T' group is an obvious example of this method of training, but there are others including encounter groups, psychodrama, and sensitivity groups in general.[6]

In broad terms the aim of the feeling method is to increase the individual's awareness of his feelings about himself and his resulting impact on others. This awareness is developed through the course participants exchanging perceptions of each other and giving and receiving feedback.

The participants are thus frequently encouraged to say what they feel about themselves and others. The trainer's role is to encourage feedback, help people identify alternatives in the ways in which they behave and relate to others, and to support and confront as the need arises. The trainer will be looking particularly for those occasions where the participant refuses to listen to feedback or dismisses it as irrelevant. Another characteristic of this approach is the stress on the 'here and now'. Participants are asked to examine incidents and feelings in the group as they occur and not to escape into talking about the past. This clearly contrasts with the 'thinking' method which is, by definition, all 'talking about'. With the 'doing' method this time focus can vary quite considerably: it could be very much 'here and now' if the trainer, for example, focuses on what somebody is doing with the feedback he receives; alternatively, the analysis of an exercise would move the time focus more into the past and make it less threatening (for further elaboration of this point see Chapter 6).

Since in this type of training the participants are given total, or almost total, responsibility for learning, there are implicit or explicit expectations that they be proactive and take the initiative in giving feedback, asking for feedback and expressing feelings and meeting training needs. With the 'doing' approach the responsibility for learning can vary depending on the extent to which the trainer encourages the participants to set learning goals for themselves and manage events, e.g. the feedback sessions. Because of the 'unstructured' nature of the feelings approach, the management of conflict, to continue with the example, would not be identified prior to the course, as a specific topic to be dealt with. However, it is probable that, in the search for structure and purpose, conflict would arise between members of the group and this would then be regarded as a legitimate subject for examination. It could lead into the exploration of stereotypes which may have developed, or the poor quality of listening or in many other directions, all concerned to get the group learning about itself. (An important aspect is how much the trainer intervenes. This is dealt with further in Chapters 2 and 5.)

This area of training is sometimes called 'process work' – a term requires some explanation as it will subsequently be referred to quite extensively. In IST an important distinction is made between 'content' and 'process'. 'Content' is to do with the words actually used, process is concerned with the 'real' or psychological message behind them, this normally being indicated non-verbally, especially through voice tone. Some examples are, 'With all due respect' (without any respect at all); 'Well, I suppose I could do it' (I really don't want to do this at all); 'Oh . . . I see' (I don't understand what on earth you're on about). In examining relationships it is valuable for people to be aware, and assess the implications of, the psychological messages they are sending and which are being transmitted to them. We believe that generally these double messages get in the way of effective communication because the person sending the message is not being 'straight' and those on the receiving end may simply be aware that 'something funny is going on', but not really know what is being said. Alternatively, both parties may collude in not achieving clear and direct communication. Building on the last example given above, 'Oh . . . I see' could be said by a new member of staff who is being told by his boss how to work a machine and is afraid that he will appear stupid if he says that he does not understand. His boss may accept his comment at face value because he does not really want to be bothered with training.

There are two types of process – external and internal. So far only external process has been described. It is external because it reveals itself in communication to other people through gestures, voice tone and other non-verbal means. Internal process is to do with the fantasies, imaginings, beliefs and values which prompt the external message e.g. when Fred says 'Well, I suppose I could do it' (sulky tone of voice), he might be saying to himself, inside or outside awareness, 'I must not say what I really want otherwise there will be conflict and people will not like me'. The 'feelings' approach is concerned with both internal and external process. Some of the 'doing' approaches explore process, but only external process.

One of the main advantages of the 'feelings' approach is simply that it values the importance of feelings in relationships. Feelings and intuition, or more colloquially 'vibes', 'chemistry', 'gut reaction' are important. We imagine that a manager would normally find it difficult to engage in rational problem-solving with a colleague whom he disliked intensely. The origin and nature of these feelings are clearly crucial and the manager needs to develop skills in handling them.

Another advantage is that as the participant is responsible for his learning he is likely to be more willing to take the initiative in resolving difficult relationships and avoid 'ain't it awful', i.e. futile moaning, sessions. However, the converse of this advantage is that the values of the feelings approach may be counter to the manager's organisational culture. The organisation may not value those who take the initiative in exploring and possibly expressing 'bad' feelings, (or even 'good' ones). Related to this, the job relevance of the training may be unclear: 'How does my telling Fred here what I really think about him help me to be more effective in managing my subordinates?'. The lack of right answers may be seen by some as liberating, while others would view it as frustrating and ridiculous. Finally, among a number of methods which constitute the 'feelings' approach', there is usually no clear-cut conceptual framework that the participants can use as an aid to transferring learning from the training room back to work. Allied to this is the problem that in 'feelings' based training it is difficult to set specific training objectives prior to or even during, the training programme. Training needs among the course members are likely to vary so much that it would not be realistic to say that by the end of the training everybody will, for example, be more assertive or less autocratic; some may need to be less assertive and others more autocratic, and others may have needs that are nothing to do with assertion or autocracy. We have discovered that even if course members have, at the beginning of the training, been strongly urged (told?) to be specific about their needs, the problem of specific training objectives remains. There are several reasons for this. Firstly, the stated need may merely be a symptom: the statement that 'I want to express myself more clearly and concisely', could for example, mask a broader and probably deeper problem to do with handling authority figures. Secondly, the need as stated may be a diversionary tactic because the person is afraid to be open. Thirdly, many people are genuinely unused to identifying and stating their needs. In other words, they have not learnt how to learn. However, as people learn how to learn and trust develops in the group, then the participants may be more willing and able to be specific about what they want from the training. The trainer frequently has a key role here as one of the ways in which people stop themselves learning is by not being specific (see Chapter 3).

Reverting to the idea of identifying training needs prior to the course,[7] certainly this would be possible with a considerable amount of work, probably consisting of several in depth counselling interviews. Specific objectives might emerge from these. However, we imagine that most trainers and training organisations do not have the resources for this in-depth analysis. Also, if it happened it could become a substitute for the training itself. (This would not necessarily be a bad outcome except that the training group can be a powerful vehicle for learning.)

With the 'thinking' and 'doing' approaches it is much easier for the trainer to set specific objectives if he wishes, e.g. 'Each course member will know and be able to state the difference between motivators and hygiene factors', or 'Each course member will be able to formulate different types of interviewing questions – "open", "closed" and "hypothetical" '.

The three main approaches to IST, together with their strengths and weaknesses, are summarised in Table 1.1. These various approaches offer the trainer, training adviser and manager a wealth of opportunities either for self-development or managing the development of others in interpersonal skills. However, the training

Table 1.1   Overview of approaches to IST

	Thinking	Doing	Feeling
Training methods	Lecture. Case-study. Guided discussion. Films. Programmed learning texts. Tape/slide presentation.	Role-plays. Structured exercises, e.g. group problem-solving.	'Sensitivity training' – focus on individual and/or group processes and feelings.
Approaches*	Traditional classroom education.	**Action-centred leadership. Coverdale. Interaction analysis. Managerial grid.	**Tavistock. 'T' group. Encounter. Gestalt. Psychodrama. Bioenergetics.
Time focus	There and then.	Immediate past.	Here and now.
Chances of trainee feeling uncomfortable	Low.	Variable.	High.
Responsibility for learning	Trainer.	Variable.	Trainee.

* This is exaggeration for the sake of emphasis. These approaches do not fit neatly into a category but they reflect general orientations.
** These and other approaches are described in more detail in Appendix 1[8]

can lose a lot of its effectiveness if the approaches are not regarded as part of a spectrum.

We now want to integrate the divisions made between 'thinking', 'doing' and 'feeling' and stress that each course and training event can be designed to help people learn in a variety of ways (Table 1.2).

The spectrum in Table 1.2 is based on the assumption that the training group consists of strangers attending an IST course; however, it is being used to illustrate a general point which, to reiterate, is that IST does not have to be *either* 'thinking' *or* 'doing' *or* 'feeling' in its scope. For example, giving people the chance to express and explore feelings does not necessarily mean adopting a totally 'unstructured' (e.g. 'T' group) approach. The trainer can modify his approach as the course is taking place and adopt a more 'thinking' or 'doing' or 'feeling' orientation, in order to give people the best chance of achieving the training aims. The trainer has many choices about how or whether he blends his approaches (see Chapter 2).

Alternatively, the training can be designed in such a way that the trainer can move in a controlled and deliberate way across the spectrum, with the participants learning in a variety of ways. For example, an interviewing programme could be designed with the following broad sequence of events:

1. A fairly general discussion on 'What skills does an interviewer need?'. This could then be backed up by some theory (non-personal, there-and-then time focus, and probably a low level of risk because nobody is being directly challenged on their interviewing skills).

2. Self-assessment of interviewing skills to be shared in small groups, followed up by a large group review. (Probably a fair increase in risk level because people are being asked to think about and assess themselves, but as the discussions are initially taking place in small groups it is likely that trust will start to develop, especially as they begin to learn that others have similar problems.) The small groups have the choice about how open they are in the large group.

3. This stage could be interviewing practice using artificial role plays, (e.g. 'You pretend to be Mr Smith who is a diffident sales representative . . .'). The risk level is being maintained, and possibly increased, because of the requirement to perform, be observed and subsequently appraised, but there is an important escape route in the artificiality of the role play. Somebody who believes, or is told, that they have performed badly can always say that they were not being 'natural' (because they have never been a sales representative, or they tried too hard to be diffident etc.).

4. Then the group could role play and review difficult interviews they have personally experienced. (Here the escape routes referred to above have been closed). The trainer can encourage 'opening up' by asking increasingly probing questions, 'What were your alternatives?', 'How did you stop yourself from taking the initiative at the time?', 'Is that a pattern for you?', 'Has it happened during this course that you wanted to take the initiative and stopped yourself?'

It must be stressed that this should not *necessarily* be the design, so much depends on the contract, the nature of the group and many other points which are referred to in Chapter 2. The example is intended to illustrate the way in which a training programme can be designed to move gradually across the training spectrum. At any point the trainer can 'pull back' and modify his approach if he feels that the session is not going well, (e.g. pressure from the trainer leading to resistance in the trainee).

Clearly a dominant factor in moving across the spectrum is managing the degree of risk. This cannot be quantified, as the amount of risk and degree of threat anybody feels will be largely dependent on

Table 1.2   Spectrum of training methods

	1	2	3	4
General approach	Course members thinking and talking about others.	Course members thinking and talking about themselves in the past in general terms.	Course members thinking and talking about themselves in the immediate past, in specific terms.	Course members thinking and talking about themselves having played clearly artificial role.
Training methods	Lecture, film, case-study; full/small group discussion.	Trainer encouraging group to share their experiences.	Trainer encouraging the group to 'open up'. Probing questions.	Scripted/semi-scripted role-play; then analysis and feedback.
Example: based on the topic of 'Handling conflict'	Course members are shown film about an industrial relations conflict and are then asked to comment; theory might then be used to summarise.	Trainer asks course members to talk about conflicts they have experienced in past at work; discussion going on to explore way in which conflicts were handled and the alternatives; possibly concluding theory.	Course members are asked to talk about work conflicts which they are currently facing. After discussion problem-solving groups could be set up to identify courses of action.	Two course members might be briefed to role-play a manager and a subordinate who frequently comes to work late; manager's handling of the 'disciplinary interview' can then be analysed and teaching points drawn from it.
Additional points		The group might feel uncomfortable if its members were from the same organisation.	May cause arguments in which individual's personal competence is questioned.	Course members can, if feeling threatened, 'escape' responsibility by blaming the role. CCTV can increase the penetration of the feedback.

THINKING ◄───
◄ ─ D O
◄ ─

5	6	7	8	9
Course members thinking and talking about themselves having played semi-artificial role.	Course members thinking and talking about themselves having played semi-artificial role.	Course members analysing themselves as group in 'here and now'.	Course members analysing themselves as group in 'here and now'.	Course members discharging long stored-up feelings, e.g. anger, grief, (frequently referred to as therapy).
Practical activity followed by generalised *group* feedback (e.g. 'The group seemed to lose motivation').	Practical activity followed by specific individual feedback (e.g. 'Bill, you seemed to lose direction').	Individuals are encouraged to examine own processes and give and receive feedback; trainer makes *group* level interactions (e.g. 'The group is refusing to take any responsibility for its own learning').	Individuals are encouraged to examine own processes and give and receive feedback; trainer makes *individual* level interventions (e.g. 'Bill, you are refusing to take any responsibility for your feelings')	Encouragement of catharsis. (See Chapter 3.)
An exercise can be run where conflict is almost inevitable and can then be analysed. Course members given roles in simulated organisation which has problems of time pressure, role ambiguity, limited resources etc.	An exercise can be run where conflict is almost inevitable and can then be analysed. Course members given roles in simulated organisation which has problems of time pressure, role ambiguity, limited resources etc.	Participants encouraged to identify and work through any conflict which emerges.	Participants encouraged to identify and work through any conflict which emerges.	Participants act out any conflict they experience; this could be conflict reflecting childhood issues; as a consequence there might be an activity in which the participant acts out an imaginary dialogue with his father.
Course members have less chance of escaping adverse feedback because they have largely played themselves However, since feedback is generalised the threat is likely to be low.	If any course member feels too threatened then trainer can make feedback more general, e.g. 'One of the problems most of us will face at some time or other . . .'	Trainer may need to analyse events to enable participants to understand their experiences more fully.	The trainer may use 'hot seat' technique, i.e. spending considerable time working with an individual in the group.	

N G --→

--→ F E E L I N G their internal process. Nevertheless, certain training approaches are likely to increase the risk level and consequently increase excitement, the basic precondition for learning. People need to touch the boundaries of their knowledge, skills and awareness, even if it is simply to gain confirmation that their existing behaviours and values are right. In our experience, designing the training or colluding with trainees to make it absolutely safe, (the implicit psychological contract being – 'We won't ask you to do anything you are uncomfortable with and in return we expect you to say nice things about us at the end of the course') has backfired with the trainees expressing disappointment about the lack of excitement.

To summarise, stating the obvious – there is no best training method. Rather each choice of method will lead to certain *fairly* predictable consequences, some positive and some negative. What is important for those involved, whether directly or indirectly, in training, is that the choice should be informed and that expectations should be realistic.

It is hoped that the manager, bearing in mind the spectrum and the table on page 8 will be able *either* to identify more clearly the type of training that is being offered *or* clarify in his own mind the type of training he wants for himself or his subordinates. He might also want to think about his organisation's culture and its attitude to training and learning. The manager will also need to think about what sorts of risks are acceptable or even desirable in the training.

The training adviser will probably ask similar questions in relation to his client organisation. Additionally, he might want to reflect on his own expectations of IST and their realism.

To take some extreme examples: A half-day seminar with theory and discussion is unlikely to generate strong personal awareness. Equally, a one or two-week personal awareness (or feelings-based) programme is unlikely to produce a wealth of theoretical models or skills-based techniques for handling people.

The trainer will probably acquire some additional options in course design and management, which will give him greater flexibility. Also, this and subsequent chapters are intended to encourage all, directly or indirectly involved in training, to think about their boundaries – the limits they set for themselves and others – and the basis on which these boundaries are set. These boundaries may be in exactly the right position – on the other hand they could have become obsolete or based on prejudice or fear. Either way they merit further examination.

References

(1) For an overview of the case-study approach see: *Personnel and Training Management Yearbook 1980*, Kogan Page, London, pp 143.

(2) C. Elgood, *Handbook of Management Games*, 2nd edition, Gower, Aldershot, 1981.
(3) N. Rackham and T. Morgan, *Behaviour Analysis in Training*, McGraw-Hill, Maidenhead, 1977.
(4) For a brief description of R. Bales's work see: W.J.H. Sprott, *Human Groups*, Pelican, Harmondsworth, 1966 (Chapter 8).
(5) P. Honey, *Face to Face*, IPM, London, 1976.
(6) For a fuller explanation see Appendix 1 and P.B. Smith, *Group Processes and Personal Change*, Harper and Row, London, 1980 (Chapters 7 and 8).
(7) For a description of ways of identifying training needs see V. and A. Stewart, *Managing the Managers' Growth*, Gower, Aldershot, 1978 (Chapters 4 and 5).
(8) See also N. Rackham, P. Honey and M. Colbert, *Developing Interactive Skills*, Wellens, Northampton, 1971 (Chapter 1).

2 Designing IST programmes

A successful training programme rarely comes into existence overnight – it must be designed and developed over a period of time. This chapter examines the most important considerations in IST design and is intended to help the trainer or manager to do the job himself or to help him monitor the work of others. The review, based on our own experience, looks at the design process not in order of priority but approximates the sequence of events and options to that likely in practice.

Formulating a contract

The awareness of some kind of training need can emerge from a variety of sources: company results; labour turnover; review of company/departmental objectives; performance appraisal; individual experiences; top management decree; changes in company structure and operation, or more conventionally as a result of a training needs analysis by an internal or external training agency.

Clarifying the training need, defining it and turning it into a set of aims or goals are the first important steps in training design. This is not to say that the resulting formula should be enshrined as fixed and permanent, but that having a clear base from which to work allows assumptions to be tested and data to be collected.

An example of training aims in the IS area are:

1　To develop human relations skills in graduate engineers with 2–3

14

years' experience as a means of enhancing their current work performance and future potential.

2 To improve communication skills (expressing, listening, exchanging feedback, observing) in a number of contexts: one to one – small group – inter-group.

3 To encourage the development of assertion and influencing skills.

4 To develop awareness of the elements of supervisor/subordinate relationships, including an understanding of the problems in authority relationships and skills in managing these problems.

5 To increase self-awareness and sensitivity to others, both as an individual and as a member of a department in the broader context of the corporation.

It can be seen that these are not highly specific and behavioural objectives. The main reason for this is that the needs are likely to vary significantly from one individual to another. For example one person may learn to be more assertive by altering his posture and tone of voice; another might change at the level of how he formulates questions.

Aims such as these are normally arrived at as a result of extensive needs analysis which can be conducted on the basis of a number of techniques:[1]

1 Critical incident
2 Self report questionnaires
3 Structured interview (performance appraisal, training needs questionnaire, development plans)
4 Diary method
5 Performance questionnaire
6 Content analysis
7 Behaviour analysis
8 Psychological tests
9 Repertory grid[2]
   etc.

The depth and breadth of any training needs analysis should be related to the resources that are available for monitoring and evaluating the results and the prospects for committing time and money to subsequent training. There is little point in conducting elegant and elaborate reviews of staff development needs if the sponsor is unwilling or unable to invest in the training requirements that are likely to emerge. An investigation of training needs, by its very nature is more likely to confirm than deny the requirement to do some training, so it is worth making sure that the resources available match those devoted to the needs analysis.

In formulating the aims, the designer should bear in mind the culture of the target population, and the organisation. It is helpful if they all understand and agree with the purpose of their training. Therefore the aims are best presented in an acceptable form which makes sense to them. In fact, the prospective trainee's commitment to a programme is substantially enhanced if he has had the opportunity to review and shape it in its early stages. It is helpful therefore to follow these steps:

1 Formulation of felt need by: trainee himself – superior – subordinate (?) – training adviser – training consultant.
2 Training needs analysis within the assumed target population, plus consultation with relevant superiors and subordinates.
3 Definition of training needs and definition of training aims, by the investigator or training agent.
4 Consultation with (at least some of) the trainees, their supervisors and/or managers, about the relevance, significance of the proposed training.
5 Revision of training needs and programme design.

These steps require that the investigator is sufficiently involved in the organisation to understand the work of the prospective trainees and their environment. At the same time a degree of detachment is necessary in order to avoid the distortions caused by such things as organisational politics, ambition, the need to conform or simply being too involved in the issues to see things objectively.

An important factor in the training needs analysis, and indeed the total training event is whether it is being carried out by an internal or external trainer/consultant. There are potentially considerable differences in their power and influence. The internal trainer will be more knowledgeable about the power and communication system (formal and informal) operating within the organisation, and who the key individuals are. He may be mistrusted for fear that he passes on confidential information as a basis for enhancing his career within the company. He may have to work harder to establish his credibility, especially as he is probably not charging for his services. It is likely that the external trainer can divorce himself more easily from organisational pressures and also avoid the dangers of tunnel vision. Another important factor will be the hierarchical status of the internal trainer and the extent to which training is regarded as important.

A likely solution to these problems is a partnership between an internal agent (local manager or training adviser) and an external agent (central office trainer, external training consultant etc.) to conduct investigations and design programmes.

The training proposal

This document contains a number of elements which will help all those involved to understand exactly what they are letting themselves in for. As sections of the proposal may be used to inform and consult with participants and their managers it is important that the proposal should use as little jargon as possible. The main components of a proposal should include:

1 Title and initial statement of the purpose of the proposal.
2 Target population. (See pages 18–24 on selecting participants.)
3 Aims of training (it is useful to include the supporting evidence provided by the needs analysis).
4 Methods: this section will include an account of the work already conducted and statements concerning subsequent stages e.g. further consultations, pre-course briefings, individual preparation, a training event, follow-up and evaluation.
5 Timing: including completion dates for each stage.
6 Location of each stage.
7 Training event details: this section will normally include information concerning: group size/mix; duration and detailed daily timetable; and training methods.
It will also contain a provisional programme which spells out session by session the purpose, method and timing of each part of the programme.
8 Training staff: including information about each staff member.
9 Likely outcomes: for the participants and other areas of the organisation which may be affected.
10 Possible outcomes: for those concerned, including consequences which may not be so welcome (see Chapter 3).
11 Administrative aspects: this segment to include statements concerning the facilities required for each stage and who will provide them; costs; cancellation arrangements and the names of the 'client' and the 'training agent'.

Group size

Once the aims and target population have been identified one of the next considerations in formulating a training design will be the overall size of each training group. Decisions about the numbers in a group will be based on a number of interrelated factors: duration, aims, methods, intensity, and trainers in relationship to group size. These factors are examined in detail in Table 2.1.

Table 2.1 The relationship between group size and other design factors

Group size	3–6	7–12	13–25	25+
Duration	2–3 days' residential or repeated short periods of ½ day or less.	3–5 days' residential or repeated short periods of ½–1 day.	3+ days' residential	½–1 day non-residential.
IST aims	Suitable: Team building. Interviewing. Counselling. Interpersonal relationships Unsuitable: Group membership. Leadership. Negotiating. Intergroup relations.	Suitable: Most types including Team building. Interviewing. Interpersonal relations. Negotiations. Selling. Advising. Influencing group leadership/membership. Intergroup relations. Group decision making. Creativity. Assertion. Motivation etc.	Suitable: Negotiating. Selling. Group membership. Interleadership. Intergroup relations. Understanding human relations. Use of structured presentations. Unsuitable: Teambuilding. Interviewing. Interpersonal relations. Selling. Advising etc.	Suitable: Understanding human relations. Some selling. Unsuitable: Most skill development.

Methods	Effective for some 'feeling' approaches, few 'doing' approaches.	Effective for *all* approaches: 'thinking' 'doing' 'feeling'.	Effective for 'thinking' and some 'doing' approaches.	Effective for some 'thinking' approaches.
Intensity	Likely to be high, little time for withdrawal. Therefore need frequent breaks to avoid 'hothouse' effect*. Contact with outside world.	Variable – likely to include periods of involvement and withdrawal. Can be increased or decreased by the use of syndicates. Informal 'social' time still important for learning.	Variable – low. Little possibility of dealing with 'feelings'†. Primary aims concerned with 'thinking' and some 'doing'. Risk of slow pace‡ and low involvement.	Low. Can generate enthusiasm/high morale.
Number of trainers	Up to 1 day: one. 2–5 days: two. 5+ days: three.	Up to 3 days: two. 3–5 days: three. 6+ days: four. With a group of up to 12 trainer can just keep track of content and process of learning in group.	3–5 days: three/four. 6+ days: four/five. Depending on aims.	2–6 trainers making lecture-style presentations.

---

* Learning occurs rapidly in an 'artificial' environment, but exposure to the real world kills off growth leaving the subject exhausted and vulnerable.
† Exceptions to this include the Grubb Institute Programme in which participants experience a variety of group sizes.
‡ This can be overcome by ensuring that:
  (a) Group members see each other as main source of information and feedback
  (b) Challenging activities are structured to balance periods for absorbing theory or information
  (c) Different individuals are encouraged to take key roles in the course at different times
  (d) Group members are encouraged to look after and support each other
  (e) Conflict is acknowledged and handled constructively.

Group mix

It is not always possible to be selective about who attends which particular training event. When a programme is planned, much depends on the availability of money, work schedules, the interest of nominating managers and participants etc. Most IST events however depend on the willingness and ability of participants to learn, and particularly to learn from each other. This consideration varies in importance according to the methods and aims of training but is of considerable importance for training in the 'doing' and 'feeling' areas. Assuming then that it is possible to have some influence on the group mix, what are the variables which can be considered as likely to affect the learning process?

Age
Sex
Time in current position
Time in the organisation
Career path and potential
External/internal training
Status
Previous experience of IST and other training
Attitude

Age

Each generation grows up with different attitudes, values and fashions. This variety of ages and experience can enrich the training event considerably. It is not helpful however to have a group in which sub-groups can easily identify themselves and each other, leading to 'us and them' stereotyping which inhibits learning.

Sex

We have experience of all-male, mixed and all-female courses. A training group without a woman tends to have a heavy, competitive 'be strong' atmosphere in which softness and tenderness are avoided. A training group entirely composed of women (especially when the trainer is male) tends towards passivity, accepting the man's world myth, with a certain reluctance to take themselves seriously. A mixed group with more than one of each sex seems to create the permission for a wider spectrum of attitudes and feelings which encourages experiment, fun and creativity. Mixed groups are certainly more enjoyable to work in as trainers and often are more effective.

Time in the job and organisation

The transfer of learning and level of interest depends to a great extent on the relevance of the training experience to work. There is likely to be an 'ideal' time at which to offer a manager training after his induction. One–two years' experience seems to match the general consensus of opinion between nominator, trainer and delegate. Earlier than a year and the trainee is unlikely to have the necessary experience to draw on; much more than two years and he may be too set to change or may already be aiming for his next job change. While a long-service person may gain less from any particular training this is not necessarily a contra-indication. However someone who sees himself as having only a few years to 'endure' before retirement is likely to be a difficult training group member and will seldom learn much.

Career path and potential

Some organisations, often successful ones, invest considerable time and money in their young staff who they see as having potential. Being talented, energetic, technically able or intelligent does not by any means correspond with having interpersonal skills. The basic skills in communication, group membership and leadership, self-awareness and sensitivity will form a sound basis for future responsibility. This argument is conventional wisdom for most managers although many begrudge the investment in a future in which they may not share. For those who have reached the limits of their competence or beyond (by their own or someone else's standards) there is still a strong argument for some IST if not to the same level of investment. The world, society, technology and organisations are changing at an exponential rate. No supervisor or manager is going to escape the new demands these changes bring with them. Flexibility and adaptability are needed to meet the new styles of relationships which the changes will bring. In any event the manager with potential and the individual at the top of his/her career ladder will have significantly different approaches and attitudes to training. A good mix of these will enhance the learning of each: a group entirely composed of those starting in their managerial careers is likely to be a lively and stimulating event if exhausting and demanding for the trainer. A training group of experienced managers with little scope for advancement may need approaching carefully and gently. However, providing the training is well managed and relevant, it is likely to yield excellent results.

External/internal training?

There is no simple answer to the question of whether it is better to train groups whose members come from the same department or organisation (sponsored) or better to use an external trainer with a group composed of members sponsored by many different companies (open). Obviously for team-building work the 'team' will form the training group. Equally if the organisation is undertaking training as a response to a particular event, such as reorganisation, technical change, or union membership, then it makes sense to sponsor the training. Although it is usually cheaper to use sponsored training the decision becomes less clear for IST of a more general kind (see Table 2.2).

A compromise between the two extremes (that is an open course with a large minority of the group from one organisation) creates many of the disadvantages of both types with few gains to offset them.

Table 2.2   Comparison of sponsored and open training groups

	Sponsored	Open
Advantages	– Cheaper. – Many organisational members trained quickly. – Tailor-made programme can be adapted to suit the current organisational needs. – Participants quickly understand the problems of others. – New relationships provide support on return to work. – Can lead to team building element. – Can help to establish a common language and culture.	– Much of learning derived from talk among course members. – Trust builds more quickly, reaches higher level with stranger group. – Individuals can be nominated on a course meeting a particular need. – New ideas/approaches more likely to emerge.
Disadvantages	– Problems with confidentiality. – Organisational 'games'/ 'Ain't it Awful', 'See what they made me do', 'If it weren't for them' etc. – Narrower view of options – lack of creativity. – Trainer sometimes seen as saviour or enemy. – A course may take on a reputation which is hard to change.	– Less opportunity for post-course support from other group members. – Takes a long time to train a work group unless training events take place very frequently.

Status

A mix of status is nearly always an advantage on open programmes. The projections, assumptions and curiosity of one status group about another can be explored, tested and revised or abandoned. Where the status mix includes managers and subordinates or members of departments that are related within a single organisation, the learning process becomes complicated. A sponsored event of this kind needs careful planning and the relationships between the status groups need to be raised explicitly as a part of the course, even if this is not the main purpose of the programme. If successful, the combining of managers and subordinates in a training group can open channels of communication, reduce tension and defensiveness and create enthusiasm. If unsuccessful the opposite results can be expected.

Previous IST experience

Someone who has attended IST (in whatever form) will probably have acquired some basic skills such as distinguishing between 'content' and 'process' and will have some experience of giving and receiving feedback. He is likely therefore to be able to learn more quickly on a subsequent programme and (unless his experience was a bad one) to accept a more open, higher risk atmosphere. Basically, he has some idea about what to expect and will probably jump in enthusiastically.

Someone with no experience is likely to be uncertain about the concepts and their value and will certainly want to 'hold on to the side of the pool' for a while to make sure that it is safe; being pushed, pulled or hurried is likely to make him hold on tighter.

Bearing these different attitudes in mind, it is sometimes better to ensure some similarity of previous training experience when selecting participants: particularly for less structured or more feelings based programmes.

Attitude

Many managers have heard something about 'T' groups or Encounter groups or CCTV and what they have heard often puts them off. Most trainees arrive at a training programme with mixed feelings. At best the trainer can expect everyone to be hoping to learn something and enjoy themselves; at worst those trainees who expect to be 'analysed' by the trainers and 'torn to pieces' by the group are, not surprisingly, hostile and defensive. There is a spectrum of attitudes to IST which can be represented as a line (see Table 2.3).

Table 2.3   Attitudes to IST

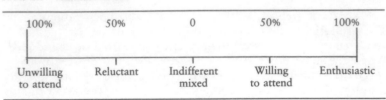

100%	50%	0	50%	100%
Unwilling to attend	Reluctant	Indifferent mixed	Willing to attend	Enthusiastic

Depending on the type of training certain combinations of attitudes are counter-productive. Any group with a significant number of members who are unwilling to attend is likely to have a difficult start. Higher risk, less-structured or feelings based programmes should not have anyone who is in the range from reluctant to unwilling. More structured events can accommodate a greater proportion of people who start off in this band.

It is rare for a trainer or nominating manager to be in a position to select his trainees and yet results of training will vary considerably according to the group mix. What can the nominator and trainer do?

1   Before selecting, gather information about potential trainees concerning age, sex, time in job, organisational relationships, status, willingness to be trained and previous IST experience.
2   Exclude combinations that are going to inhibit seriously the learning process and go for combinations that help learning.
3   Consult and brief participants carefully about intended/proposed future training plans.
4   At the start of every programme double check issues about organisational, departmental or status relationships, willingness to attend, expectations about the course etc. and assign time to resolving uncertainties, fears, hostilities.
5   Agree that any participant is free to leave whenever he or she chooses.

Location and facilities

There is considerable evidence to support the view that interpersonal skills training is most effective when conducted in a residential setting.[3] Ideally then, the location should provide a 'cultural island' but with a frequent 'ferry-service' to 'the mainland'. The best type of location then will be a purpose-built training centre with a range of facilities for relaxation both within and outside its boundaries.

The most important considerations in choosing (or for that matter building) a venue are likely to be:

Main training room – Size? overhead projector/cine-projector screen – flip-chart – white board – pin boards – ventilation/temperature control – power-points – noise – lighting/curtains, facilities for CCTV – flexible layout – suitable furniture – privacy – security.

Subsidiary rooms – Number (approx. 1:4 participants) – size – proximity – flip-chart – power – CCTV facilities – lighting – noise – privacy – security.

Other facilities – Coffee and tea-breaks flexible – meals served and taken within 1 hour – comfortable public rooms (e.g. lounge and bar for exclusive use of course members) – opportunities for exercise (e.g. swimming, squash, golf, tennis etc.) – personal privacy and comfortable sleeping accommodation – easy access to telephones, newspapers etc.

In our experience, few hotels offer these facilities and where they are available they are expensive. Training centres are a luxury in which few companies invest and management colleges rarely lease their premises to 'outsiders'. Nevertheless, these last two are likely to provide the best facilities with hotels inevitably requiring a compromise.

Timing of training

An individual manager may undertake training for many different reasons and there are a variety of views about when, in terms of career and experience, certain kinds of IST become most effective (see 'Group Mix' above). The ability to work effectively within a group, to communicate and express oneself adequately, to listen and observe others, and to conduct a good interview (e.g. for appraisal) are all important foundation skills on which a manager will draw throughout his career. Some companies recognise this fact and provide general training for relatively inexperienced staff who may have technical expertise and are looking forward to management positions. The disadvantage of this timing is that the trainees can only imagine the sort of problems that they will face and cannot bring their experience with them to enrich the learning process. On the other hand, groups composed of prospective managers are usually highly motivated and adventurous, seeing the course as an opportunity to advance themselves and enhance their prospects.

Providing training very shortly after a person has taken up a management position seems the most sensible option at first thought. The need is clear and understood; the motivation is likely to be strong and immediate. One drawback, however, as with the previous group, is that the individual usually does not have much job experience to go on. Secondly, the trainee may feel he has a lot to learn to enable him to do the job, and this may well be his primary priority. Taking him away for IST is likely to be thought of as an interference. Thirdly, because individuals are rarely promoted in groups, and the timing of the course is likely to be within a narrow band of weeks or months, the organisation will have to send the manager on a public course, away from the company which entails the merits and problems discussed above (page 22).

As suggested earlier in this chapter, there is much to commend sending a manager for training after he has had some period of experience in the position for which he is being trained (6 months – 2 years). Having said that, there is still the case of the manager or supervisor with many years of experience who is confronted with the different demands on his role brought about by technological or social change. It may also be that because of a change in policy in the company it is now considered worthwhile to invest in IST for a group of managers with many years of experience. Such groups, provided their experience is respected and used in the training, can be among the most rewarding to work with. Having, as they see it, been neglected for so long the very act of selecting them for training can bring out forgotten commitment and enthusiasm for the job as well as eagerness to learn. There is little evidence to support the saying 'You can't teach an old dog new tricks'.

Among the least auspicious circumstances in which to nominate an individual for training is after things have gone wrong. Remedial training is likely to be conducted against a background of fear, resentment and despair. Much of the allocated training time will be spent overcoming the resistance and resentment created when the nominee is told of his deficiencies. A training remedy is often seen by both parties as the last resort, so that an air of desperation or resignation will offset much of the value of the learning offered. (An important factor affecting the outcome of 'remedial' training is the skill of the trainer in avoiding the role offered to him by the trainee. The trainer will usually be expected to act as agent for the nominator. If, instead, he can sustain the position of a neutral with no prejudices, then a high degree of trust can develop and produce a useful outcome.)

Time-table

Apart from breaks for meals and breaks for tea and coffee during the morning and afternoon, it is useful to be able to find reasons for other five-minute pauses in the day. These intervals serve to reduce the intensity of the learning process and allow time for the integration and absorption of feedback.[4] They are also useful as an opportunity to change the focus of attention from an area of tension or discomfort or to allow members of the group to retrieve their place in the group after the isolating experience of say a CCTV interview in which they took part.

A substantial amount of time is also necessary for meal breaks. Sitting without exercise for long periods can be frustrating and unusual for many managers; resulting agitation is a sign that the individual is not involved in learning but is probably using up all his energy in resisting the urge to get up and do something. The meal breaks then also become an opportunity for exercise and hopefully some facilities will be available.

Whether or not to work in the evenings (after the evening meal) is a subject often raised by course members. Most nominating companies like to feel that precious time away from work is used intensively by their nominees. Some encourage trainees to spend their whole time, apart from sleeping, engrossed in the course activities. Evening sessions can be particularly useful in say syndicate discussions preparing for presentations or in enjoyable activities connected with the training but not requiring learning at the thinking level. However, these events should not be allowed entirely to take the place of social time.

Much of the most valuable learning from courses takes place 'out of hours'. During the social time individuals can find privacy for thought and reflection, seek out individuals for help or guidance. Sub-groups can form and identify themselves and create mutual support. Individuals can gain confirmation of their ideas or feelings. Group members can exchange information about how their environment and problems are similar or different. Above all, the social hours are for group integration and relaxation essential for the development of trust. It is at these times that the advantages of a residential setting can be most clearly seen.

Providing time for social contact is one reason for limiting the number of daily programme hours. A second reason is the limit on an individual's ability to maintain interest and concentration. Providing that the course design includes a mixture of theory and activity, eight hours can be taken as a useful daily learning period. This might be divided into three hours in the morning, three and a half hours in the afternoon and one and a half hours in the evening. If the evening is excluded, then perhaps a more realistic limit might be seven hours.*

A further consideration in determining the length of the training day and indeed of the complete programme is the availability of competent trainers (see also Chapter 3, Ethical and professional issues). Trainers have a responsibility to take care of themselves and to maintain an adequate level of competence. Each individual will have different limits (depending on such factors as type of training, type and size of group, physical fitness, concerns outside the training event, other commitments, amount of sleep etc.) after which he becomes less effective. In order to guard against this, the trainer should have limited contact with the group. A reasonable guideline would be:

Maximum: 6 hours contact per day.

Average (over say 5 days): 4 hours contact per day.

With a schedule of this kind the trainer will still gradually lose his alertness and involvement so that longer breaks away from training events every 4–5 weeks can be planned. These periods could be devoted to self-development and programme design preparation.

The implication of these guidelines is that in order to provide training for a group over say five days two or three trainers will need to be involved. To sustain this over a substantial number of weeks would take four individuals, one of whom would have a no-contact week every fourth week.

Duration

There is no simple answer, but as already described, duration can be related to group size, objectives and type of training, as well as the need for group development (see Chapter 5). For example, a stranger group which begins a relatively unstructured training programme (Tavistock, 'T' group, Gestalt group etc. see Appendices) normally would require between 3–12 hours group time for the ice-breaking process in which the minimum levels of trust and some basic ground rules are established. It is likely therefore that the minimum period for an effective training intervention under these conditions will be 16–20 hours. Even then, with these short time periods there is little time for integration and the transfer of learning so that the cost-effectiveness of interpersonal relations (feelings based) programmes lasting less than say 3 days is marginal.

For more structured, skill-oriented training, the duration of an event is less critical as long as the skill elements are broken up

---

* These estimates are based on our experience of running training programmes and are intuitive rather than stemming from rigorous research.

logically and time is available for practice and review of performance. Therefore an appraisal interviewing skills programme for an in-company peer group of say 6–8 participants who are willing to attend can usefully be conducted within 12–16 hours. This time period being spread over one and a half days and not necessarily residential.[5]

Another option for introducing IST is to integrate it with other management training (e.g. financial procedures, production planning, stock control, computers etc.). In this case some of the problems concerned with group development and transfer of learning become less acute and the time periods can be reduced. The placing of the periods concerned with IST needs to be carefully considered so that firstly, the group has been together sufficient time to develop some trust (at least one day) and secondly, so that the IST elements are not seen to predominate or leave unfinished business.

As far as a maximum period for effective IST is concerned there is little systematic evidence available. Like many other fields of training however, it is useful to assume diminishing marginal returns. After, say, two weeks of intensive residential training it is likely that a manager will benefit more from a period of at least 6–8 weeks back in his normal work environment than he would from further training. This period can be used to try out his learning, to check the validity of feedback and effectiveness of any new skills he may have acquired. In so far as the intensity of the experience is reduced, such training can be valuable over an extended period.

The ideal circumstances for broad spectrum IST might be a combination of intensive periods with regular and frequent supplements, for example:

5 *days intensive*
2 *hours per week* peer group follow-up *for 3–6 months* followed by a further 5 *day intensive*

Course design

Up to this point this chapter has been concerned with decisions that can be made in advance of the course. The contract, the pre-course training investigation, decisions about group size, mix, location, facilities, timing and duration are all about getting the context right. This section is concerned with the choices and consequences related to the conduct of the programme as a whole.

It has been stressed throughout this book that there needs to be a close relationship between training design and the needs and aims to which they relate. There is also a set of requirements which will be common to most IST programmes and it is this that is reviewed here.

Getting to know each other

It is well understood that individuals arrive in a new situation (such as the start of a training event) with a number of needs and questions[6] (see also Chapter 5). One of the first tasks that needs to be undertaken, then, is some form of ice-breaking. This process is likely to have a number of elements: 1. Welcome and administration in which participants are informed about the arrangements for basic needs, food, drink, etc., given a time-table and encouraged to feel at ease in their surroundings. 2. Introductions – of which there are a number of different types and styles. The nature of the introductions, the questions asked and how the responses are received will be a key factor in determining the atmosphere and style of the relationships within the group, and also help establish norms about the nature of the training in terms of: formal or informal; 'thinking', 'doing' or 'feeling', approach, structured/unstructured.

Perhaps the most basic form of introduction would involve each individual saying something about himself. (Sometimes called 'creeping death'!) More interest can be created by having pairs talk to each other and introduce their partners to the rest of the group. There are also a variety of start-up activities which provide still more contact and exchange of information. Issues to be considered are types of questions, whether or not the trainer takes part, degree of self-disclosure, how closely the information is related to the course material.

Examples of introductions we use are given in Table 2.4.

Establishing learning objectives and methods

In introducing a learning programme, the tutorial staff will inevitably be setting ground-rules for the course method from the first moments of contact. Factors such as appearance, voice quality, use of humour, warmth, vocabulary etc. will begin to direct the course members' thinking and feelings about the type of experience they can expect. These first impressions, formed by both trainers and trainees, are based on guesswork leaving much to be resolved before the participant (or the trainer) is likely to feel settled.

The trainers can decide in advance the extent to which they want to help the participants to feel secure and cared for (see also Chapter 5). The more that the context and methods are explained (provided that they are not threatening) the more the participants are likely to

Table 2.4 *Examples of introductory sessions*

Type of course	Format	Information requested
Skill development based on thinking/doing. Structured.	Paired	Name, job, career background, personal interests.
Thinking/doing plus some feeling. Structured.	Paired	Name, job, interests, needs/ wants of the course, what I can contribute to the course.
Doing/feeling. Unstructured. Skills and personal development.	Paired	Name, three things I like about myself, anything I do not like about myself, what I can contribute to the group, something I would otherwise conceal.
Thinking/doing/feeling. Structured. Skills and personal development.	Individual	Draw a picture of your life (portrait gallery).
Structured thinking/doing/ feeling.	Small group	Hopes, fears and expectations regarding the course.
Feeling. Unstructured	Large group and individual	'Magic shop' fantasy*. 'Journey to the course' fantasy.
Thinking (large group)	None	List of delegates' names and job titles.

* A guided fantasy in which participants enter a magic shop and exchange attributes which will help their learning (e.g. curiosity, enthusiasm etc.) for attributes which hinder learning (anxiety, pride and cynicism).

feel comfortable although this may not produce optimum learning conditions. The types of issues that can be raised here are:

Level of formality
Degree of participation
Pace and time-table
Methods
Purposes
Contexts (e.g. plenary group, syndicates, one to one etc.)
Varying outcomes (e.g. different individuals will learn different things)
Handouts
Jargon
Having fun
Support and development vs. judgement and evaluation
Confidentiality

Having reviewed some or all of these issues the trainer may, before embarking on the training proper, want to orient participants further by spelling out in brief terms the content and purpose of each session or module. This procedure will normally* reinforce the sense of security and predictability of the training event for the participants.

How much time is spent in preparing the ground will depend on a number of factors; but it is important to consider the question of control and responsibility. As the trainer spells out the nature of the week, so by implication he takes control of the group and responsibility for the learning,† (see also Chapter 5 and Chapter 3).

Building trust

The development of trust between participants is an essential ingredient of IST if people are to take the risk of practising, experiment and exchanging feedback.

In terms of macro-design, trust building will depend on whether or not the participants have a sense that:

1   They are able to cope with what is being asked of them.
2   The learning goals are worthwhile and there is no ulterior motive.
3   They have a chance to work together as a group.

It is useful therefore to provide tasks and activities during the early phase of a programme (particularly those based on the doing approach) which are fairly straightforward, which have obvious relevance to the training aims and which require the participants to make contact with one another (see Table 2.5).

Developing skills

All IST is obviously aimed at developing skill and may also include developing understanding or awareness or some combination of them. The training design must therefore as a priority, provide opportunities for this learning to take place. The Kolb learning cycle is an excellent guide to the design of learning experiences.[8] In terms

---

* Occasionally participants become nervous at the prospect of having to make presentations or appear on closed circuit television.
† Assertiveness training and personal development programmes are conducted on the assumption that the individual is responsible for his own life and behaviour and is not a passive recipient of the demands of others. To begin such a training with the definition by the tutor of how to behave and what is to be learned places the participant in a 'double-bind' i.e. 'You are here to develop your ability to assert yourself and this is how to do it!'

Table 2.5   Trust building (early phase)

Training approach	Possible method
Thinking	Syndicate discussion (e.g. What factors determine whether communication is effective or not?).
Doing	Straightforward group tasks (e.g. Structured group decision-making exercise e.g. NASA).[7]
Feeling	Leader draws attention to the problem of trust building and suggests group explores ways of dealing with it.

of the whole programme it is essential that enough time, opportunity, tutorial staff and facilities are available to enable each member of the group to prepare, practise and receive feedback if the learning aims include skill development. Learning to interview would therefore require a briefing, preparation, the interview and then a review, with feedback. The first occasion provides valuable feedback and key learning goals. Having another go and, hopefully, doing better and feeling better provides encouragement and incentive for the individual to continue his learning.

For less structured programmes, the individual is likely to be left to set his own learning objectives and to determine his own timetable and methods for doing so. Feelings-based programmes vary according to the amount of theoretical background provided as a learning framework (see Apendix 1).

These types of skill development programmes also lay great emphasis on the need for practice and experience as the basis for learning.

Integrating learning

It is very useful to provide, towards the end of a structured training event, one extended activity which brings together all the main learning points of the programme. Such an event will:

1 Require the participation of all group members.
2 Simulate the 'real world' reasonably closely (e.g. an organisation, a negotiation, a sale, etc.).
3 Bring together in one exercise the need to use all the skills and understanding referred to during the programme.
4 Be sufficiently flexible to allow the participants to experiment and test out new ideas or behaviours.
5 Be seen as the 'climax' of the course.
6 Require a thorough review and examination to help participants to understand themselves and others as well as how much (or little) they have learned.

Planning the return to work

This phase of a training event improves the ability of trainees to take what they have learned away from their normal environment and apply it on the return to work. In many cases the intensity of the learning experience, the sense of trust and mutual understanding creates a kind of special and unreal environment on intensive IST programmes. Planning for the return to work helps to refer individuals to the reality that they will have to face the following day or week. Much can be done to provide a bridge of support and encouragement so that the new possibilities are realised and are incorporated into work practices. For in-company programmes, peer groups or support groups can continue to meet or agree to provide each other with counselling or guidance. For those who have experienced a sense of failure or come to terms with themselves in a painful way during the training event, this period can serve to plan to 'put things right'.

Participants can use this period to acknowledge what they have learned and evaluate themselves against their self-image and then compare with others' perceptions of them.

Ideally, each individual will emerge from a back-home planning session with: a detailed plan for the application of learning; the commitment to carry it out; the support necessary to do so; and a plan for further self-development, continuing to develop using the insights, skills and understanding which have already been gained.

Closure

At whatever level the training has been aimed, the feelings of participants for each other and the trainer will have been involved. In order to close these relationships in a satisfying way, it is helpful to provide the chance to make these known whether implicitly or explicitly depending on the design of the preceding events. In any event saying goodbye is a frequent experience for all and the ability to do so gracefully is a worthwhile skill. Equally for those who are regularly involved in leading training courses, finishing with each successive group becomes important so that a fresh start can be made with a subsequent one.

Examples of some closing activities are:

1   Course evaluation by group members.
2   An evaluation of the group's learning by trainers.
3   Expressions of appreciation and regrets.
4   Sharing of memories of the programme.
5   Statements of what has been learned and plans for further development.
6   Exchanges of gifts, telephone numbers, addresses, offers of support, invitations.

Evaluation (see Chapter 7)

Course design – further choices and considerations

As the ideas, training needs and design content become clearer, the trainer is faced with a series of choices and considerations which will form a back-cloth to the programme. Often the issues are dealt with without considering the alternatives. In practice the decisions and approach to these matters can crucially affect the outcome and consistency of the training.

Amount of structure

This question has been the subject of references in this and other chapters (see page 4). A training programme that is highly structured is one of which the aims, style, content and activity have been determined in advance and are closely managed by the course leaders.

Unstructured training in its extreme form (e.g. 'T' Group or Tavistock Group. See Appendix 1.) takes place in a setting where the only controls provided by the trainer are:

1 A statement of the time-table
2 Provision of the essential facilities
3 A statement of the purpose of the training (e.g. 'The purpose of this group is to develop a greater understanding of relationships.')
4 A statement of suggested ground-rules (e.g. 'Please refer only to events in this room and concern yourselves with your experiences here and now.')

The trainees' experiences in these different settings are vastly different and yet often the proclaimed training objectives are very similar. How can that be? Which type of training is most effective?

As with most answers to do with people and their relationships, they are neither straightforward nor reliable.[9,10] In so far as there are choices, there are also consequences, some of which are summarised in Table 2.6.

It is probably fair to say that the more structured programme focuses explicitly on the combination of skill and understanding so that the outcome in terms of feeling is never clear. As a result, the trainee may complete his training knowing how to do what he has been taught but still hostile to doing it or incapable of applying it. On the other hand, the participant in unstructured programmes, which are likely to focus strongly on insight, awareness and feeling, may, as a result, understand himself and others and feel much better about both and yet not have learned any new behaviour!

Table 2.6 Consequences for structured and unstructured training

Structured (The set menu)	*Unstructured* (À la carte)
Learning goals largely pre-set by designers/tutors	Learning goals largely determined by the individuals
Learning goals the same for all group members	Learning goals vary from individual to individual
All participants are expected to take part	Participants determine the level of their involvement
Limited time available on any one topic	Time available can be used as participants wish
Learning content and method controlled by leaders	Learning content and method controlled by participants
Leaders initiate and take responsibility for activities and learning	Participants initiate and take responsibility for activities and learning
Outcomes, in terms of behaviour changes limited and fairly predictable	Outcomes in terms of behaviour changes not predictable
Expression of feelings likely to be limited	Strong feelings likely to be expressed
Relevance to work likely to be seen as high	Relevance to work likely to be varied
Level of intensity likely to be low or moderate	Level of intensity likely to be intermittently high
Opportunity for evaluation in terms of behaviour change greater.	Opportunity for evaluation in terms of behaviour change fewer.

These are the rather extreme effects often pointed out by the critics of both sides. On the positive side, a good structured programme will be sufficiently enjoyable, interesting and relevant to gain the commitment of participants so that learning takes place at the level of thinking, doing and feeling. A well-led unstructured event on the other hand, will help the participants to understand their experience in common-sense terms and to be able to put their learning into practice.

Sequencing

Like a good story, a training programme needs a beginning, a middle and an end. The content of these elements has been discussed in an earlier section. It is usually important that these events occur in a logical sequence and that trainees have a sense of direction. In structured events, linking the content of each learning session and setting it in its context is the first task of the trainer. In terms of

Table 2.7   Designing IST to include thinking, doing and feeling approaches

	Early phase	Middle phase	End phase
Structure	HIGH. Takes care of needs, concerned with orientation and security.	MODERATE. Participants know each other and are better able to structure their own time.	LOW. To allow 'space' to absorb, reassess and integrate (may need some structure for back-home planning).
Theory	LOW. Participants unlikely to absorb theoretical concepts.	HIGH. With development of trust, full attention can be given to new theory and concepts.	LOW. Participants are likely to make sense of their experience so far. New concepts should not be needed.
Practice	HIGH. To help build trust. Provides common experience to which to relate theories.	HIGH. Putting theory into practice. Developing new skills. Experimenting, generating feedback.	LOW. After integrating activity this is the time for reflection and planning.
Self-disclosure and feedback	LOW. As people 'feel each other out' and try to avoid risks.	MODERATE. Trust grows, activities lead to exchange of feedback which leads to self-disclosure.	HIGH. Participants learn to treat feedback as information and are willing to share feelings as well as thoughts.

process and relationship there are a large number of developments taking place concurrently at different levels. Table 2.7 illustrates four design parameters and guidelines for an IST event which is intended to involve thinking, doing and feeling approaches.

Pace

A well-designed learning programme provides for a variety of pace. The effects of changes in pace are to maintain interest and involvement, provide for relaxation and reflection and to take into account the different learning preferences present in the group.

Activities that slow the pace down are:

CCTV review of group discussions or interviews.
'Here and now' awareness exercises[11]
Process based learning
Relaxers: guided fantasies, breathing exercises, meditation

Complex theory
Abstraction, conceptualising
Discussion without clear end objectives
Transfer of information

Activities which speed the pace up are:

Concentrating on doing
Physical construction projects [12,13]
Goal oriented discussions with time limits
Energisers (activities which involve physical movement, competition and loud noises)
Competitive activities
Simulation exercises with tight time constraints

A blend of short theory inputs or introductions, with purposeful discussions; exercises with a process oriented review (including CCTV) and summaries which combine the opportunity to conceptualise and generalise should produce a variety of pace which will enhance the learning process.

Relevance

It is often thought that in order for learning to be transferable to the 'real world', the exercises and activities must simulate that environment accurately. The relevance of each exercise is not however mainly a question of its ability to simulate organisational demands. It is more important that an experience comes to grips with the areas of immediate concern to the trainee and in particular:

1 The training encourages the understanding of individual behaviour and its consequences.
2 The experience encourages an evaluation of current behaviour patterns.
3 The training elicits 'new' behaviours as realistic alternatives for trainees.
4 The trainee concludes with a belief that his current range of skills is adequate to meet his needs or that he now knows how to develop the new skills he requires.

So long as these points are achieved, then the trainee will feel that the training is relevant to himself. This will be the case no matter how different the learning process is from his normal experience. Making this relevant to work is a matter of learning at the thinking level and can be done by generalising from the particular experience.

The person who says, after a role play, 'That wasn't really me' or 'I would never have done that in real life' appears to be questioning or denying the relevance of the event to his normal work context. In reality he may have a real need to defend himself, and it is important to respect this. Nevertheless, a person cannot be anyone else but himself and unless one believes in alternative realities there is only one 'real life'. The issue is what was it about *that* reality which made him behave differently and what can be learned from the experience?

Flexibility

A well constructed training plan is an excellent guide but each group of trainees is unique and the best plans sometimes need to be abandoned. Occasions when this might be necessary are when the relationships within the group or between the group and the trainers become an obstacle for learning; (evidenced by tension or low energy, see Chapter 5) when the majority of course members see the learning as irrelevant or in some way too difficult; when the group express an overwhelming interest in something else; when group members are frustrated with a slow pace or when it is late and everyone has had enough for the time being.

For such occasions apart from just stopping, it is very useful to be able to draw on contingency plans already available and as trainer, to offer alternatives.* Alternatives are to confront the group members with some direct feedback ('It looks as though you're not interested in doing this') or a question, ('Is there something going on in the group that we need to clear up?') or asking people if they have any unresolved issues they wish to raise or for some feedback for the trainers. In these events, silence and over-emphatic denial are nearly always an indicator that the matter is worth pursuing and that the set programme should be put to one side. Being responsive to the current needs of the group is a demonstration of social skill, failing to do so may be seen as lacking in sensitivity.

The trainers

Chapter 3, Ethical and professional issues, takes up in detail the need for co-ordination between trainers and the maintenance of clear relationships between them. In terms of design, it is important to take into account the fact that each trainer has his own style, personality, interests and experiences.

From the designer's point of view this means that unless he is to lead the training programme on his own, then he will have to take these differences into account. Serious problems can arise when a

---

* In feelings based programmes this may be counter-productive.

trainer is asked to present material with which he does not agree or is not familiar. In the same way, designs which require sensitivity at a feelings level may be inappropriate for a trainer whose expertise is primarily at the conceptual, thinking level, and vice versa.

The other side of this concern is that trainers who have particular skills or styles should have the opportunity to use them. This argues against rigid, step by step instructions on the conduct of any particular session and requires a greater emphasis on main objectives. The trainer is then free to use his own methods, provided they are acceptable to the other team members. When we prepare for one of our regular joint programmes, the period immediately before the start is devoted to exchanging perceptions of the purpose of the course; particular personal concerns which may affect the attitude to the programme; and any particular new interest or approach that is likely to be used.

Session design

While there are many different approaches to session design, the recognition that learning needs to take place at all three levels, thinking, doing and feeling, carries with it some guidelines which are outlined in the following paragraphs.

Checking for 'unfinished business'. Right from the start of training, individuals carry with them quantities of unfinished business. For example, feelings of tension after a difficult journey, resentment because the training takes them away from other higher priorities, worries about leaving the family for a time. Later as the course develops and participants become more involved with each other the unfinished business may be concerned with concepts not fully understood, conflicts not resolved, feelings not expressed.

Any of these may clutter the field of attention so that the individual does not allow himself to participate fully in the forthcoming session. By inviting the expression of unfinished business, some of this clutter may be raised and consequently removed. (Liaison with colleagues if they have been leading previous sessions is also important.) Certainly, serious obstacles will become clearer.

Linking. This helps trainees to make sense of the logic of the programme and to register their learning so far.

Outline of the purpose of the session. Knowing where he is going and why, the participant is more likely to be able to learn at the level of thinking. Equally a clear sense of what is about to happen probably creates a feeling of security and confidence.

Introduce concepts, activity and establish observation/feedback methods and make clear any expectations in terms of content, method and timing. Apart from ensuring that everyone is clear about how they are going to learn, the introduction of theory and a framework for giving feedback can provide the necessary conceptual background.

Select participants and observers. This process in preparation for an activity can have a significant effect on the outcome. Among the things to consider are:

1 How much any individuals have been involved or the subject of attention until then.
2 The willingness of individuals to take up particular roles.
3 How they are likely to undertake the task, role etc. (this will be influenced by their personality, attitude to other group members and the training, status, and skill level).
4 The prospect of useful learning being derived from their participation.
5 The chances of discomfort arising.

Conduct the activity.

Check perceptions of participants. Before asking for feedback from observers, it is valuable to bring out the feelings of the participants and their perceptions of what they have been doing.* This information then provides a starting point against which the observers' comments or feedback can be compared. It also helps to bring any strong feelings that may have been stirred up during the activity.

Take feedback from the observers. In using observation frameworks and the participants to do the observing the trainer can structure the feedback in several ways (see Chapters 1 and 6).

Summarise and close. It is very important in order that learning be transferable that the main learning points are summarised and their implications acknowledged. Finally at the feelings level it is worth checking again for unfinished business.

---

* If some of the participants feel bad about their experience, this gives them an opportunity to put some distance between themselves and their behaviour. Far from having to confront the process, the trainer can (if necessary) help to establish this safety margin. Once having been established this leaves everyone free to learn.

Summary

The design of effective interpersonal skills training requires consideration at the levels of thinking, doing and feeling. The early phase of the design requires that attention be given to clarifying the contract by means of agreed objectives based on a review of training needs. Decisions can then be made concerning the size and composition of the group to be trained, the duration of the programme, the location and the overall intensity and methods. Having made these decisions, the designer can turn his attention to the more detailed work of establishing how the various learning objectives can be met. While developing the content he needs to bear in mind some of the 'process' considerations from breaking the ice at the start to ensuring a satisfying close. At each stage the designer has a considerable range of choices, and each carries with it particular consequences. Perhaps the most important thing is that the process, content and method of training should work together and not in opposition so that the course takes on a consistent flow in its chosen direction.

References

(1) V. and A. Stewart, *Managing the Manager's Growth*, Gower, Aldershot, 1978.

(2) A. and V. Stewart, *Tomorrow's Men Today*, Institute of Personnel Management & Institute of Manpower Studies, London, 1976 (Chapters 4 and 5).

(3) P. Smith, *Group Processes and Personal Change*, Harper and Row, London, 1980.

(4) T. Buzan, *Use Your Head*, BBC Publications, London, 1974.

(5) E. Singer, *Effective Management Coaching*, Institute of Personnel Management, London, 1974.

(6) E. Schein, *Process Consultation: its role in organisation development*, Addison-Wesley, Reading, Massachusetts, 1969.

(7) D. and F. Johnson, *Joining Together: group theory and group skills*, Prentice-Hall, Englewood Cliffs, N.J., 1975.

(8) D. Kolb and R. Fry, 'Towards an applied theory of experiential learning' In: *Theories of Group Processes*, C. L. Cooper (Ed.), John Wiley and Sons, Chichester, 1975.

(9) 'Small Groups and Personal Change' P. Herriot (General Ed.) P. Smith (Ed.) *Psychology in Progress*, Methuen, London, 1980.

(10) C. Cooper, *Learning from Others in Groups*, Associated Business Press, London, 1979.

(11) J. Stevens, *Awareness: Exploring, Experimenting, Experiencing*, Bantam, New York, 5th Edition, 1976.

(12) J. Pfeffer and J. Jones (Eds.), *A Handbook of Structured Experiences*

for Human Relations Training, Volumes I–IV, University Associates Publishers, La Jolla, 1974.
(13) J. Adair, R. Ayres, I. Debenham and D. Després (Eds), *A Handbook of Management Training Exercises*, BACIE, London, 1978.

3 Ethical and professional issues

As mentioned in the Introduction, an important distinction between technical training and IST is the fact that the latter raises many ethical issues. This chapter describes these issues, particularly with the trainer and consultant in mind. However, we hope that others (e.g. training advisers, management development managers and generally those responsible for making suggestions about training) will be encouraged to examine their own values and beliefs and consider afresh what is, and is not, acceptable to them in this type of training. It is also possible that those who have had or heard about 'good' or 'bad' experiences on IST courses will have a better understanding of the events concerned.

The early stages

Ethical considerations are raised well before the training, whatever form it may take, actually starts. In Chapter 2 the more technical aspects of contract development between the trainer and the client were discussed. In this chapter a different perspective is taken reviewing, for example, some of the 'soul-searching' which may be required.

An important point, for all the parties to be aware of, is the danger of a culture clash. This can reveal itself in many ways, but is particularly likely when the training is based on the feelings approach and consequently is likely to have some roots in humanistic psychology. Its principles, described on page 183, are frequently not supported in a lot of organisations. Some organisations operate quite rigid control systems and 'personal growth' (e.g. somebody wanting to be creative) can be seen as disruptive. If the training encourages people to develop skills which are not supported or valued by the organisation then the scene is set for a battlefield of recriminations. Consequently, as training needs are identified the trainer should be open about any basic assumptions or values he has if he feels these may conflict with the organisation. For example, the trainer may have a strong belief in the importance of assertiveness (i.e. people being 'open' and direct with everybody, *including authority figures*, about wants and needs). If he does not make this clear then the organisation, which may function on the basis of its staff *not* being assertive, could be faced with a culture clash where the recipients of the training become very frustrated. Another possible outcome is that the organisation will have great difficulty in coping with its newly trained and assertive staff and that it will lose some of its effectiveness. Sub-groups might also develop consisting of those who have been trained and those who have not.

Also IS I frequently leads to different learning outcomes for different people, particularly where the training encourages some fundamental self-appraisal. In the same training group one person might decide to work less hard and devote more time to his family; another might decide he wants a complete change and to press for a move to another part of the organisation and yet another might decide to leave the organisation altogether. If these are some of the potential risks and the trainer is aware of them they should be discussed before the training starts. It is also at this point that time scales should be considered ensuring that the aims of the training are realistic in view of the time allowed. For example, two days of non-residential training is totally unrealistic for helping managers carry out the type of self-appraisal mentioned above (see also Chapter 2). Under such circumstances the dangers of culture clash are greatly increased.

The trainer will also, in these early stages, need to state his attitude about confidentiality. Whatever happens on the training course should be confidential, and there should be no feedback to the organisation on specific individuals. If this confidentiality is lacking then the chances of people taking risks and therefore learning (see later in this chapter), are reduced.

It is likely that in-company trainers will have more difficulty in taking this line, because they will be more subject to political, organisational and financial pressures.[1] Where the trainees all come from the same organisation and additionally may have among them hierarchical relationships (e.g. as with some team-building programmes), then the need for confidentiality within the group is even greater because of fears that events on the course could be used later on against the participants either by each other or the trainer. We believe that there is a need for confidentiality regardless of whether the training is based on 'thinking', 'doing' or 'feeling' approaches. In all cases, the trainer's own decision must be made clear to the parties involved including, obviously, the course members, who should also be told of the course objectives and methods.

Another ethical point is the extent to which the trainer should be willing to work with the need as stated by the client, even though he may believe that it is a small part of a much larger problem. For example, one of us was invited into a company to examine the need for customer contact training. It rapidly became clear that different parts of the organisation had different attitudes to, and policies on, customer contact. To obtain a unified and agreed statement of customer contact policy would have required an intervention looking at policies throughout the organisation. The project never really got off the ground because of lack of money, but it provides a classic example of where an apparently 'small' need ('How can we train our staff to handle angry customers?') was linked directly to a large need ('What type of an oganisation do we want to be?'). The moral dilemma for the trainer is that the client organisation may be daunted by being faced with a large, and unexpected problem, and may decide not to do any training at all. Generally, it is not worth pursuing a 'foot in the door' policy, i.e. working at the level of the stated problem and then letting the client see from the results of the training that there are other areas to be considered. If it appears to the trainer that there are larger problems and that the need as stated is a symptom rather than cause, then this should be made clear to the organisation even at the risk of losing the work.

It is misguided and dangerous to seek entry to the organisation at any cost and to carry out training which is unlikely to be relevant. An example, which is described in broad terms because of its generally recurring nature, is where problems of morale and communication are seen by the client to be lodged in the lower part of the organisation ('What they need is to be told how to communicate more effectively'), when in fact a key cause is with middle or senior management, who are ineffective in their communication down the line. If the trainer leaves the client's assumptions unchallenged then his training programme will, to say the least, be 'difficult'. ('We aren't the ones who should be on the course!')

The trainer, even at the risk of losing his client, should make it clear where, in the final analysis, his loyalty lies. This should be with the trainees, rather than the client organisation. This requires some explanation. It is not being suggested that the trainer should lightly dispense with an agreed programme. However, the training needs analysis does not always produce totally accurate information and it may have produced generalisations which are not applicable to a particular training group. For example, one of us was engaged in running an in-company course on the management of change and the participants' responsibilities in introducing change. Soon after the course started it became evident that morale was low because these managers felt that they had been unfairly treated by their bosses who, they believed, had not given them enough resources to manage the change effectively. The managers on the course were therefore very unwilling to consider their own responsibilities until problems further up had been dealt with, at least partially. Consequently, the course programme was ignored for a day whilst the group was helped to identify specifically its grievances which were subsequently presented to a member of senior management. It is almost certain that any attempt to keep rigidly to the previously agreed time-table would have generated considerable resentment. Obviously, each case has to be taken on its merits and it would be immoral, for example, for a trainer to agree in his contract to run a tightly structured skills-based course and then use the slightest excuse to make it unstructured and sensitivity-based.

A key skill for the trainer, most particularly in the early stages, is in being a part of, and at the same time apart from, the organisation. This applies even with in-company trainers. There is a need for the trainer to be in touch with the realities of the organisation and yet sufficiently distant not to be seduced into seeing them solely from the client's point of view. The IS trainer will need all his interpersonal skills to manage these contrasting pulls. To be effective he needs to push some boundaries and yet not push so hard that the organisation pulls back and excludes him.

Two fundamental questions each trainer needs to ask are firstly, whether there are any types of organisation that he would, on principle, refuse to work with; and secondly, whether there are types of training which, on moral grounds he would be unwilling to carry out. Certainly these questions involve highly individual decisions. Regarding the first one, there are trainers who would refuse to work with the armaments industry; there are others who would not work for an organisation which they saw as somehow being concerned to exploit or manipulate the public.

In terms of the second question, regarding types of training, the authors would suggest that necessarily the trainer should not carry out training which he does not feel competent to handle. (This is referred to again later in this chapter.) Also, there are grounds for morally objecting firstly to training which is being used as punishment, rather than problem solving or personal development, and secondly to training where important information is being withheld from those who should have it. An example of the latter occurred when a trainer was invited to carry out a team-building programme and was told that a particular member of the team would be required to leave the team *after* the training had taken place. This person had not been told of these plans. The trainer refused to go any further with this work. It is also possible, particularly these days, that some trainers would refuse to carry out any training which could lead to people being made redundant. At the very least they should think about it carefully.

One can summarise this section of the chapter by saying that the trainer and his client need to beware of any training activity which generates too much unfinished business, i.e. creates more problems than it solves. Where, for example, the organisation is left with skills or expectations which it cannot handle; where the course members are left feeling resentful, frustrated or confused; and where the trainer feels exploited or manipulated.

Self awareness

Just as trainers in the technical field need constantly to update themselves so IS trainers need to keep themselves informed of new approaches and techniques as they arise. Beyond this, and possibly even more importantly, the IS trainer needs to look after, pay attention to, his own self-awareness. This does not mean that he should be devoutly introspective, but that he should be regularly checking how he feels about himself and finding out how others perceive him. For example, it has frequently been stressed that giving and managing feedback is a key skill for the trainer. We would suggest therefore that the trainer make it his business regularly to receive feedback from others. It is possible that the trainer will get feedback from course members during a training programme, and certainly at the end. It is worth the trainer's while going beyond this and making sure that he asks for and obtains feedback from his co-trainers on the course, and quite possibly from colleagues who have not been working with him on that particular programme, but with whom he has been in contact.

There are a number of reasons for suggesting this. Firstly, it helps the trainer to keep in touch with what it is like to receive feedback. He can then more readily identify with course members when they are receiving feedback. (We imagine that most people feel apprehensive when they hear the words, 'I want to give you some feedback . . .'.) Secondly, the feedback might well provide some valuable information regarding training techniques and the management of the group, e.g. 'You might have been more effective if you had used syndicates rather than trying to stimulate a full group discussion'. Thirdly, the feedback might help the trainer to assess how effective he is in his own interpersonal skills and management of relationships, e.g. 'You seemed to be rather detached and uninvolved during this course'.

The trainer can then use this feedback for making decisions about his own training and development. With time and experience the need to concentrate on acquiring basic training skills may diminish, but the need to examine one's own interpersonal skills and interpersonal processes is likely to continue. The trainer might frequently receive feedback from various sources that at certain times, or with certain courses, he becomes detached, or unenthusiastic or aggressive or patronising etc. The trainer may then decide that he needs to attend some training sessions or groups to understand his behaviour and what he can do about it. This would seem to be the case particularly for the trainer who spends a lot of time operating at the 'feelings' end of the training spectrum. A trainer needs to know what he feels about himself if he is to help other people cope with their feelings. This does not mean that the IS trainer should have solved all his problems about himself and his relationships — this would be impossible — but that he should be clear in his own mind about the sort of person he is and how people are likely to react to him. He should have acquired the groundwork of skills he wants his trainees to acquire. If the trainer is very uncertain about the key factors within him that affect his relationships with others, then there is a danger of his unwittingly allowing some of the 'negative' elements of his own processes to impede his work with the group. For example, as part of his personality the trainer may have an over-strong urge to look after others and protect them from 'unpleasant' experiences. As a result he may be less effective as a trainer because he avoids confrontation at all costs. It is likely that the trainer will only learn about this aspect of himself through feedback; naturally it is only then that he can start to make new decisions about his behaviour and then increase his effectiveness.

Another way in which the trainer can obtain feedback is by tape recording some of his sessions (with the permission of the participants!). He can then, if he wishes, involve some of his colleagues in reviewing the tapes. This can provide a rich learning opportunity by not only covering the content of the tape but also reviewing the feedback skills which are being used during the analysis of the tape.

Almost as a matter of principle there is a lot to be said for trainers being trainees once in a while. Trainers can become blasé about the power they have and not realise that, for example, an exercise being presented for the fiftieth time may seem easy to them, but is not necessarily seen to be easy by the course members. Certainly trainers should experience the type of training they are carrying out and go a little beyond it in terms of risk in order to clarify their boundaries. Relating this to the overview of training approaches our suggestion is that, for example, those carrying out training based on the 'doing' approach should have experience of it as course members and should have 'a taste' of 'feeling' based training so that they are clear about where they can establish a boundary for themselves. In this way the trainer can develop a sense of the limits of his competence and, if wanted and needed, gradually expand beyond these limits.

Observing other trainers in action is a useful starting point for developing some degree of self-awareness. This would largely be through comparison – 'I would not do that', 'I need to develop a lot more skills before I could get involved in that type of training'. However, there is no real substitute for experience and testing out, in a practical way, skills and limits. Also the role of the observer on an IST programme can be a difficult one, complicating the relationship between the training group and the 'active' trainer and reducing the chances of people taking risks. The more the training moves into the 'feelings' area the more difficult becomes the role of the observer.

Involvement and detachment

One of the reasons why the trainer should look after his own training is that it will help him manage the fine balance between involvement and detachment with the group. Involvement is evidently a positive and necessary quality in IS, or any, training. The training will be much more effective if it is obvious that the trainer cares. However, the trainer can care too much and feel that he has to help *everybody* solve *all* their problems. In extreme cases he will try to solve everybody's problems for them and give himself sleepless nights! A consequence of caring too much is that the trainer burns himself out. It can mean that he is too exhausted to handle subsequent work effectively and that he does not give his personal relationships enough time and attention. The trainer needs to have enough caring left over for his spouse and children and for himself. Therefore, a degree of detachment is important in terms of the trainer looking after himself and seeing the total picture of group interaction; it also helps him to be aware of the relationship between himself and each member of the group. However, too much detachment can lead the trainer to appear to be uninterested or too clinical, or seemingly believing in his own superiority.

There are a number of ways in which the trainer can take care of himself. One, which has already been mentioned, is for the trainer to devote time to his own training and development. A second factor to be considered is the manning of the course. It is useful to have one or two colleagues who can share the training load, confer with each other, and express their doubts, fears and good feelings (see Chapter 2). It is at such meetings that giving feedback can be valuable, for the reasons mentioned earlier. The total workload of the trainer is also important. The trainer needs to practise his skills sufficiently to keep them well developed, and yet too much work can lead to tiredness and his becoming jaded. When considering the manning level for a particular course it is important that a balance be struck between giving the trainer enough time with the group so that he is closely in touch with the individual processes, and yet enough time away from the group so that he can rest, reflect and 're-charge his batteries'. We find that more than 20 contact hours per week with a training group reduces a trainer's effectiveness. (Particularly if he is involved in leading training events almost every week.)

For a trainer to look after himself he needs to have realistic expectations of the course and himself, recognising that in the final analysis he cannot change anybody but only help to establish conditions where people *might* decide to change. Expecting too much of the course, the course members, and himself can lead the trainer to frustration and exhaustion, which results in his antagonising people. It is worth recognising the value of one small step at a time. Sometimes IS trainers believe it is their responsibility (vocation?) to help people make 'life decisions' which will require of the course member a fundamental reappraisal of his attitudes to himself and others. If a trainer has this belief then he may well try to go too far too quickly and then become frustrated through not meeting his own unrealistic expectations. It may be that on occasion there will be course members who need *and want* to make some profound changes to their lives, but it is much more likely that they simply need and want to become a little more effective in managing their relationships. If, at the end of a day's, or even a week's, training a trainee has, for example, learnt to listen more carefully, then that might be as much as the trainer could or should expect.

There are a number of very specific ways in which a trainer can look after himself and allocating definite times for them can be helpful. Here are just a few suggestions: spending time playing with the children; having a long lie in bed; having a bath to wash off all the 'bad' feelings which may have accumulated during the day and then taking great pleasure in watching them go down the plughole; massage; having a bean bag to hit, shout and scream at – it can represent a difficult course member! Finally, since IS training is normally highly sedentary, the trainer would do well to make sure he is physically fit.

Confrontation

In managing the balance between involvement and detachment a key skill is the ability to confront constructively and with caring. Much learning on IST courses can take place through people being challenged to examine and re-evaluate their existing patterns of behaviour and their perceptions of themselves and others. Nevertheless, if this challenge is made without apparent care and concern, then the trainee is likely to see the relationship with the trainer as a win/lose contest and will be more concerned with simply rejecting (actively or passively) what is said, rather than assessing its validity. If the challenge or confrontation is made with evident concern then it will probably 'hold' the trainee and he will be prepared to listen. Powerful and penetrating comments are not in themselves effective interventions, they must be accompanied by caring. Without this there is the paradox that the more penetrating the comment, the more the trainee may be driven into defensiveness and rejection, and thus lose awareness of some choices. The main aim of confrontation as a training method is to increase the trainee's choices; not necessarily to stop doing something, because this then removes a choice, but rather to realise that there are *additional* choices.

It is also important to realise that the trainer can confront explicitly or implicitly. Some examples of explicit confrontation are where the trainer gives feedback (e.g. 'I noticed that when you said "yes" you shook your head'), questions (e.g. 'Why did you choose to set up the interview in that way?'), or invites other course members to give an individual feedback. Examples of implicit confrontation could be the course itself ('Why did they choose me?'); modelling from the trainer: e.g. his being 'open'; or even the furniture arrangements in the training room: e.g. a lot of courses in the 'feelings' area are designed to take place without desks being used and this can be the first 'shock'.

At a broader level the confrontation may exist in terms of the assumptions the trainer makes about responsibility for learning. As was explained in the Introduction the more the training is designed to be based on feelings, then the greater the reliance on the trainee being proactive and taking the initiative, for example in giving and receiving feedback. The more the training is based on thinking, then the more the trainer will take responsibility for providing learning, although obviously he cannot learn on behalf of others. In this latter instance the trainees will probably feel less confronted because the trainer is likely to be living up to their hopes and expectations.

A valuable concept drawn from transactional analysis is the importance of 'permission', 'protection' and 'potency'.[2] These are directly related to confrontation. 'Permission' means saying, explicitly or implicitly, that it is alright to try something different and that it is possible to replace an old and obsolete rule about relationships with one that is more satisfying; 'protection' means the trainer saying that he will act as a 'back-stop' and make sure that the trainee does not physically or emotionally do harm to himself or others; and 'potency' means acting in a congruent, credible and genuine way. We suggest that the trainer would benefit from regularly reflecting on his relationship with group and considering the permission he is giving, the protection he is offering and the potency he is demonstrating. Clearly the trainer needs to be aware of the positive and negative recognition he is giving and how it is being accepted, i.e. the behaviour and attitudes he is encouraging or discouraging, whether by smiles, frowns, words of praise or adverse criticism.

Frequently the aim of confrontation is to help the person be more specific, since one of the ways in which people stop themselves from exercising new choices is by holding onto vague generalisations as rules for relationships. Here are some examples, with some possible trainer responses given in brackets: 'Everybody knows that you have to be firm with young people these days.' ('Everybody?' or 'What do you mean by "firm"?') – 'Sometimes I feel really scared about getting close to people.' ('At what times?' or 'What does "getting close" mean for you?' or 'When was the last time this happened?'). Teasing is also a means of confrontation. It can be powerful if it works but does need careful handling. When encouraged to be specific then the person often finds that his problem is more manageable. Usually, some element of positive thinking also emerges, which can be built on. A person who starts by saying that he can *never* get anything right frequently remembers, when questioned, some past successes.

One of the paradoxes in confrontation is that if the trainer over-confronts and tries to corner the group then he can corner himself. An example of this occurred when one of us tried to set up an exercise which would 'force' the group to look at its own process and relationships. The group's resistance to this was so great, and yet not directly expressed, that it was difficult to retrieve the situation which had degenerated into win/lose: 'If we do what the trainer wants we have lost.' If there is the slightest doubt about the wisdom of a confrontation then the trainer should offer an escape route, since by doing that he will be giving himself one at the same time. The case cited above would have been better handled if the group had been given more choices about what they could do. The irony is that they would quite probably have been willing to look at their process if they had not been 'forced' to!

If there has been some dramatic confrontation, frequently involving a high degree of openness and the expression of emotions, then the group will generally need some time to wind out of it, for example by having a general discussion about nothing special.

In confrontation the time dimension is important, 'here and now' confrontations normally being more challenging and risky than 'there and then' ones (see Chapter 6). A particular example of where 'here and now' confrontation can be valuable is where the content of a course member's question reflects his process. This happens quite often e.g. 'How do you handle somebody who does not have much self-confidence?' – the question being asked in a self-effacing and unconfident way. It parallels the story of the patient who goes to the doctor and says 'I've got this friend . . .'.

The importance of confrontation in IST cannot be underestimated since it is a sound basis for learning (see also Appendix 2). People frequently reduce their effectiveness in their relationships by clinging to old and obsolete images of themselves ('I am the sort of person who always loses'). A challenge to these images can be painful because they are long-established and provide the comfort of predictability. Yet underneath it all there is a real possibility of a better and more fulfilling life and the trainer would do well to retain confrontation as an option. Confrontation, or any other intervention, should not mean the trainer scoring points or seeking to gain a one-up position. If he does and becomes concerned with self-glorification then he will lose touch with his own process and the process of the group. He will no longer be credible.

Constructive and destructive discomfort

The authors do not subscribe to the view that learning needs to be a painful activity. Nevertheless, the process of 'unfreezing' is likely to be accompanied by some discomfort as the course member re-evaluates his existing attitudes and behaviour, decides whether to change or not, and finalises any decisions he may take. In all this the trainer, if he is to be effective, has to help the course member through problems and achieve a 'reasonable' degree of equilibrium by the end of the course so that any discomfort is felt to have been constructive. It is important that any training leaves the participant with a way forward and being clear on his next step(s). It can happen that the training raises problems and generates experiences which are not resolved sufficiently and then the course member suffers from destructive discomfort. This means that he is in a 'no-man's land' where the past seems unsatisfactory and the future seems uncertain and forbidding. In other words, he is not clear what makes sense for him, and feels inadequate in dealing with this uncertainty. The trainer needs to be on the look-out for where this has occurred. It is to be distinguished from those situations where the course member leaves with food for thought and is clearly going to be able to resolve the matter to his own satisfaction sooner or later. The 'no-man's land' is an impasse where the person seems to be lacking the internal or external resources to deal with the problem he faces. For example, somebody may have received feedback that he is difficult to get close to and isolates himself. This feedback may disturb him quite considerably, especially if he has never had similar feedback before. The trainer should make sure that the person has the time, either in the group or outside it, to 'work through' the feedback. This process of 'working through' does not necessarily mean having a complete understanding and it certainly does not necessarily mean incorporating the feedback as 'true'. What it does mean is making decisions (probably tentative) about its validity and the action which may or may not be taken.

The discomfort associated with IST can be due to its impact extending into the home. That is, while examining relationships skills to do with work, the trainee may begin reflecting on his relationships at home. This happens more frequently as the training moves further into the 'feelings' area. Some theories, e.g. transactional analysis, deliberately stimulate the exploration of a wide range of relationships, not just those at work. It may also be that the participant is attending at a time when he/she is facing up to some deep personal problems e.g. mid-life crisis, marriage breakdown.

One cannot always easily identify the person who is having difficulty in coping with their actual or potential learning. If somebody has been the focus of attention and feedback, then the trainer, probably as a matter of routine, will be watching him closely. However, sometimes people not directly and obviously involved in an exercise or exchange can be disturbed by it. When watching the person receiving feedback about isolation they may be thinking, 'I'm like that too . . .' or 'I'm really angry that they should say that to her . . .'. Sometimes the simple act of the trainer presenting some ideas and theories (e.g. the notion 'scripts' in transactional analysis) can generate considerable introspection with which the trainee may have difficulty in coping.

There is no easy solution to this problem, but there are several things that can reduce the chances of its happening. The first is to generate an atmosphere where people feel free to express what is troubling them. Indeed this may be a vital part of the design and content of the course. The trainer might want to do some 'modelling' and give his opinions and feelings about how the course is going. Secondly, the trainer can make the offer of individual discussion and counselling for anybody who feels they want it, stressing, where appropriate, that significant personal change may have an impact on domestic relationships. Thirdly, the informal contacts which are established between trainers and course members outside the training room are a good source of information about how the course is being received. Also it might be worth experimenting with small group review sessions where the course splits into groups to review how the course is going, whether training needs are being met and what needs to be done next. It is frequently helpful if the trainer is willing and able to explain the rationale of the course and his own behaviour. This is particularly important in the early stages of a course which is operating at the 'feelings' end of the training spectrum. For example, if the trainer is pushing responsibility back to the group to decide what it wants to do during the week then it probably helps if he explains why that is his strategy. In the 'doing' approach also there is usually a need for the trainer to explain his training philosophy, especially if he is asking the group to undertake apparently meaningless tasks such as assembling toy brick towers.

Another possible intervention is to explain different types of feedback and ways of handling them. This could then be used subsequently for a 'here and now' examination of somebody's reaction to feedback. One of the crucial aspects of relating to people is the ability to distinguish between information and adverse criticism. On many occasions a course member's discomfort is more to do with his own internal processes and imagination than external reality. Once he becomes aware of this then, almost by definition, his discomfort begins to decrease. The trainer can develop his intuition and use it to identify those who are in distress and to discover appropriate interventions. The question of constructive and destructive discomfort can be usefully reviewed and summarised by reference to Kolb's learning cycle.[3] He states that there are four stages in the learning process. The first is concerned with direct experience, e.g. participation in a practical activity (tower building). This experience is then followed by a review and analysis of the activity where people have the opportunity to think about what has happened (e.g. 'I remember feeling excluded'). This stage of thinking then leads to generalisations in which people decide what makes sense for them (e.g. 'I think that next time I'm in a work group I'll make sure of a contribution and I'll do this by . . .'). The fourth stage is where the people test out their learning and generalisations in a new practical activity.

Ideally the trainees will go round this cycle many times during a training programme. In terms of managing possible discomfort it is probably best if the trainer does what he can to ensure that his group has gone through stage three as they prepare to leave the course. The new situation in which they can test out their ideas will then be at work. If the group is left 'hanging' at an earlier stage in the cycle then there may well be a considerable amount of unfinished business , e.g. people having been through an experience that generated many feelings and yet uncertain about their own performance or its implications. Ideally, people should leave the course ready to try out some new things and in a position to provide much of their own impetus for getting themselves round the learning cycle, i.e. energy without agitation.

Individual and group focus

When working at the 'feelings' end of the training spectrum the trainer can increase his effectiveness if he is fully aware of how he is dividing his time between looking at individual and group processes. Sometimes trainers will spend the vast majority of their time working at the level of individual process (sometimes known as the 'hot seat' technique). This has the advantage of helping the individual to make considerable progress, but it can mean that not enough time is spent examining the group as a whole – each person takes it in turn to be 'done', but it is a lonely process if the members of the group do not take any responsibility for looking after each other. The focus on individual process can become too intense and the individual may be under too much pressure. A rigid pattern of individual work may not so much lead to the exclusion of the rest of the group who are not 'working', but may generate a lot of group pressure to 'say what you're really feeling'; 'the rest of us have been open and feel much better for it'. Once the group, quite possibly following the lead of the trainer, has developed a set of norms (i.e. the price of membership) then they can be used to exert a lot of pressure on individuals.

Trainers can, if they choose, focus largely on the group process (e.g. Tavistock).[4] This means that attention is paid much more to the effectiveness of the total group rather than to specific relations between its members. Yet the learning can lack penetration because it is not so readily transferable. The individual is the most important common denominator between the training environment and work, therefore the transfer of learning is more likely to take place where the course member has been focused on himself, rather than on himself as part of a group phenomenon. There is, therefore, a lot to be said for the 'hot seat' technique, assuming it does not get too hot! It can stimulate a considerable amount of deep personal learning which the individual can take away and use. Where the emphasis is on the group then certainly individuals learn about themselves, but it is likely to be in relation to that particular group and parallels between the course and work may not be explicit. If the trainer chooses to work on individual process it may accentuate his position of power within the group and he will need to beware of compliance masquerading as learning, i.e. where the course member is concerned to please the trainer rather than doing or saying what makes sense for him. The rest of the group will usually be quick to notice this and should therefore be encouraged to give frequent feedback.

Relationships with colleagues

Reference has already been made to the relationship between the trainer and his colleagues in terms of giving and receiving feedback, and sharing the work load. Additionally, when two or more trainers are working on a course their responsibilities to each other, and to the course members, are to ensure that they are working in the same direction. This obviously should not, and could not, mean that they handle the group in exactly the same way, but it does mean that their interventions and approach should be broadly similar. As an example, it would almost certainly be disruptive and destructive if on the same course one trainer worked largely with theories and concepts while his colleague generally operated with feelings. In the same way, there could be difficulties if two trainers were working at the level of feelings, but one was making group-focused interventions and the other individual-focused interventions. A likely problem stemming from this would be where a group member was making progress on an individual issue in one session and then was not followed up because a group-focused trainer took over the following session.

However different styles can combine to produce a powerful combination with one trainer, for example, taking the lead in support and the other providing confrontation. Nevertheless there may be some 'good-Daddy' 'bad-Daddy' stereotyping following from this, particularly if it is highly contrived with each trainer becoming locked into a role which does not match his personal inclinations.

Where trainers are running a session jointly it helps if they can develop a 'sixth sense' for the direction in which each of them is moving. This is particularly important where the training is 'unstructured' and it is not possible to agree in detail beforehand the approach or style to be adopted throughout each session.

It is also useful, and perhaps a necessity, for trainers to discuss before the course or session the options they have in managing the group and to identify the factors that could arise and require a change of approach. Equally they should meet to keep each other up to date in the developments: a day in IST is a long time! The trainers need to have common concepts and frameworks which they can use to communicate with each other and possibly with the group. This does not mean that the trainers should always agree with each other in front of the group. It can be a great help if the group is aware that the trainers do not see the same things in the same way: people on IST courses can have problems because of the scarcity of 'right' answers, and there can be learning for them if they see the trainers disagreeing and yet accepting the validity of each other's point. (Of course, it is a matter of degree and the sight of trainers having long and intense arguments in front of the group could be highly entertaining but not very constructive.)

However, trainers should not work on problems about their own relationships in front of the group. As an example, questions of trust and competitiveness between the trainers should be worked on outside the group for the simple reason that they are being paid to spend time on other people's problems, not their own. It could also mean that the trainers become too closely indentified as members of the group and the difficulties of over-involvement, referred to above, are likely to occur. Additionally for this reason the trainer should not work directly on his own personal problems and issues in front of the group (e.g. 'I'm afraid I'm not going to be able to cope'). It can be a dramatic and unproductive diversion since the group is likely to have plenty to deal with already without the authority figure identifying so closely with them. This is a fine distinction and it is being made rather more on pragmatic than moral grounds.

It is worth considering how far the values and objectives of the course should reflect the relationship between the trainers. It is a matter of the trainer practising what he preaches and 'modelling' the values that he is articulating. There would seem, for example, to be little point in the trainer explicitly or implicitly stressing the benefits of openness (assuming that to be a tenet of the course) if he refuses to be open with his training colleagues. The greater the 'feelings' element within the training, the greater the need for the co-trainers to work on their own relationship. Failure to do so could mean that they spend time, wittingly or not, in front of the group trying to score points over each other and therefore divert the group's energy away from examining its own process.

Manipulation

A common complaint or concern about IST is that it is, or may be, manipulative. This can mean many things, including 'putting people down' and/or getting them to do things which are sometimes not in their best interests. Certainly this is possible, because interpersonal skills are tools, neither inherently moral nor immoral, but capable of being used in a moral or immoral way. If the IS trainer uses his skills in a moral way then it is probable that the trainees will acquire some of his moral values, but there can be no guarantees, it has to be a matter of personal choice and belief. A work study trainer may face a similar moral dilemma since those he is training *may* eventually be responsible for putting people out of work ('rationalisation') or making their job much less interesting. It is unlikely that IST can 'make' people manipulative. They are likely to be that way inclined anyway. At the very worst the skills acquired through IST add to their armoury.

Also in discussion about manipulation, it is sometimes said that people are being taught not to be themselves, but to put on an act or be 'unnatural'. This is true to the extent that the process of acquiring new skills can be difficult and feel awkward. It is something that usually has to be worked on, but it does not make it either more or less natural, it just makes it different. We would rather deal with somebody who was 'unnaturally' caring than 'naturally' boorish! A large part of how people relate to one another is what they have learnt over the years, and IST is simply another step along that road.

The aim of IST is not to make everybody cool and calculating, but rather to add to their choices about how they are in the world. So long as this is its major direction then people's options, *including* the option to be cool and calculating, will be increased and it cannot be said that any manipulation is taking place.

Conflict

In most groups, especially those being formed for the first time, some degree of conflict is inevitable as people start testing out limits and establishing 'norms'. The conflict may manifest itself in direct or indirect ways, for example challenging the authority of the trainer, coming in late, withdrawal. The word conflict is being used here to refer not to 'genuine' differences of opinion, but to actions intended to prove points about relationships.

It can be seen from what has been said earlier in this chapter that a willingness to face up to and engage in conflict is an important skill for the IS trainer. It is one of the bases of confrontation, challenging trainees to re-examine their values and attitudes, and has a particularly useful role to play in the 'feelings' approaches. Consequently where it occurs in 'unstructured' training it should be seen as a legitimate subject matter for exploration. This could be done in a variety of ways including the presentation of solid evidence ('I notice that whenever I say anything you disagree') or sharing feelings ('I feel uncomfortable about what's happening in this group and I can't clearly identify what that is'). Under these circumstances the trainer's credibility may well rest on his dealing openly with conflict even at the cost of being accused of encouraging it.

In the 'thinking' and 'doing' approaches conflict is not so clearly something that has to be faced up to openly. For example, if the training has been designed on structured theory sessions and exercises then it would probably be unwise for the trainer to focus directly on the conflict he sees. He would be making a dramatic switch into the here and now and might well be breaking his contract. Obviously there are exceptions, one instance being where there is a rebellion or direct challenge ('I think you're talking a load of rubbish', or 'I don't want to be here').

A rough generalisation is that the more structured the training the less likely that conflict will 'get in the way'. This means that the conflict will not be obtrusive, although it may be evident. In structured training the trainer normally accentuates his position of authority and will usually be met with a fair degree of deference. The trainer can also take a fatherly role in smoothing over conflict between course members, for example, putting them into separate groups.

The IS trainer, whatever his style and philosophy, will need to manage conflict. This management may mean containing or controlling it, or meeting it head on, or even, as part of a tactical withdrawal, avoiding it. Here, a knowledge of group development is valuable, allied to a self knowledge so that the trainer can know how he responds to conflict and establish more clearly the boundary between his process and the process of the group.

Training and therapy

In Chapter 1 brief mention was made of the relationship between training and therapy and this is now explored in more depth. The first point is whether a valid distinction can really be made at all. John Heron's view[5] is that no differentiation can be made since they are both simply part of an educational process. In terms of a definition we would support this view. Therapy can be seen as assisting in a healing process and this process can take place in almost any IST activity. For example, a manager who had tended always to think the worst of himself might go on a strongly techniques-based interviewing course, receive plenty of positive feedback and develop greatly in his self-confidence. He could then build on this to make dramatic changes at work and even at home. It is not stretching a point to say that his experience was part of a healing and therapeutic event. Indeed, many IS trainers would regard a growth in self-confidence as an important and probably essential part of their aims for the participants.

Some of the recent developments in psychotherapy have grown out of the humanistic psychology movement and do not entertain the medical model of man, i.e. the notion of man actually or potentially a sick animal needing to be cured. Consequently, the dimension becomes one of growth and education rather than training for the normal and therapy for the abnormal.

Nevertheless, there is clearly a concern about trainers somehow exceeding their terms of reference. At one level the simple and common question, 'Isn't all this amateur psychology dangerous?', can be a reflection of this. Certainly one of the issues here is competence. If the trainer goes beyond his ability to cope then he may leave the trainee with a considerable amount of 'unfinished business', i.e. feeling disturbed, upset and possibly suffering marked distress.[6] As the trainer moves across the spectrum and becomes more involved in the 'feelings' approach, then he is likely to require skills which are not part of most training for trainers' programmes. It is therefore when the trainer seeks to explore feelings in depth and 'fails' that he is likely to be accused of engaging in therapy. ('Failure' can be regarded as leaving somebody in 'no-man's land' at the end of the training programme – see above.) Yet it is 'success' or 'failure' rather than the trainer's behaviour itself which leads to the designation of training or therapy. Taking due account of the aims and agreements associated with the training the authors suggest that it does not matter whether the trainer is perceived to be engaged in training or therapy as long as he is 'successful'; or, more accurately, does not fail, i.e. recognises the warning signs in himself and others and thereby stays within the limits of his competence, deciding not to probe further. The basis of this ability has already been described in the section on self-awareness. Additionally, the trainer will need to have some basic grounding in psychodiagnosis[7] in order to identify psychotics and others whom he is not competent or trained to handle. Certainly this is not easy, but what is being described is not detailed clinical analysis but a very rough and ready guide. Psychotics will be few and far between on most IST courses, but it is useful to have an agreed policy for handling them, considering particularly whether the person should be guided to other sources of help.

Since 'feelings' based training can be seen as going against the rules of Western culture we would strongly recommend preliminary contact with the participants, clearly outlining the training method and ensuring as much as possible that attendance is voluntary. Obviously this is not fail-safe but it does help sift out those who would have found it difficult to benefit from such training, e.g. being compelled to attend, totally rejecting the course method. (See also Chapter 2.)

Sometimes training is seen to have moved into the realm of therapy if somebody in the group cries. The fact of this happening may well be therapeutic and, in our experience, it rarely means that something has gone wrong. On the contrary, crying is usually a healthy activity, if sometimes uncomfortable for the observers, and usually leads to a clearer understanding of self, (see Catharsis, below). Any trainer working in the 'feelings' area is bound regularly, though not frequently, to experience people crying; this is due to the simple fact that the training method encourages the expression and exploration of feelings and that generally in Western (or at least in Anglo-Saxon) culture there are a lot of pressures not to do this. Consequently, some managers coming on 'feelings' courses have been holding on to their eotions for many years ('Big boys don't cry'), and their release can be momentous.

It will be evident from what has been said so far that we believe no clear distinction can be made between training and therapy. However, there are certain interventions which are more likely to be carried out by a psychotherapist and as such would be out of the ordinary on an IST course, i.e. firstly, the active encouragement of catharsis. This is very different from the offering of support when somebody cries. Secondly, regression work, i.e. taking somebody back in time and helping them re-enact the past. More general, and thus less clearly defined, guidelines are that the trainer should be more concerned with the trainee's work, rather than domestic, relationships. Also, for the majority of the training the trainee should be invited, explicitly or implicitly, to keep his thinking and problem-solving processes engaged. One way for the trainer to encourage this is by regularly explaining the reason why he is making or not making, certain interventions.

Catharsis

Catharsis is a healthy process, a purging of distress, a way of finishing unfinished business. It can consist of the discharge of any one of a whole range of feelings including fear, anger, guilt and grief. In the context of management training these feelings may have been accumulating in a number of ways — coping with a 'difficult' boss, doing a boring job, overwork, or the legacy of an unhappy childhood. The person may have been able to do a 'holding operation' e.g. playing sport or being with his family but these would not resolve the underlying problems which would continue to re-emerge and finally provide the need for catharsis.

Catharsis does not mean a complete loss of control, but a lessening of controls sufficient to allow the expression of feelings previously suppressed. Crying would be a typical manifestation of catharsis, others would include laughter and the expression of anger. What distinguishes catharsis from an unthinking and unfocused emotional explosion is the insight and sense of relief which follow. The internal process which provides the need for catharsis is energy being directed towards holding down a particular feeling. This holding down consists of and leads to a shutting down of internal awareness ('I'm not really angry') and external awareness. The latter happens because the person is preoccupied with self and is 'wasting' energy which could be used to make or enhance contact and relationships with others. The person is likely to have a number of conscious or unconscious ways of justifying the suppression of the particular feeling:— obsolete rules ('I must never get angry') and old memories ('I remember when I got angry once and the person refused to speak to me ever again').

In catharsis the energy which was directed inwardly, to 'hold on', is directed outwardly. Thus the insight comes from seeing and accepting the feeling for what it is — a natural human response to current or past events. What is achieved is an increase in personal power, a realisation that certain feelings can be expressed without disastrous consequences and, by definition, an increase in options. The energy which is now turned outward rather than inward can be used almost immediately to reflect on the catharsis which has just taken place and to understand it. It can be understood now because the interference or 'noise' of repression has been removed. The trainer and others can help in this process of understanding in ways already referred to above (see section on constructive and destructive discomfort).

On a management training course a number of factors could lead a person to the point of catharsis:

1 A course design which 'legitimises' the expression of feelings.
2 A supportive atmosphere in the group.
3 Another group member who represents or resembles the person's unresolved issues (e.g. is like his mother, or his difficult boss).
4 The training may come just at a time when the person has 'reached the end of his tether', and realises, at some level or other, the basic ineffectiveness of his holding operations.
5 The trainer may have encouraged catharsis by, for example, asking the person to repeat or exaggerate a particular phrase which seems crucial ('I'll never get what I want'), or through physical touch. This is not to say that every time these events occur catharsis is being encouraged.

Thus, the expression of deep emotions is a 'normal' though not frequent occurrence on a number of IST programmes. It usually leads to a feeling of closeness as it is one of the most dramatic signs of high trust within the group.

Saying goodbye

As the training draws to a close there are several important items which need to be covered regardless of whether the training has been largely 'thinking', 'doing' or 'feeling' in its approach. Firstly an offer of continuing support from the trainer. This can be backed up by book references, and the addresses of places where further learning and development can take place. An offer of individual counselling is normally important so that the trainee feels encouraged to renew contact should some unfinished business relating to the course re-emerge at a later stage. It may be necessary to stress confidentiality.

Secondly, the trainer needs to encourage the group members to 'take it easy' when they get back to work, i.e. not to evangelise and attempt the introduction of dramatic changes. These would normally only succeed in antagonising many people. A small step at a time is usually a good motto as the items of learning begin, hopefully, to slot into place. The trainer also needs to beware of setting somebody up to have a fight when they get back to work. Thirdly, there is the activity of saying goodbye itself; closing the relationship whether temporarily or permanently, and expressing whatever feelings or appreciations seem to be appropriate. Saying goodbye is a way of finishing business and being ready to say hello to the next relationship.

Conclusion

By definition ethical and professional decisions in IST will be highly individual and personal. Ultimately each trainer has to construct his own moral code, deciding what makes sense for him. This is the only way of achieving congruence, a sense of internal coherence which reveals itself externally as consistency. There are a number of fundamental decisions to be made: e.g. Is the trainer to be an agent of social control or social change?; Is he to seek organisational evolution or revolution? What matters is not so much what decision is made, but that a decision is made at all. The trainer, not just in IST, should not be a technician deciding in a clinical way what sort of adjustments may be necessary for the organisation to function more effectively. At a more fundamental level there is the matter of the type of society he wants to live in.

References

(1) For a fuller explanation see D. Schwartz, 'Similarities and Differences of Internal and External Consultants', *Journal of European Training*, vol. 4, no. 5, 1975.
(2) M. James (Ed.), *Techniques in Transactional Analysis*, Addison-Wesley, Reading, Massachusetts, 1977, p. 39.
(3) D.A. Kolb, I.M. Rubin and J.M. McIntyre, *Organisational Psychology: An Experiential Approach*, Prentice-Hall, Englewood Cliffs, N.J., 1974, p. 21.
(4) R. de Board, *The Psychoanalysis of Organisations*, Tavistock Institute, London, 1978, p. 78.
(5) J. Heron, *Dimensions in Facilitator Style*, University of Surrey, Guildford, 1977, p. 2.
(6) See also S. Kingsbury, 'Dilemmas for the Trainer' in *Modern Theory and Method in Group Training*, W.G. Dyer (Ed.), Van Nostrand Reinhold Co., New York, 1972.
(7) A brief overview is contained in M. Brown, *Psychodiagnosis in Brief*, Huron Valley Institute, Michigan, 1977.

4 Body language

A surprisingly large proportion of communication (perhaps 70 per cent) between people takes place in the form of body language; yet this area rarely receives as much attention as its importance might lead one to expect. Body language is an exciting, enjoyable and fruitful area of study for the IS trainer. Some insight into non-verbal communication provides the opportunity for understanding oneself, for generating feedback and for managing groups. Observing and making sense of body language are interpersonal skills which give the trainer an additional range and depth to his work.

Making sense of non-verbal signals is frequently a part of the trainer's normal repertoire of skills. He will often respond to other's messages and get a sense of what a group feels or wants without the need for words. This chapter is designed to help the trainer to build on what he is already doing, to increase his awareness of body language and also to offer some ways of using this awareness to support his training work.

The first section of the chapter presents a definition of body language and its elements, and goes on to explore the possibilities and limitations that the observation of people can provide. The second section sets out a framework for the trainer to enable him to choose how to handle what can sometimes be a sensitive issue. Photographs provide analysis and the basis for discussion of the choices and consequences of trainer interventions.

A final section explores the use of body language as a means of self-development and personal understanding. This approach may be valuable to the trainer for himself or as a means of facilitating the development of others.

Bodily communication begins as soon as two (or more) people are aware of each other's presence. Of course only occasional parts of the communication are deliberate messages in the sense, for example, that turning one's back on someone may be intended to convey a meaning. Nevertheless most actions carry a message which is often unclear to others and yet is a part of the communication process. Almost all of these interactions happen at great speed and simultaneously at a number of different levels. Table 4.1 sets out the channels of non-verbal communication and suggests the great variety of dimensions and qualities involved.

Table 4.1 The elements of body language

Physical appearance
colour, sex, age, height, weight, shape, build, hairiness, cleanliness, hairstyle, smell/scent, clothing (colour, quality, fashion/style, neatness)

Physical position
distance (near, far) depends on such things as: sex – status – activity and circumstances

Physical posture
slouched – straight
rigid – flexible
'open' – 'closed'
turned towards – turned away

Movements
Whole body (walking, running, dancing, swimming)
Part body (arms, hands, fingers, legs, feet, toes, head, face, eyebrows, eyes, nose, cheeks, jaw, mouth, tongue, chin.)

Necessary functions (breathing, blinking, swallowing)

Sounds and voice tones (loudness, sharpness, softness, rate of speech, rhythm of speech, intonation, accent.)

Other activities
blushing, looking, smiling, crying, laughing, hand-shaking, touching, kissing, smoking, nail-biting, scratching, tapping, picking, stroking.

All the channels listed in Table 4.1 carry messages to anyone who looks for them. Signals vary in their direction, some being more constant and sustained, while others are momentary.

It is useful to think of all aspects of non-verbal communication as providing information about the sender and work from the assumption that much of this information is deliberate. Most people choose their own hair-style, long or short, neat or untidy, sometimes even curly or straight! Clothes are also carefully selected; people consistently choose particular colours and styles. These choices may not seem the result of a premeditated attempt to project an image, yet in effect the choices are rooted in the personality and attitude of the individual.[1] Taking little trouble over appearance in itself is a message to the rest of the world, just as a carefully prepared image is. Similarly, the habitual gestures and postures that form the repertoire of an individual, while not necessarily consciously selected, reflect and represent attitudes and personality. These repeating patterns also play their part in forming the shapes and features of a person leaving some permanent evidence. Examples of this would be the highly-developed jaw muscles of someone who clenches his teeth frequently or the fairly permanent stoop of someone who lets his arms and shoulders hang. Two of the most common examples are the stiff military bearing of a lifetime military man and the laugh lines on the 'happy face'.

It would be marvellous if someone could produce a 'dictionary' in which each of the features was given a definite meaning so that we could easily translate body language. In reality there are almost infinite variations in humanity and corresponding variations in their means of expression. Interpreting body language is therefore best approached from a position of exploring possibilities and testing ideas rather than labelling gestures or expressions with a specific meaning. There are some body language messages that have a clear and definite meaning within the culture of North West Europe and North America.[2] Some examples of gestures with clear meanings are:

Shaking fist = 'I am angry with you'
Wagging finger (to children) = 'You are not supposed to be doing that!'
'Two fingers' = 'Go Away!'
Raised eyebrows and shrugged shoulders = 'I don't know'
Tapping feet = 'I'm feeling frustrated or impatient'.

Even with these, however, the context and individual process are likely to help the receiver to confirm or modify the initial interpretation.

In pointing out the complexities and uncertainties of body language it is not our intention to discourage the reader from exploring and understanding body language. It is true that there are no simple formulae for precise interpretation but there is much to be gained from awareness and observation. Simply by paying attention to

physical expression the observer has available much more information which can enhance the quality of the communication process.

Often a trainer will already do this effectively. For example when
he notices course members frowning and glancing at each other, he
may assume that they have not fully understood what he has been
saying. Having become aware he has a number of choices: to check
this assumption with the group by asking if something is unclear; to
go over the point again; to provide an illustration; to tell the group
not to worry if they do not understand. These are just a few examples
of the many choices open to the trainer.

Similarly the trainer may be able to make some guesses about how
involved different individuals are in the learning process. Having
made the guess (based perhaps on such observations as the proportion of time the individual gazes out of the window) he can check it in
a number of ways and then choose what if anything he wants to do as
a result.

One of the complications in understanding body language is that
there is so much information available at any one time. This fact can
be better understood by reviewing a CCTV recording, say of the first
three minutes of an interview. By watching the same three minutes a
number of times, it is possible to focus at different levels (e.g. seating
positions, eye contact, facial expressions). Each piece of behaviour
carries a message and much of it is normally lost on the participants,
who are initially concentrating on the content of the words spoken.
The glances, movements, smiles, voice qualities, postures, breathing
patterns happen very quickly and are followed by more data in the
next instant. Even more perplexing is that much of this is not directly
relevant to the content and meaning of the verbal communication.
Nor have the problems of identifying the meaning of signals ended;
because many messages have no clear meaning (e.g. crossing legs or
resting one's cheek in one's hand); because one person may be sending two conflicting signals at the same time (frowning and smiling).
Some messages are confusing (gazing into the distance). Other problems concerned with identifying meaning arise when messages are
ignored because they are taken to be 'mistakes' or unintentional or
meaningless or hostile. A final barrier to understanding is created by
social convention which teaches us that it is not polite to take
obvious and explicit interest in what someone does with their body
and why.

As a result most body language remains outside awareness. Rather
like driving a car, it all seems to happen without the need for thought
and only becomes the focus of attention when something unusual or
striking occurs. Most trainers recognise that non-verbal conversa-
tions are often happening alongside or instead of the verbal ones.
Some of the messages 'go straight in' and are understood without the

awareness that this is happening. Here the message is sent, received
and creates a response without either party giving it their conscious
attention. An example of this are the signals which prevent people
from bumping into each other while walking in a crowded street or
the breathing signals associated with starting and stopping talking
during a discussion.

While it may not be possible at first to understand very many of the
messages, it is possible to bring most of them into the conscious
mind. There is nothing magical or inherently obscure about body
language. The ability to recognise that there is more to people than
the meaning of what they say is a skill, and, as with other skills,
improvement comes with practice.

A fascinating aspect of learning by discovering one's own body
language and even encouraging others to provide feedback about it is
the idea of 'leaks'. A leak happens when some meaning or feeling is
transmitted clearly but unintentionally. Obvious examples are the
change in eye-contact during a deliberate attempt at lying or decep-
tion, impatience which leaks out through twitchy fingers and tapping feet and the hurt glance of someone who would rather not show
his tender feelings.

People leak most through their eyes, legs and feet, fingers and
hands. These are the parts of the body which in some circumstances
seem to take on a life of their own and refuse to comply with a need
for self-control. The eyes seem indeed to be 'the windows of the soul',
while fingers tremble without regard to the need to appear calm.
Similarly feet can dance with impatience or excitement at most
inopportune times. Of course the reality is that the leaks are no more
and no less part of the real person than other aspects of non-verbal
communication. Often the leaks are the key element in a relationship
keeping it alive and open, and far from damaging a person's image
the leak creates understanding. Hence the loyalty to a gruff and
apparently uncompromising boss (who dare not show how much he
cares) and the consideration offered to a colleague who wants to hide
his disappointment at failing to gain promotion.

In order to develop high levels of interpersonal skill, it is invaluable to be able to recognise and respond sensitively to one's own and
others' leaks. This will often mean respecting the other person's need
to conceal the real feelings or message and yet at some implicit level
offering an appropriate response.

For example, it is quite common in the early stages of any course
('thinking', 'doing' or 'feeling' based) for individuals to feel embar-
rassed about speaking in front of the group. This embarrassment
probably shows itself through such leaks as a reddening of the cheeks
and the frequent breaking, or even complete avoidance, of eye contact. If the trainer were to encourage the person to focus on his

embarrassment it would probably just lead to a dramatic increase in discomfort. An implicit handling of the leaks in this example would involve the trainer in smiling, nodding in encouragement and taking care not to put the other person down.

In 'thinking'/'doing' based programmes the trainer would probably want to exercise additional choices. As an illustration, a participant might come back into the group having completed a closed circuit television interview and 'leak' the fact that he feels very disappointed about his performance e.g. downcast eyes which directly contrast with his attempts to laugh off the whole affair: 'My first step towards stardom!'.

An implicit approach to these leaks would be for the trainer simply to ask the person what he liked about his performance. If the trainer were to deal with the leaks explicitly then he might openly share his concerns, 'I've got a hunch that you feel pretty bad about your performance'.

In courses which are firmly based in the feelings area then leaks are the legitimate subject matter of the programme and will more often be handled explicitly than implicitly. Somebody whose foot is tapping might be faced with the comment, 'I notice that your foot is tapping, what is your message to the group?'. Somebody whose eyes are glistening with sadness could be encouraged to express their feelings or examine their process which seems to require that they control their feelings.

Leaks are an invaluable source of information about individuals and groups and the trainer reaps a rich reward if he trains himself to be aware of them and exercise a wide and flexible range of choices in dealing with them.

Body language for the trainer

Those who have developed their observation skills to the point where both obvious and fleeting language becomes noticeable are often tempted to make pronouncements about the 'true' state of mind or feeling of their subject. In some cases as has been illustrated, non-verbal signals do have fairly clear meanings and these are interpreted as a matter of routine in perceiving others. Body language in these circumstances can be a kind of social dance in which the steps are known and the rhythms familiar. In a particular culture some non-verbal exchanges are expected or required so that their absence, deliberate or otherwise is considered insulting or rejecting. For example, on meeting a business acquaintance from another organisation it is expected that there will be a handshake, that each will meet each other's gaze and probably return the welcoming smile all within an acceptable physical distance.

Realising the difference between what can be seen (i.e. observation) and what is interpretation is crucial to developing interpersonal skills. In the course of normal dialogue, most people believe they can actually see things like anger, frustration, disappointment, confusion and *know* how others are feeling. To say that these are just assumptions based on inadequate observation is not just making a pedantic distinction between observation and interpretation. The fact is that one person simply does not *know* what is happening inside another nor can they *know* how or what the other feels just by looking at them.[3]

A good way of testing this process is by conducting an exercise in which two people observe each other and take it in turns to describe what they see and then to say what they imagine is happening inside the other person. For example, 'I see you are frowning . . . I imagine you are puzzled', 'I see your eyes narrowing . . . 'I imagine you are concentrating', 'I see you fold your arms . . . I imagine you are impatient'. This exercise usually demonstrates quite clearly that sometimes the interpretation is 'right' and sometimes it is 'wrong'. Interpretations can sometimes say a lot more about the interpreter than the interpreted.

Much communication is based on guesswork about body language and usually a precise understanding is not needed. It is simply necessary that responses are appropriate. Mistaken assumptions which are used as facts can create a fertile environment for misunderstanding and futile conflict. Examples are where a frown is taken for disapproval where it might be an indicator of confusion; a break in eye contact might be taken as an indicator of thinking when it reflects hurt; a sigh is seen as boredom when in fact it is self-doubt. For the trainer this understanding is important since much of the feedback that comes from trainees is likely to be non-verbal. This feedback will concern the level of interest, comprehension, discomfort and impatience that the trainees feel in response to the trainer, fellow trainees and the events of the course. In the context of IST either failing altogether to notice the feedback that is being transmitted through body language, or noticing but misinterpreting it and continuing under a false understanding, can lead to problems.

Table 4.2 lists some of the more common cues together with suggestions about the possible underlying processes.

It must be stressed that any attempt to label examples of non-verbal behaviour with definitive explanations is fraught with danger. The trainer needs to look at all non-verbal behaviour (including the examples above) within its context and accumulate evidence from a range of sources.

When drawing attention to the behaviour of an individual in a group the trainer can choose to intervene at different levels of risk.

Table 4.2   Non-verbal cues and possible underlying processes

Non-verbal cues	Possible processes
Furrowed forehead, knitted brows.	Thinking, rehearsing in an internal dialogue; giving self a bad time.
Tapping foot and/or drumming fingers.	Impatience; irritation; anger; agitation.
Avoiding eye contact.	Discomfort; anxiety; suspicion; confusion.
Intense eye contact.	Anger; concern; sexual attraction.
Rapid, light breathing.	Anxiety; fear; distress.
Irregular breathing.	Approaching an important issue; forcing self; controlling feelings.
Deep, slow breathing.	Supporting strong feelings – often precedes catharsis.
Physical stroking of face, arms and neck.	Comforting self *or* holding back from stroking others *or* holding back the need for comforting.
Scratching, pinching, gouging, severe pressing.	Punishing self, reflecting self-criticism or holding back from provoking or punishing someone else.
Controlled, low, quiet voice.	Suppressing energy/interest; excitement.
Fast, high voice.	Excitement; tension; fear.
Tightness/rigidity in jaw, neck, shoulder.	Holding back anger, sadness.
Clenching fists, tightness in arms.	Holding back anger, sadness.
Body leaning forward in chair.	Interested; concerned; about to 'happen'.
Body leaning backward in chair, sprawling.	Detached; uninvolved; unconcerned.
Arms tightly folded; legs tightly crossed.	Defending; putting up barriers; resistance.
Lounging extravagantly in the chair.	Detachment; cynicism; discounting.
Hand covering mouth.	Hiding; playing games; uncertain.
Finger jabbing.	Critical; putting down; fencing with.

His choice of risk level at any one time will be determined by many factors. Perhaps the most important consideration is the training objectives in terms of 'thinking', 'doing' and 'feeling' (see Chapter 1), the overall training design (see Chapter 2), the relationships within the group (see Chapter 5), the type of feedback available (see Chapter 6) and the competence of the trainer (see Chapter 3). It is important to adapt the type of feedback to the individual's needs and his ability to receive and use it.

'Risk levels' are distinguished by the degree to which defensive behaviour of the trainee is provoked by the trainer. The following steps offer a sequence of interventions that a trainer might work through in helping a trainee examine his own body language. It is of course important to leave the trainee to decide whether or not he wants to make the next step and to monitor signs of serious discomfort. In exploring body language, small steps are often enough and stopping sooner rather than later is a useful guideline.

Increasing awareness of behaviour (DOING level)

For example, when the trainer is reviewing a CCTV tape of an interview he might say to one of the participants, 'Notice your facial expression at this particular moment in the interview', but does not at this stage carry out any analysis.

Increasing awareness of behaviour (FEELING level)

The trainer might intervene at the level of 'Pay attention to what you are doing'. This intervention leaves all of the responsibility for exploration with the course member. The risk level can be increased slightly by asking the individual to report on his experience or behaviour 'What goes on?' or 'What are you doing?'.

Exploring the behaviour (DOING level)

Here the trainer might encourage the observers of a management exercise to give feedback on the participants' non-verbal behaviour and then to explore it further: 'Fred, you've just agreed with Bill that you were getting flustered and unable to concentrate on the exercise. What were you feeling at the time?'.

Exploring the behaviour (FEELING level)

At this level the trainer encourages the individual to explore his behaviour. Such invitations may be: 'Repeat the gesture and notice the feelings that go with it', or 'At whom would you like to direct that expression', or 'Continue with the gesture and allow it to develop and vary', or 'How could you express that gesture/posture in words?'.

Experimenting with behaviour (DOING level)

For example, 'In the exercise you found it difficult to assert yourself. How about experimenting with this next time, for example by maintaining eye contact with the person role-playing your boss?'

Experimenting with behaviour (FEELING level)

Here the trainer is offering the trainee a chance to develop new choices in extending his repertoire of behaviours. Examples of giving permission to experiment are: 'Find new ways of expressing your disappointment', 'Experiment with letting your shoulders relax', 'Try the opposite of what you are doing now'.

Exaggerating the behaviour (FEELING level)

At this level the trainer is encouraging a sharpening of awareness at the level of feelings. The intervention 'Do it more!' or 'Exaggerate that expression' may lead to clarification and insight or catharsis or both.

Making contact (FEELING)

In the sense that is used here this process involves communicating directly and with the minimum of words. This approach is typical of Gestalt, encounter and bioenergetics (see Appendix 1) where an introductory exercise might be 'Find out as much as you can about someone else here, without using words'. The implication is that participants will explore with their other senses as far as their rules and inhibitions allow.*

Other aspects of making contact might lead to a participant stroking, scratching, picking at someone else instead of himself.

Whether or not a trainer decides to draw attention to body language depends on many considerations. Given that body language is an appropriate area for learning, the trainer has to distinguish between the more and the less significant aspects. Some classification of behaviours to inform these choices is helpful and some essential dimensions are set out below:

Internal

Body language can be differentiated according to its function. A physical sign of an internal process is a different phenomenon from the normal signals which regulate conversation. Body language which is predominantly a reflection of inner experience is called internal. For example, a momentary wince as a painful memory is recalled.

External

This category contains messages for the outside world. These mes-

---

* There is normally a restriction on violence or sexual contact in these settings.

sages may not be clear or translatable directly into words but they are intended to convey meaning to others. For example a stern glance at someone who is trying to interrupt. (Internal may be more significant when training specifically involves feelings. External may be more significant when training is concerned with communication skills.)

Congruent

It is clear that body language operates simultaneously through many channels. Meanings are clear when all the channels (e.g.: physical appearance, clothing, posture, gesture, voice-tone) harmonise to produce a coherent and congruent pattern. When this happens physical behaviour serves to emphasise, elaborate or enrich any words that are spoken.

Incongruent

Frequently the body language and the verbal message are in some way incongruent.[4] Thus:
'Oh how awful' (with a smile and a twinkle in the eye)
'How nice to see you' (with a forced smile)
'Can't you take a joke?' (with a malicious smile)
'Oh yes . . . (pause) . . . now I understand' (said doubtfully with puzzled expression)
'How interesting' (said flatly with an inanimate facial expression)
'Go away' (with a sad pleading look in the eyes)
'Oh, by the way . . .' (with a trace of a smile sometimes followed with devastating news like 'we're sending you to our branch in Saigon' or 'your new boss arrives tomorrow')

The incongruence often indicates some ulterior or second messages and is a good clue to manipulations or what is called, in transactional analysis, 'games' (see Appendix 1).

Secondary

Mostly the body is used as a means of providing emphasis or depth to verbal communication. In performing this function body language is clearly fulfilling a secondary role, while the verbal content and meaning provide the primary communication. For the purposes of IST non-verbal messages (internal or external) that are both congruent and secondary are less likely to warrant attention than incongruent or primary ones.

Primary

These are the signals which convey the most important message of that moment. They are often dramatic and emotion-filled. Examples of these are thumping the table, eyes filling with tears or the facial glow that comes with pride, love and pleasure. There are occasions when these signals dominate the communication process so that words seem, and often become, unnecessary. The trainer can encourage awareness and sensitivity to these occasions and is likely to enhance trainees' interpersonal skills when he does.

Infrequent

In helping a trainee to increase self-awareness the trainer selects priorities. One criterion for selecting a particular aspect of body language is the frequency with which it occurs. A seldom occurring piece of non-verbal communication, other things being equal, is less likely to provide important insights than a frequently occurring one. It is likely therefore to be more effective for the trainer to concentrate on helping the trainee to discover the implications of his more frequent expressions, postures etc.

Frequent/persistent

Some aspects of body language are relatively enduring for example, physical size, body shape, hair style, facial lines, bearing etc. Both these and the frequently used non-verbal postures and gestures will probably yield important self-understanding.

The photographs are included to provide an opportunity for applying these classifications and to explore their implications for trainer interventions.

The three individuals shown in Figure 4.1 are taking part in a training event, each of them is clearly conveying a message, although not consciously, to the other group members and to the trainer.

Take the person on the left of the picture. There are obviously some strong messages concerning his identity and character reflected in his style of hair and clothing and in his body size. This (persistent) image becomes the sort of back-drop against which any particular non-verbal message can be interpreted. When the photograph was taken, he was leaning slightly forward with some of his weight on his

Fig. 4.1

forearms. What message does he convey to the trainer or group? His
attention is directed outwards to the world rather than inwards to
himself (external), and he is interested in what he perceives.

This external orientation is also recognisable in the individual to
the far right of the picture.

The central figure seems to be less involved with external reality
and shows some indication of withdrawal (internal). The evidence is
that he is tilted back on his seat, his hands are interlocked on his
head, his eyes are not focused and his lower jaw and mouth are 'set'.
Certainly this pose reflects some internal process that is connected
with his relationship with the group, the trainer and the subject being
discussed. Some possibilities are: that he wishes to withdraw from
the group; that he feels threatened by what is being said; that he is
bored and frustrated or that he has withdrawn to think over an idea
etc.

The withdrawal as a momentary and isolated event (infrequent)
need not concern the trainer. However, if the withdrawal is persistent and perhaps defensive then the trainer may decide to intervene.

In deciding to do so the trainer might take into account such
factors as the training objectives, recent events which might have
triggered the response, the individual's patterns of behaviour and
feelings, the trainer's own feelings toward the individual. Some of the
ways of handling the central figure in the photograph include:

Intervention type	Example
Hooking out	'I'm interested in your views' 'What do you think?'
Gentle enquiry	'Is there something you're not happy with?' or 'What goes on with you?'
Descriptive feedback (see Chapter 6)	'You're tilted back in your chair with your hands on your head and you don't seem to be focused on us'
Gentle confrontation	'Be aware of your body/face' 'Pay attention to what you are doing right now' 'What is your message to us?'
Mimic, mirror	Use the person's name and copy his posture and expression.

Depending on the setting and circumstances these interventions may help both the trainer and the individual to understand more about what is going on. This new understanding can provide the basis for choice – to continue behaving/feeling as before or to change to something new.

Figure 4.2 seems to suggest strongly that the woman is oriented toward an 'internal' process. Before either leaping in with an interpretation or passing on without doing so, the trainer would perhaps momentarily consider the context and whether the expression is 'primary' or 'secondary'. In this instance the communication

Fig. 4.2

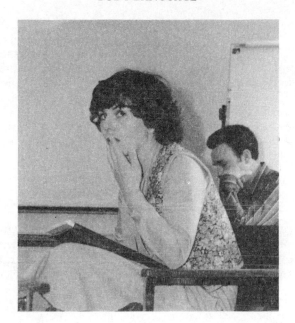

Fig. 4.3

is evidently 'secondary' and it does not 'demand' attention and a verbal intervention from the trainer.

In the event that the mood of the individual contrasts with that of the rest of the group and that the expression is frequent or persistent the trainer may nevertheless choose to intervene:

Intervention type	Example
Offer interpretation	'You seem sad or preoccupied'
Check data	'Tell me what you feel'
Offer support	'Is there anything you want from me?'
Encourage catharsis	'Stay in touch with your feelings'
Offer counselling	'Let's talk outside the session'

The same individual in Figure 4.3 is probably engaged in a memory search. The clues to this are that her eyes are not focused on events in the room but are directed upwards to the left. The fingers of her left hand are lightly touching her mouth.

In terms of the framework the body language is 'internal', 'congruent' and 'secondary'. While it may not be important and the trainer is unlikely to intervene in order to help develop insight or self-awareness, there is nevertheless something of interest here for the trainer to consider.

NLP (neuro linguistic programming – see Chapter 8 and Appendix 1) states that eye-positions are an important and surprisingly accurate clue to the frame of reference and orientation of a person. In this photograph the up/left glance suggests a 'visual' frame of reference; the previous photograph of the same person looking downwards to the right (Figure 4.2) suggests a prime concern with feelings.

Based on NLP the trainer would intervene using the same frame of reference as the individual. So in Figure 4.3 the intervention would contain a visual reference:

Intervention type	Example
Ask for information	'How do you see it?'
Ask for opinions or views	'Tell me your view'
	'How do you look at it?'

By using a common frame of reference the trainer quickly tunes in to the person and in doing so encourages confidence and trust.

Figure 4:4 illustrates body language which is also 'internal', 'congruent' and 'secondary'. The individual's attention is on some aspect of the environment, but his body language is a reflection of his (internal) concentration and effort. In the context of theory input

Fig. 4.4

during a training programme, the behaviour is congruent and clearly the message is secondary to the overall learning process and does not force itself on others.

The interesting aspect of this picture is understood best in terms of the Gestalt approach (see Appendix 1). From Gestalt comes the idea of retroflection, which literally means turning back on oneself. The subject of this photograph is literally pushing and putting pressure on himself with his thumb. Although the trainer may not make any intervention, it may help him to know those who typically retroflect their effort and energy are less likely to express themselves openly. For example the retroflector will often blame himself for not understanding rather than ask questions and will try to drive himself on when he is tired or unwell rather than ask for help or a break. Since much of this energy is turned inwards the retroflector is often quiet and unresponsive and is therefore less likely to be noticed.

Simply by observing the patterns of body language a trainer can begin to identify those who are holding in their energy. Depending on the type of training programme the trainer may offer a variety of interventions:

Intervention type	Example
Permit/offer encouragement toward self-expression	'I would like to hear your reaction' 'It is alright to express how you feel'
Descriptive feedback	'I notice you are putting pressure on your self with your thumb'
Encourage self-awareness	'Notice what you do with your thumb — exaggerate the pressure — how does that feel?'
Check on level of comfort/understanding	'How does this make sense to you?'

Figure 4.5 illustrates a very clear example of 'primary' non-verbal communication. It is a dramatic gesture which, if ignored by the trainer, is likely to generate a lot of 'unfinished business' ('What do I have to do in order to get people to pay attention to me!').

There are a number of interventions which could be made in this particular instance:

Intervention type	Example
Open ended enquiry	'I can see you feel strongly about something, do you want to talk about it?' 'What do you want?'
Copying the gesture	'When I do this I feel some sense of despair — what does it mean for you?'

Fig. 4.5

Offer feedback about self	'When you did that I felt . . .'
Encourage catharsis	'Let your feelings go'
Offer interpretation	'Your eyes seem sad and I don't know what your hands are saying'

The non-verbal communication shown in Figure 4.6 is external in that it is being used to make a point (literally and metaphorically) to the rest of the group. If the gestures were supported by a firm and judgemental voice tone then the whole communication would be congruent. All evidence would indicate, using a transactional analysis perspective (see Appendix 1), the 'critical parent ego state'. Incongruence would occur if the individual had a whining or vulnerable quality to his voice (in transactional analysis terms, the 'adapted child ego state') for here a double message is then being sent: on the surface, 'You must listen to my really important point', but underneath it, '. . . but I don't think you will'. Assuming that the message in this example is incongruent then some of the possible interventions are:

Intervention type	Example
Ignore the underlying message	'My understanding of what you are saying is . . .'
Offering implicit support	Checking understanding, this accompanied by smiling and nodding (basically conveying the mes-

Fig. 4.6

Offering explicit support

sage 'I *really* do think what you have got to say is important').

'Your voice tone leads me to believe that you are feeling uncomfortable in some way. If I am right then I would like to give you some support.'

Some additional interventions would be playing back a tape recording of the individual's comment, so that he could listen to the quality of his voice tone.

The final photograph (Figure 4.7) graphically illustrates the richness of non-verbal communication and the range of opportunities it offers trainees and trainers to learn about themselves and how they relate to others.

The three figures are reacting very differently to the same situation:

Figure on left of picture
Half smile and yet his eyes not laughing (incongruent).
An intent gaze which he is using to convey a message (external) but the message is unclear; it is probably not one of approval!
Steepled fingers which are probably a reflection of internal pro-

Fig. 4.7

cess (e.g. 'I and others must always do everything perfectly'??).
Head at an angle which once again is probably a reflection of
internal process (e.g. 'I must look for all the angles or somebody
will catch me out'??).

Figure in the middle

Face down and shielded and sitting on crossed legs in the chair. He
is literally turned in on himself and this is probably the result of
internal process – insight, or possibly 'There I go making a fool of
myself again'. It is also a primary communication 'demanding'
attention and comment unless, of course, the individual concerned starts to talk about it himself.

Figure on the right

Full bodied laughter which is clearly demonstrated in the face and
posture.

Body language and self discovery

Not only are the messages that others convey sometimes not noticed
but most people miss much of their own bodily expression. The
easiest way to confirm this is to point out to someone whom you
know well that, for example, he is stroking his forearm, or has just

held his breath for a few seconds, or has his hands behind his head. It becomes quite apparent that most people do not realise what they are doing with their bodies. Yet by paying attention to non-verbal behaviour it is possible to discover a great deal about oneself and one's feelings.

The assumption here is that very little behaviour is 'accidental'. Actions, while not taken deliberately, are nevertheless meaningful. The ability to maintain some additional awareness (not control) of bodily behaviour, when coupled with a curious and open mind, can bring about an enhanced understanding of self and the environment.

For example, many managers may have finished management meetings with a stiff neck and the beginnings of a headache. Some of these consequences will be the result of tensions set up during the meeting. By becoming aware of how and when these tensions occur an individual may be able to achieve important insights into his needs and relationships.

Perhaps more obvious illustrations are the manager who discovers that he has clenched both fists so that he can see 'the whites of his knuckles' and had not realised that he was angry; or the person who finds he cannot see clearly because his eyes have inexplicably filled with tears. In these circumstances a person actually discovers his emotions through awareness of his body.

It may even be true that it is not possible to have certain feelings without the corresponding internal bodily feedback. Body language may, therefore, be an integral part of the process of experiencing feelings.[5] In this sense, for example, sadness does not *cause* crying and a 'heavy heart', but that is what the experience of sadness *is*. In other words people's emotional and physical beings are not in reality split but are probably part of a single integrated experience. This argument can be taken one step further. If it is true that certain body movements release and express emotions it may also be true to say that by holding in certain non-verbal messages about one's state of being, by muscle tensioning (e.g. clenching jaws), the emotions are trapped. As a result it becomes impossible not only to express them, but also to feel them and the opportunity for emotional release is lost. An example might be that the refusal to cry stifles the expression of sadness and locks it inside the body. The consequence may be a lasting decrease in responsiveness for that person in which the ability to feel that emotion is lost. (See Appendix 1 – bio-energetics, and Chapter 3 – Ethical and professional issues)

Whatever the truth of this issue, the body is a valuable source of information which an individual can use to gain personal insight. Most people, once they become aware of, or even have pointed out to them, a particular gesture or posture will stop and revert to a more 'neutral' position. While this behaviour may preserve self-image, it is not a good way to discover self or understand relationships.

Particularly for the IS trainer there is likely to be considerable benefit in becoming aware of his own body language and to develop a familiarity with the messages that he is conveying implicitly or explicitly, deliberately or by chance. As discussed in Chapter 3 the trainer is often taken as a model and is most likely to generate messages to trainees about his thoughts, feelings and concerns. These messages can directly affect the trainee's response to learning so that it is useful for the trainer to have some idea of how he is seen.

The first step is to generate awareness of one's own non-verbal communication. The most fruitful way of generating awareness is likely to be from the feedback gained from others. Most probably, in order to get the feedback he wants, a trainer will have to make some particular arrangements with colleagues, trainees or the use of closed circuit television, or a combination of these.

In gaining self-awareness by these means it is worthwhile attending to the large and obvious gestures or behaviour and momentary bodily events. In terms of fleeting or less obvious events, eye-contact patterns, self-stroking or scratching, jaw or leg muscle tensing can prove to be important guides to internal experience.

The most interesting of these events are likely to be those that, at first, the individual was not aware of, but which occur frequently. Once identified by the individual he can enlist the help of others in becoming more familiar with how, why and when he does it.

An example of such an exercise might be a trainer who discovers from feedback that he has a habit of tilting back his chair from time to time. His first response to having this pointed out is that he was aware of doing it on occasions but not aware of the internal process that sets it up or of the impact (if any) it has on others. By encouraging more feedback the individual will begin to become aware of the point at which he changes position. In learning about the movement it is worth noticing if there are external events linked with it (e.g. course members asking awkward questions,) and whether these form some recognisable pattern (e.g. dealing with a particular type of individual/group, type of task, social setting etc.).

Similarly, and of equal importance, it is worth attending to internal events which precede or happen at the same time as the body language event. These might be emotions, thoughts, images, associations. In the case of the chair tilting, the trainer's internal experience might be of carefully maintaining a precarious balance.

This initial insight opens up the possibility of exploring further. The trainer can ask himself what he is balancing and attempt to connect the inner experience, the body language and what is happening around him. This process of exploration is likely to be exciting and productive. In the above example the trainer may find that the issue of the precarious balance is between the demands of his work as a professional trainer (which require that he behaves calmly and reasonably) and his personal needs (which encourage him to express his anger and frustration). As he tilts his chair back he is withdrawing momentarily from the group's discussion and conducting an internal dialogue in which the two sides argue it out. On some occasions he may lean forward abruptly and express his impatience in an outburst as his feet and the front legs of the chair hit the floor. On other occasions he may suppress his feelings and (while still tilted back) with a skilfully placed question carry the discussion to a new area. As the group take up a more productive stance, the trainer involves himself again and discovers that, without noticing when, he and his chair have returned to a stable position, squarely on the ground.

The growing awareness of this process is likely to help the trainer to make new choices about his approach to training. He may ask himself about alternative ways of expressing or managing his feelings, or how they arise in the first place. He may want to make choices about which should take priority – his needs or the group's? Each individual will have his own criteria, but often body language can provide clues about the issues and the underlying thoughts and feelings which otherwise remain outside awareness.

In some cases the clues are more obscure and the connections less direct and obvious. For example, a particular and habitual gesture of the hand and wrist, as though tapping the air, accompanies the trainer's presentation of theory. Asking the trainer about the significance of this gesture produces no meaningful answer, yet the same movement occurs frequently and always under similar circumstances. Again the first step for the individual who is curious and wants to develop awareness is to become familiar with the movement and as far as possible notice internal experience and external events. The next step is to exaggerate the gesture a little at a time, without forcing, in order to discover what it turns into and what thoughts and feelings come into focus. In the example of the hand gesture, the movement might turn into an aggressive jabbing in the direction of the training group. When asked to express this gesture in words the trainer might say 'Don't you dare challenge me or my ideas . . . just shut up and listen!'

Again the process of exploration produces new insights which can be used for self-development. The insight or understanding may be sufficient and satisfying in itself, indicating a new set of choices. Alternatively it may give rise to a sense of discomfort and the need for support and counselling to achieve clarity and resolve the difficulty or concern.

Observing and making sense of body language is an interpersonal skill and its development has an important place in any IST.

The development of the skill is very worthwhile and quickly brings with it a wealth of additional information about oneself and other people. With observation comes the recognition that most relationships exist at a number of levels. From the recognition can be developed self-awareness as well as guesses or hypotheses about other people which can then be checked explicitly or covertly in reality. Awareness of body language provides raw data but not always a directly usable language and needs careful analysing if it is to be used positively in the context of IST.

References

(1) M. Argyle, *Bodily Communication*, Methuen, London, 1975.
(2) D. Morris, *Manwatching*, Jonathan Cape, London, 1977.
(3) R. Laing, *The Politics of Experience*, Penguin Books, Harmondsworth, 1967.
(4) S. Feldman, *Mannerisms in Speech and Gesture in Everyday Life*, International University Press, 1969.
(5) A. Lowen, *The Language of the Body*, Collier-Macmillan, 1971.

5 Managing groups

It is very useful for anyone involved in IST either as trainer, nominator or participant to understand something about group development and group management. Often, events occur in training groups that do not make sense solely in terms of the individual relationships or the learning process. For the trainer, course design and choices about interventions require a background understanding of group development.

In the first half of this chapter, the main stages of group development are described together with their implications for training design, the participant, the trainer/group relationship and the management of group boundaries. The second half concentrates on the choices for the trainer in terms of group management, some of the more common problems and responses that can be offered.

Phases of group development

The experience of meeting a new group of people in a new setting is filled with some uncertainty and anxiety for most people. There are many questions to be answered from the straightforward concerns about finding one's way around, to the prospects of new relationships and the purpose of the group's coming together. These unanswered questions become more urgent if the context is some kind of training event where one's ability or competence may be tested 'in public'.

The difficulty of getting answers is made that much greater

because the questions are difficult to formulate (for example: how does one ask someone if they have the same needs and expectations as you do?) and the very process of asking is a form of risky self-disclosure. In unstructured programmes it is harder because the process of group development is part of the subject matter to be considered in the learning event and the leaders are not likely to be 'helpful'.

This process of sorting out who is who in the group, what kind of group it will be, who will have authority, what rules of behaviour apply etc. is called 'forming' by Tuckman,[1] or 'Dependency' by Bennis and Shepard.[2] In these circumstances most people ask each other questions which are indirectly concerned with these issues and often receive guarded replies e.g.: 'Have you been on anything like this before?' (implicit: Do you have any inside information?), 'No, nothing *quite* like this' (implicit: Maybe I have!).

In training concerned with 'thinking' and 'doing', the trainer may well want to help the group to pass through this period of orientation as quickly and comfortably as possible. The programme will therefore begin with a formal welcome, a briefing on such things as the geography of the facilities, meal-times etc., and continue with a structured pattern for introductions. Paradoxically, this managing of the process actually inhibits the group's development so that the group is likely to settle into a comfortable state of 'dependency'. This may be very appropriate to the circumstances of say a short skill-based event. Apart from the obvious value of information, the structured beginning will take care, at the process level, of concerns about:

Who is in charge? What is he/she like?
How much/little am I to be managed?
What status do I have in relation to others?
What is expected of me in terms of self-disclosure?
How well will I be taken care of?
Will there be any fun or humour in the group?
Who is there here that I might like, dislike, fight with, keep clear of, be friends with?

Two further elements of an introductory phase will help to provide answers to the awkward and usually unspoken questions. Firstly, a briefing on the nature of the week in which the trainer can explicitly and will implicitly set some of the norms and standards of behaviour and continue to define the kinds of relationships he expects to prevail in the group. In this presentation messages about the degree of formality, responsibility for learning, participation will be conveyed and some modelling of acceptable behaviour will occur (e.g. warmth and intimacy, concern for others, listening and self-disclosure). Secondly, an opportunity to tackle a task, the outcome of which has little significance at the content level. For example, a syndicate discussion on the meaning of the word 'authority' or 'management' or 'communication'. During the syndicate discussion group members can express themselves and find their place with each other rather than in relation to the leader(s). The trainer can use a subsequent plenary discussion to encourage differing views and demonstrate implicitly how conflict will be handled as well as activating or suppressing sub-group rivalries and identities.

One of the consequences of a structured start is that it cuts down the possibility of participants' learning new ways of coping with the stresses of joining a group. There is an alternative of a less managed opening together with an intervention which directs attention to the process (e.g. 'Notice how you cope with the uncertainty of joining a new group') and an invitation to learn (e.g. 'Try out some other options to deal with this situation'). The consequences of this type of design will probably be to increase the level of uncertainty (and therefore the level of discomfort). At the same time, provided group members can develop enough self-support, it increases the possibility for participants to develop interpersonal skills in this context.

At the implicit level, by referring participants to their experience 'here and now' and to the possibility of alternative ways of behaving, the course leader is defining learning methods and some aspects of the relationships within the group. For example by making these two interventions the leader is taking responsibility for defining an area of learning and in suggesting that participants try out some options is providing support and encouragement. He is also, by omission making it clear that participants must learn by initiating and from their own experience. Clearly in this second type of opening, participants are more likely to have to deal with their own feelings as well as other people's.

Whatever the approach taken, the issues for the 'forming' group will take up a great deal of the available energy during the first hours of a group's development. There is no particular time limit to the process, nor will the whole group move along in unison through each phase. In leading a group, however, the phase is recognisable and the majority of the group will be seen to move on to a second phase. If this does not occur then much of the attention that would otherwise be available for learning and skill development may be taken up in seeking to settle the unresolved problems of 'forming'.

The second phase of group development is what Tuckman called 'storming' and Bennis and Shepard called 'counter-dependency'. This phase is characterised by the emergence of more overt and direct expressions of concern about leadership, membership and authority.

A highly structured 'thinking' and 'doing' based training event will

provide little scope for these to be dealt with directly in the relationship between the course members and the leader. The bids for
leadership and the conflicts are therefore likely to emerge among
group members or may become apparent as an underlying process
between group members and the trainers.

Examples of the way in which the group will direct their energy
during this phase include attempts by individuals to dominate discussion, attempts to ridicule others or sharp competitiveness between sub-groups. There is likely to be some show of feelings and
sometimes the group may polarise into 'camps'.

Attacking the trainer can give the group its first sense of common
identity but is also a means for avoiding the internal problems of
leadership and membership. Equally the course method and course
material may come in for criticism. We have experienced training
groups at this stage who vehemently refuse to try an activity on
principle even though they have little idea of what could be learned
or what it is about.

The first problem for the trainer is to decide whether the group's
behaviour makes more sense in terms of the content of what is being
said (e.g.: 'This interviewing exercise is irrelevant because we never
do any interviewing nor are we likely to!') or at the level of the group's
process. Unfortunately, there are not likely to be many obvious clues
about which is which and the rapidity of events is likely to make it
even more difficult to clarify. For the trainer perhaps the best advice
is don't panic!' A more detailed look at handling counter-dependency
appears later in this chapter (p. 110).

In terms of training design a number of factors can be considered.
The more structured the training and the more the group are managed, the slower will be the move through counter-dependency. In
some cases the opportunities for the expression of conflict or for
making bids for leadership are 'managed' out and the result is that
the group stays in the first phase. This can be desirable for training
which is aimed at 'thinking' and 'doing' where time is rarely available
for developing the group. On the other hand excluding the possibility for the group members to come to terms with each other and the
trainer means that the participants may identify little with group or
the training process. Because their feelings have been suppressed,
there is less likelihood of the experience having a significant impact
and less durability for the learning since it will not have been inter-
nalised.

'Feelings' based training does not suffer these difficulties although
there are equally awkward issues that need thinking about.

It is not uncommon for trainees within a few hours of starting a
feelings based training event (e.g. 'T' group) to begin to challenge the
competence and authority of the leaders[3] as well as the training

methods. Often these challenges are direct and provided that the trainer is not 'hooked' into unnecessary defensiveness, the concerns of the group can be explored and resolved. Indeed this process provides a fertile learning ground in which skills can be gained in self-expression, listening, assertiveness, handling conflict and coping with ambiguity.

The problems that arise through the acceptance and encouragement of counter-dependency can result from individuals being put down or hurt and consequently withdrawing psychologically or physically from the group and the learning process. In this event it may be counter productive for the trainer to 'rescue' the individual or to 'punish' the group members (see Chapter 3). Nevertheless, the group leader can usefully confront all the group members with the consequences of their behaviour and encourage them to look for new ways of resolving conflicts.

Typically the learning that takes place during the counter-dependency phase is in the 'doing' and 'feeling' modes and it is thinking that is neglected. It is in this area that the trainer can help to integrate the learning. Training which relies solely on the open expression of conflict or anger and typically involves extended periods of hostility is not likely to provide useful learning.[4] However, the process of counter-dependency (whether focused between group members or between the group and the leaders) if it is channelled wisely, provides valuable opportunities for learning and a spring-board to the next phase of the group.

The third phase of group development is what Tuckman called 'norming'; it is also called 'cohesion'.[5] By now, instead of splintering or attempts to dominate, the aftermath of the conflicts is a process of reconciliation. Participants begin to look for ways of coming together and establishing the cohesion of the group through a common identity. Some of the feeling of belonging comes from having worked through the conflicts to a new sense of understanding. Each individual is likely by this time to have created a role for himself which is acceptable to others as a claim to, and basis for, membership.

The learning activity is now examined with a sense of responsibility for learning shared between the participants and the leaders. The purpose and methods of learning are likely to be reviewed, discussed and largely agreed. Often the group begins to monitor these for itself to ensure that no individual gets in the way of others or avoids particular issues. Individuals are likely to ask for feedback and to accept feedback when it is given. There is, as a result, an increase in awareness and sensitivity and a growing sense of relaxation.

The remaining tender spot is likely to be loyalty. For example, challenges to the group consensus or a decision to opt out are likely to be taken as a sign of disloyalty and the individual may be punished or the group close ranks to maintain their new found but delicate identity.

The trainer will be relieved when this phase is reached as the worst is over and now the group can get on with the task of learning and skill development without turmoil. In this phase it is often helpful to give the group some choices about how they want to use their time and energy. They are more likely to be receptive to suggestions and guidance rather than a set syllabus and instructions. Certainly this is not a time during which to impose a tight time-table with heavily controlled exercises. Indeed sudden changes in the degree of control either way are likely to create problems at the level of group process. Particularly during the stage of 'cohesion' the trainer needs to be flexible and provide support and facilities for the group.

The final phase of the group's development is called 'performing' by Tuckman and 'interdependence' by Bennis and Shepard. As the titles imply this is a most productive stage and reflects the optimism that these authors share about the power and potential of the group. While we largely accept this view, the implication that the group has now 'arrived' in a permanent state of grace, does not match with our experience. There are, during the performing phase problems, difficulties and tensions concerning the group's task and process. The difference between this phase and the previous ones is the way in which the group tackles them. Tasks and relationships are approached on the basis of a high commitment to and acceptance of individual and group action.

Individuals are less likely to have their motives or actions questioned. The leader begins to be seen as a possible resource on which the group can draw without feeling threatened or patronised. As trust develops participants feel free to take risks by engaging in new types of relationships or behaviour. The group's work of learning will now continue rapidly until the group is broken up by the departure of one or more members, or a complete change in the tasks, environment or leaders.

Group development and the 'thinking', 'doing', 'feeling' model

It may be helpful to look at the group development model and see how it relates to the learning at the three levels of thinking, doing and feeling (Table 5.1).

During the dependency stage, the group members look to each other and particularly to the leader to help them cope with uncertainty. Feelings are suppressed until the individual understands enough about his environment to decide whether or not to express them. If the training event is structured and managed, the trainee will not have the opportunity to express his feelings openly. He will be occupied with absorbing knowledge and developing skills. Feelings that do arise are likely to be dealt with implicitly (see Chapter 4) or in a one to one setting outside the group.

During the next stage, counter-dependency, the individuals in the group are dealing with their personal needs at the level of feelings. These needs are usually concerned with such things as acceptance, membership, control and intimacy and obviously give rise to strong feelings of affection and hostility.

Table 5.1   Group development and the thinking, doing, feeling model

Phases of group development	Thinking	Doing	Feeling
Dependency (Forming)	√	√	?
Counter-dependency (Storming)	?	√	√
Cohesion (Norming)	√	?	√
Interdependence (Performing)	√	√	√

While these are being expressed, the rational thinking process is temporarily set aside.

The period of 'cohesion' gives rise to thoughtful reflection and consideration, together with feelings concerned with loyalty, identity and commitment. In this phase the group are unlikely to want to get on with a task until they have clarified their relationships and understood what they intend to do.

The final phase, interdependence, engages all three methods of learning, in which thinking is maintained alongside activity, and feelings are expressed and dealt with as they arise. It is certainly our experience that the most effective and satisfying training programmes reach the stage where the group is interdependent and learning happens in all three modes.

Factors affecting group development

There are a multitude of variables which together influence the pace and duration of the stages of group development. There are equally no known methods for ensuring that a group develops at a pace desired by the group members individually or by the leaders. In discussing the significant variables and later the options for group management it is hoped that each unique unfolding of a group will make more sense to the reader and will allow him to facilitate the processes more effectively.

Objectives and methods of the training

This factor has been considered at length in other parts of the book. Training aimed at skill and knowledge development, which relies on a series of structured events managed by the trainer, is likely in most circumstances to maintain the group at the dependency stage.* Training aimed at skills and awareness which encourage a 'here and now' focus and the expression of feelings is likely in most circumstances to support group development as far as the stage of counter-dependency. Whether the group develops beyond this stage depends partly on the extent to which participants are given the opportunity to make sense of their experience through the application of and consideration of models such as TA or behaviour analysis.

Sharp changes in the extent to which the trainer takes responsibility for the learning process by for example: (a) trainer-led introduction to theory, structured activity and review; (b) participant managed workshop; (c) further theory and structured activity; are likely to encourage counter-dependency but remove the possibility of the move on to cohesion.

Dramatic variations in the pace of the programme will have a similar effect; that is a tight schedule (1½ days) followed by a loose unstructured period (1 day) followed by a further tight schedule (1½ days) is likely to create the space for the development of counter-dependency but not for its completion.

Attitude and interventions of the trainer

The research conducted to examine the effects of IST[4,6,7] has produced widely divergent views but there seems to be a measure of agreement about the type of trainer style that is effective for learning. Similarly there are good grounds for believing that the group's ability to develop is connected with the trainer's behaviour (see Table 5.2).

The trainees

The aspects of the trainees that are likely to affect the consequences of training and should be considered are:

Personalities – level of aggression, extroversion, etc.
Needs – affections, control, learning objectives etc.

---

* Provided the motivation for learning is high for each participant, this need not have any adverse effect on the learning process.

Table 5.2 Relationship between trainer interventions and group development

Dependency (Forming)	Counter-dependency (Storming)	Cohesion (Norming)	Interdependence (Performing)
Claims high power position based on credible experience.	Claims high power without credible expertise *or* denies power.	Offers suggestions and support to the group. Not concerned with power.	Offers full extent of expertise without taking power. Will take control to facilitate learning.
Manages majority of interaction.	Does not manage interaction but may initiate and confront.	Responds to group. Does not confront.	
Evaluates participant's performance.	Refuses to evaluate: or impose values.	Shares his values but does not impose them.	Follows own interests in interaction.
Prime giver of feedback, receives very little.	Gives and receives feedback.	Withdraws from giving or receiving feedback.	Gives and asks for feedback.
Avoids ambiguity through clear and complete instructions.	Seems to encourage ambiguity gives little explanation.	Not concerned with ambiguity – follows the group's lead.	Contributes with other group members to clarifying ambiguity.
High personal investment in outcomes.	Seems to have little/no personal needs in relation to the group.	Seems concerned for the needs of the group as a whole.	Concerned for self and group needs.
Controls rebelliousness and 'rescues' effectively.	Fails to control or rescue, or does not attempt to.	Encourages group to establish procedures.	Participates and uses authority.
Rarely/never seems to make mistakes or get flustered.	Makes mistakes and *either* denies them or ignores them.	Is not concerned with doing it right, but with being authentic.	Is not concerned with doing it right, but with being authentic.

Previous knowledge of each other, the trainers, or the course.
Previous experience of training.
Motivation for attendance (voluntary/compulsory, remedial/developmental).

Clearly a group composed largely of aggressive, extroverted people whose needs do not coincide with the training, who have heard 'bad things' about the course and the trainers ('and what they try to do to you') without the benefit of any previous experience and above all who feel resentful because they have been sent to be 'sorted out', are not going to remain in a state of dependency for very long.

Whether they use their energy to develop or simply to take it out on each other and the trainer from a position of counter-dependency depends on the course design and the skills and abilities of the trainers as well as the group.

Group size

Achieving a sense of cohesion or a level of group performance is affected by group size. Groups larger than about 25 will only in exceptional circumstances be able to develop to a stable 'performing' stage within a week of intensive contact. Although with longer periods of two to four weeks this can occur, as it does on the Grubb Institute programmes. Smaller training groups of 6–12 members can pass through the phases in the matter of a few hours where conditions are conducive in terms of the variables discussed earlier.

Relationships between trainers

Many IST events are led by two or more trainers. Their relationship will be a matter of particular interest for some group members as during the early life of the group, in the dependency phase, the trainers will be set up as models for behaviour.

It is important therefore that the relationship between the trainers is clear and that the group contact time is not used as the vehicle for settling unfinished business. In that sense the trainers' relationship needs to have achieved a degree of interdependence in which disagreement does not threaten the partnership and it is based on mutual respect.

Dependence, counter-dependence or the need to maintain cohesion all create restrictions on the choices for behaviour that the trainers have. These restrictions are likely to be carried into the group as implicit norms or rules which in turn limit the group's ability to develop and grow.

Group development and boundaries

For either trainer or participant one of the most difficult aspects of group development in IST is recognising the process in the first place. The situation is not as clear cut as it is for a member of an orchestra where each movement is clearly defined and the pace and rhythm is carefully controlled by the conductor. It is perhaps a bit more like free-form jazz where patterns emerge and interweave only to the trained ear of the participants and an audience of initiates (to most of us it just sounds like noise!).

In order to understand and influence the process it is helpful to use the concept of boundaries.[8] A boundary is a line of distinction which defines the limit of a group or its activities in some way.

Boundaries can be divided into various categories and some examples are given below:

Physical
    The group's territory – the room(s) walls
    Equipment – tape recorders/CCTV etc.
    Facilities – lounge, bar etc.
    Seating arrangements – tables and chairs
    Trainer area
    Access to equipment and books etc.

Abstract
    Task and process
    Affiliation and sub groups
    Authority/power/leadership
    Status
    Attention/motivation
    Membership
    Ability
    Time
    Psychological space
    Contract
    Mind/body/feelings

The earlier phases of group development can be readily understood in terms of the progress of the group towards managing its own boundaries. During the initial phase each participant is likely to be concerned both with protecting himself and at the same time exploring the environment. From this position of uncertainty and anxiety the participant looks to the leader to define and take care of the group's boundaries.

Counter-dependency can be understood in terms of the group testing out its power and ability in managing boundary relationships both internally and externally. For example the group may attempt to control the most talkative or dominant member and in succeeding realise that the rules for behaviour can be enforced from within the group. Subsequent attempts to do this by a trainer may be seen as 'interference'. Another common example is a group's decision to manage its time boundaries and at the same time test out its power in relation to the trainer. In this event any attempts by the trainer to 'hurry' the group are vigorously resisted and the group begins to set its own schedule. Further pushing by the trainer is likely to increase tension and hostility.

The cohesion phase emerges once the power struggle is over. The group has discovered and applied its power in a limited way both in relation to the environment (e.g. the trainer, other groups, the domestic staff, 'outsiders') and itself (e.g. controlling deviants, establishing and changing sub-groups, attending to those who need support or comfort, structuring time, organising tasks). Now this process is extended and elaborated so that procedures are based on understanding and the loyalty of the membership is assured. A group that is 'performing' has established for itself either implicitly or explicitly procedures and agreements for maintaining, crossing or removing boundaries in such a way that the existence of the group is not jeopardised.

It is not necessary however for a training group to develop beyond 'dependency' for the purposes of conducting effective IST. In order to explore this further two examples are given in which the training purposes are different and therefore the approach to group boundary management will need to be different.

Example 1

A one day introduction to appraisal interviewing in which a course outline might include:

Assembly–introductions and course method.
Syndicate discussion on purpose and value of the approach
Input on appraisal system and planning and conducting the interview
Introduction to role play and preparation time in pairs
2–3 role plays using CCTV and guided observation techniques
Plenary reviews of role-plays
Summary of key learning points

Total course time   : 6 hours (excluding lunch and other breaks)
Number of tutors   : 1
Number of participants: 10–12
Boundaries managed by tutor

Physical: Group territory in terms of rooms used. The tutor will not only take responsibility for making sure that the necessary rooms are available, but will also ensure, if challenged, that the group has the right to the territory, and will uphold the right. He will therefore exclude anyone who is not part of the group (for example a cleaner) and will manage the boundary at the door (responding to a knock or taking a message on behalf of someone in the room).

The tutor is likely to set the room out to suit his purpose and may even allocate individuals to places in the room (by setting out name plates). He will therefore claim a certain amount of territory for himself (usually a disproportionately large area of the room) and his equipment, and set an implicit boundary between it and the space allocated to the group. In the same process he may well create a physical barrier (desks or tables to emphasise the boundary) and will thereby also define for each participant how much space he can have.

When they arrive the participants will perceive, from the layout of the room, various implied instructions about how they are to behave. Do not touch 'teacher's' equipment will be one of them.* That this rule has been recognised will be evidenced if a participant is 'caught by surprise' looking at or doing something with the equipment.

Abstract. The trainer in this one day event manages both task and process. He spells out the purpose of the day, causes the introductions to happen and controls the interaction. Almost all discussion will be channelled through him. The trainer will also select the syndicate groups and may nominate a chairman for each one; he will also allocate them a particular territory and define their task and time limit. The trainer may allow low-key competition and conflict within the group but is likely to see it as essential that he maintain his authority and leadership in the group as a whole. The group will in effect be consumers in which the main boundaries over which they have control are internal such as, attention, motivation and self disclosure although a powerful trainer may even try to take over some of these. By taking responsibility for managing the group's boundaries the trainer encourages the group members to remain dependent on him and not concern themselves with their relationships with each other.

Trainees are therefore free to devote their attention to the content of the learning material and to follow the procedures set before them. In this way trainees are more likely to learn what it is intended they should learn. Any resistance is likely to be overcome by the trainer since he retains a great deal of power.

Example 2

A five day programme for the development of effective personal relationships which might include:

Assembly – introductions and ground-rules
Time in large groups (flexible)

---

* More rebellious participants may write something 'funny' on the board or the OHP. Curious ones may flick through notes of OHP slides to find out what will happen.

Time in small groups (flexible)
Optional short theory input.
Boundaries managed by tutor.

Physical. For an event like this, the trainer will probably still take
responsibility for providing a territory although he may well *not*
maintain the boundary by excluding others or inviting members in.
The trainer will provide an initial seating arrangement and room
layout (it would be impossible for him not to do so) but is likely to
leave the group to use the room however they wish. He will not try to
influence who sits where nor will he claim territory as his own. If other
facilities are provided e.g. tape-recorders, CCTV, then the trainer will
not maintain exclusive control over them, leaving the group to use
them as they wish.

Abstract. For a training event of this kind, the task and the process
are likely to overlap almost entirely. The process of forming and
maintaining relationships is the subject matter of the task. With this
in mind, the trainer may set some ground-rules such as being primarily concerned with the process here and now, and may remind the
group if it is frequently ignored.

Beyond this, however, the trainer is more likely to make observations than to direct activity and will not become the 'guardian' of the
task/process boundary. Similarly, the trainer will not create or dis-
band sub-groups or attempt to delegate authority.

The group will be left to manage its own interaction, membership
and leadership. Using some approaches, (encounter, or TA) the
trainer becomes more involved in order to facilitate these processes.
With other approaches (Tavistock) the trainer ensures that the
boundary of his separateness in the role of trainer is never breached.

The group members are also left to formulate their own contract in
terms of specific learning objectives, and to allocate their time between small and large groups, attendance and absence etc. as they
wish. The leader simply is available during the contracted periods.

In this second example, the trainer avoids taking responsibility for
managing many of the boundaries. In doing so, group members are
thrown back on their own resources and are often surprised and
sometimes angry as a result. Usually this energy is expressed in the
form of counter-dependency and the group's development begins.
Once the boundaries are 'secure' the trainer is no longer seen as the
'enemy' and the task of the group can continue against a background
that is more co-operative.

The two examples represent opposite ends of a spectrum. In any training design, the trainer or the participant can choose which boundaries to manage himself and which to leave for the other(s) to manage. The process is more or less a one-way street for the leader in that having decided to let go of the responsibility for some boundaries (e.g. managing sub-groups) it is difficult to retrieve control. It is easier, therefore, to start a group with more boundaries managed by the trainer and to let go as the group gains familiarity, than it is to move in the opposite direction.

It is seldom easy as a trainer to make and implement these choices of which boundaries to control and which to leave for the group members to manage. Most managers have established patterns of boundary control in their relationships with those who they perceive as authority figures, peers and subordinates. The manager is therefore most likely to expect to be able to transfer those patterns directly into the training group. For example, many managers will begin from the assumption that the trainer will direct the group not only in terms of defining the tasks, but also in terms of acceptable behaviour. The trainee who discovers that group members will have to establish and enforce for themselves the boundaries of proper conduct is often dismayed and uncomfortable. The group's reaction may be to press the trainer to take up his 'responsibility' or to express their hostility towards him for not taking care of them. In any event, the trainer is unlikely to find it easy to resist.

Some examples of how trainees (without realising it) manipulate the trainer into managing boundaries are:

1 Saying 'Can I ask a question?' (looking at the trainer)
   Possible trainer response: 'I don't know . . . can you?' (teasing tone)
2 Saying 'I'm just going to the loo' (looking at the trainer)
   Possible trainer response: 'Do you want my permission?' (teasing tone)
3 Giving feedback to another course member but keeping eye contact with the trainer and using the third person (e.g. 'At that point he stopped participating . . .')
   Possible trainer response: 'Say this directly to him'
4 Looking at the trainer when feeling hurt after receiving feedback which felt like a put-down.
   Possible trainer response: 'I notice you look at me'
5 Keeping silent when the trainer asks the group what they want to do
   Possible trainer response: Pause . . . repeat the question

Boundaries and sub-groups

Training groups often divide themselves into identifiable sub-groups which can be recognised by themselves as well as the trainer. The sub-groups are formed by the establishing of (physical and emotional) boundaries between those who are and who are not members.

An obvious illustration of this is the claiming and 'defending' of territory within the main training room or a syndicate room. The sub-group will make it clear to 'intruders' that the territory is not to be entered except at the sub-group's discretion. The messages are usually conveyed implicitly, for example, by asking a visitor what he wants, laying claim to the territory in a humorous way or maintaining silence (while exchanging 'knowing' looks) when an intruder enters.

Emotional boundaries can also be established among participants. A typical boundary is that between participants who want to learn and those who view training cynically as wasting their time. The two sub-groups will quickly identify themselves and each other and may reinforce the barriers by competing or engaging in conflict. Other examples of sub-groups' boundaries are:

Those who have 'been through the mill' (e.g. received a lot of feedback or tried some activity in front of the group) and those who have not.

Those who have attended because they wanted to and those who are 'sent'.

The trainer can make choices about the extent to which he wants to reinforce the boundaries or to reduce their effects. The barriers are likely to be reinforced by maintaining sub-groups in syndicate discussions and introducing comparisons and evaluation of sub-group performance. Boundaries can be identified and included in the learning process by introducing inter-group exercises in which the sub-groups identify themselves and the other sub-groups. This process can be followed by an exchange of mutual perceptions.[9]

Taking this process one stage further, the trainer can encourage sub-group formation for example by a socio-drama exercise in which participants physically arrange the group members according to their perceptions.

Boundaries are likely to be reduced by a deliberate and frequent reorganisation of syndicate groups varying their membership, as well as their size, creating pair and trio exercises in which the partnerships are formed across sub-group boundaries. Another set of trainer interventions concerns encouraging group members to learn from each other rather than to compete with each other. The trainer can provide a model for this by accepting alternative views (even if they differ from his own), as valid and appropriate. This acceptance illustrates that there are no right or wrong answers and that differences can be at worst tolerated and at best welcomed.

Just as activities exist to encourage the recognition of mutual differences, so there are some that serve to integrate a fragmented group. Often tasks in which all members of the group are faced with a challenge against time or an average performance standard can help to integrate, especially if the chances for success and achievement are high. In conducting this type of task the trainer may need to provide considerable support and encouragement during the exercise as well as acknowledging enthusiastically the group's achievements. Recognition of success is itself a great integrator.[10]

The concept of boundaries can help further in the understanding of group behaviour and group management. There are examples of boundary management issues between the group and the trainer which, once recognised, allows the trainer to make his choices. One of these is the effect of a training group setting up its own informal leader who more or less covertly manages the norms which govern the trainer/trainee relationship. The controls on behaviour may be set up outside the formal training periods and reinforced during training sessions non-verbally or by 'throw away' comments. Sometimes these controls will be helpful to the learning and sometimes destructive. Once the process is recognised the trainer can decide what to do. Clearly these processes require gentle handling in order not to reinforce or create antagonism across the trainer/group boundary. It is rarely helpful for the trainer to confront the group directly on these matters.

Managing the risk level

Apart from the boundaries discussed above, the trainer will have a number of other aspects of the groups' process to manage (or not). The level of risk is one of these and has been referred to in Chapter 2.

What is the risk level in the context of IST? It is the experience resulting from not knowing what will be the outcome of our action or what will happen next. The inner experience of taking a risk varies but it often feels exciting, scary and embarrassing. Examples of actions in IST which generate an increased sense of risk are:

1 Learning a new skill which involves doing something different, understanding something new or experiencing new feelings.
2 Saying something which you believe may upset someone.
3 Asking for something important (like warmth or attention) without knowing whether you will get it.
4 Saying or doing something which you believe may make people ridicule or laugh at you.

5 Doing something instead of talking or thinking about it.
6 Acknowledging ignorance or a feeling of inadequacy.

So taking a risk means doing something without knowing what to expect, perhaps fearing an unpleasant or uncomfortable result.

From the outset, the trainer has the option to control the level of risk that the group is expected to work with. By emphasising thinking about and talking about what has happened or might happen at work and generalising, a trainer keeps the risk level low. By inviting an individual to try something (say, giving praise or criticism) here and now, with other course members, for real, the trainer generates a high sense of risk.

Table 1.2 shows some characteristic examples of the ways in which a trainer can help to keep the risk level up or down. Apart from these, there are a number of ways in which trainees can be encouraged to create a 'safe' learning environment for themselves:

1 Making explicit agreements concerning support and encouragement.
2 Getting and gaining explicit permission to make mistakes.
3 Getting and giving explicit permission to experiment.
4 Encouraging feedback that can be used and discouraging feedback that cannot be used. (see Chapter 6).

The consequence of maintaining a low risk level is that, being less anxious, participants are better able to understand and make sense of the information provided. On the other hand, they are less likely to develop skills (which take practice and therefore some risk) or to internalise the learning because their feelings have not been engaged.

If a high level of risk is maintained, trainees quickly come up against their own barriers and blocks in interpersonal relationships but may not feel safe enough to try things out in practice or to translate the learning to other situations (e.g. work).

A trainee's optimum learning at the levels of 'doing' and 'feeling' takes place when he is just on the edge of his level of self-support. That is he is just beyond the point at which he feels comfortable and able to manage the situation. At the level of 'thinking' the optimum is likely to be where the individual feels confident and secure.

By varying the type of intervention in the group, the trainer can create an optimum learning environment in which different levels of risk are encouraged according to the particular trainee's level of self-support and the type of learning objectives that apply.

From time to time, a trainee will reach the limits of his self-support, having passed the risk level too far, and may become upset and confused (see also Chapter 3). From this position the trainee's main priority may be to retrieve control by developing greater support. Here the trainer's interventions are especially important in maintaining the ability of the individual to recover and to learn from the experience.[11]

Apart from this, it is likely that the remaining members of the group will feel uncomfortable and will look to the trainer for guidance. Some useful interventions in these circumstances are:

1   Give the trainee permission to express feelings (sadness, anger etc.) e.g. 'It's OK to let those feelings go'.
2   Offer protection e.g. putting an arm around him or expressing warmth or concern.
3   Encourage the group to offer support verbally or non-verbally.
4   Directing the individual's attention to the sources of support both in himself and in the environment. (e.g. 'Look around and see if you can get what you need in this group').
5   Encourage the individual to think ('What options do you have?').
6   Remain silent.
7   Change the focus of attention to a new subject.
8   Wait until the end of the formal session and offer individual counselling.
9   Suggest the person leaves the group in order to regain their composure.

It is likely that the trainer will also be feeling upset by the event and that he should seek the support he needs from the group or colleagues. It is also worth noting that such events may bring the group to the boundary between training and therapy, and the trainer may not be expected or competent to proceed with therapy (see Chapter 3). It is important therefore that referrals to a competent agent can be made. The trainer should be able to recognise his own limitations and should not play the part of the 'amateur psychologist'.

In any event it is not likely that a trainee in these circumstances is going to be able to learn at the level of thinking or doing. Although the learning at the level of feeling may be extremely significant. It is important, therefore, that the individual be encouraged after the cathartic episode to think through the experience (perhaps using concepts and models already learned in the training) so that the processes are understood. From this point then, further learning at the level of doing can be encouraged. This may help to test the conceptual understanding in new situations.

Two common problems for the trainer

Passivity

A passive group is one in which the participants contribute little and respond with low energy to questions or activities. There is little trust and little fun in the group. Often individuals will be over-compliant, responding like automatons to the leader's instructions. Possible causes are:

1 Unfinished business with the nominator or organisation (feelings of hurt or resentment).
2 Fears based on hearsay and rumours about similar training events.
3 Course content is boring or irrelevant.
4 Trainer too controlling or confronting or viewed as 'the enemy'.
5 A powerful sub-group is controlling the group.
6 The group see themselves as inadequate, lacking in self-confidence.

Counter-dependency

One of the most difficult problems that a trainer has to face is the persistently hostile or counter-dependent individual. This person is likely to engage in generalised aggression, passive hostility, put-downs, trapping questions, pairing up, withdrawal or sulking or some combination of these. Possible causes are:

1 Unfinished business with nominator or organisation (e.g. did not want to come for training).
2 Fears based on hearsay and rumours about course.
3 Course content boring or irrelevant.
4 Does not know how to deal with authority figures (e.g. the trainer).
5 Fear of feeling inadequate (too old, too stupid etc.)
6 Conflict of values (life is about winning and losing not solving problems).
7 Personal problems inside or outside the group.

Trainer options

1 Ignore the process and keep focused on content.
2 Share perception of the group from a position of concern rather than blaming or defending.
3 Ask for feedback about course, purpose, design, development.
4 Pick up 'throw away' comments and pursue them.
5 Reduce/increase the number of boundaries managed by the trainer.
6 Suggest an interim course review. Give group the options and let them choose.
7 Clarify expectations.
8 Increase risk level/reduce risk level.

9   Ask group members what they want.
10   Take satisfaction-rating of each individual.
11   Sit down, say nothing and wait.
12   Provide lots of support and encouragement.
13   Put problematic individual(s) down sharply.
14   Ask individuals to leave the group.

Co-operation between trainers

For IST programmes than involve contributions from more than one trainer, it is important that they keep in close touch with each other about the events in the group. Each trainer has his own style and preferences for managing the group process. By capitalising on the individual strengths of the trainers, the results in terms of effectiveness, consistency and satisfaction are likely to be significantly enhanced for all concerned. (See also Chapter 3.)

For example we work together frequently and find that groups perceive us as very different and find the difference helpful to the learning process. One partner has a particular ability to confront and 'tame' the hostile, critical participants and prevent them from disrupting the learning of others. The second partner has the ability to provide special support for those in the group who may be shy or feel inadequate so that they develop enough confidence to participate.

Obviously it is necessary for each trainer to understand and come to terms with his particular abilities and his failings and it is useful if each member of the team knows them too. With this shared perception of each other, trainers can discuss their perceptions of the events in the group. There are many ways of doing this and perhaps gossiping about 'who has done what' is the least defensible but the most enjoyable.

A more professional approach would be to convene a daily tutorial meeting lasting about fifteen minutes. The agenda for such a meeting might be:

1   An exchange of generalised perceptions of the group and what has been happening. How are they doing? What's the atmosphere like? How did your session work out?
2   Agreement about the possibility of rescheduling the time-table (where appropriate) to suit the needs of the group.
3   Confirmation of the aspects of theory or types of activity that have been fully dealt with or referred to. Discussion of any additional information, handouts etc. that may be appropriate.
4   Sharing perceptions of the group's development and the factors that are contributing to a conducive learning environment. This

may include discussion about the role of particular individuals in the group, particularly those who are seen as highly positive or disruptive figures and those who seem to be especially passive or withdrawn.

5   A review of the group, one individual at a time to develop a sense of how they are responding to the training, the group and the tutors. This sharing among the tutors would include any special objectives with which the individual may have arrived or may have developed since starting the training. There may need to be some knowledge of his involvement in activities, what sort of feedback he has given and received and how he responded to it.

6   A discussion about the content and style of the next sessions and any particular consequences that may arise. This is likely to include a number of options particularly in terms of intervention strategies so that the trainer is free to make his choices.

Conclusion

It is at the design stage that the trainer will set his learning objectives and make the main decisions about the content of the training. If the background work involved in developing the course included meeting many of the prospective participants, he will also share an idea of the range of responses he is likely to get.

It is only after the course has begun, however, that the assumptions on which the training is based will be tested. It is very important, therefore, that the trainer remains flexible about how the learning objectives are to be achieved with this particular group, and indeed whether or not they are all relevant.

Flexibility is perhaps the greatest asset in IST particularly in the context of group development and group management. In the first instance this flexibility depends on the trainer's ability to recognise the source of any obstacles to learning. Are they obstacles at the content level or the process level? If at the process level, what is the trainer's contribution and what the group's contribution to the obstacles?

Once the trainer is able to come to some conclusions about these questions, he can adapt his approach to remove, overcome or by-pass the obstacles.

To respond effectively the trainer needs to understand the compatibility between his training design and the group's development. He is then in a position to decide whether to ignore the problems, to change the course content or to divert energy to develop the group process.

The real test for an intervention at the process level is whether or not the group process is seriously hampering learning for the majority of the trainees. If the answer to that question is 'yes', then it is probably time to do something different.

References

(1) B. Tuckman and M. Jensen, 'Stages of Small Group Development Revisited', *Group & Organisation Studies*, 1977, pp. 419–27.

(2) W. Bennis and H. Shepard, 'A Theory of Group Development', *Human Relations*, vol. 9, pp.415–37, 1956.

(3) E. Schein and W. Bennis, *Personal and Organisational Change*, John Wiley and Sons, 1965.

(4) C. Cooper and D. Bowles, *Hurt or Helped? A Study of the Personal Impact on Managers of Experiential Small Group Training Programmes*, T.I.P IO T.S.A. 1977.

(5) J. E. Jones, 'A Model of Group Development' in *The 1973 Annual Handbook of Group Facilitators*, J. E. Jones and J. W. Pfeiffer (Eds), University Associates, La Jolla, California, 1973, pp. 127–9.

(6) W. Bion, *Experiences in Groups*, Tavistock Institute, London, 1961.

(7) P. Smith, *Group Processes and Personal Change*, Harper & Row, 1980 (Chapter 3.).

(8) E. Miller and A. Rice, *Systems of Organisation: The Control of Task and Sentient Boundaries*, Tavistock Institute, London, 1967.

(9) R. Blake and J. Mouton, 'The intergroup dynamics of win-lose conflict and problem solving collaboration in union—management relations' in *Intergroup Relations and Leadership*, M. Sherif (Ed.), John Wiley & Sons, 1962, pp. 94–142.

(10) E. Schein, *Organisational Psychology*, Prentice-Hall, Englewood Cliffs, N.J., 1965. (Chapter 5.)

(11) W. Dyer (Ed.) *Modern Theory and Method in Group Training*, Van Nostrand Reinhold Co., 1972.

6 Dealing with feedback

Feedback is one of the main sources of learning in IST and it is worth comparing the types of feedback and how they are connected with training approaches and methods. This chapter discusses feedback in detail and evaluates the choices for trainer and participants. In the first part of the chapter the dimensions of feedback are discussed together with the implications of emphasising different aspects. In the second part some of the main methods for creating feedback are described and the problems and practicalities of using them are discussed.

A useful definition of feedback is: 'Any communication, verbal or non-verbal, which offers a person some information about how he/she affects others'. Inevitably, therefore, almost all social contact entails the exchange of feedback in some way. Normally most of these exchanges take place at a non-verbal and implicit level (see Chapter 4). In almost all IST, however, giving and receiving feedback is a key source of learning so that managing the exchange of feedback becomes an important consideration for the trainer.

The choices available which are discussed in this chapter have close links with the type of training approach and, therefore, with the intended outcomes. From the options presented, the trainer will be able to choose the types of feedback consistent with the training aims and design, and which are appropriate to the approach to learning.

The giving and receiving of feedback generates a sense of risk for both parties and much feedback offered can be wasted or even counter-productive if it is presented in a threatening way. For example, saying angrily to someone 'I get irritated with your persistent attempts to prove how clever you are!' is likely to cause considerable discomfort and may lead to both parties feeling hurt and distressed. Nevertheless, the information contained in the feedback may provide valuable learning for both giver and receiver.

Most feedback can be classified in terms which enable the trainer to choose between higher information value or higher risk value on the one hand and lower information value or risk on the other hand (see table 6.1).

Table 6.1 Dimensions of feedback

High risk or information	Low risk or information
Explicit	Implicit
Qualitative	Quantitative
Descriptive	Evaluative
Present	Past
Individual	Group

Implicit

Feedback which is implicit can be unsaid and given by gestures, expressions, voice tone and other non-verbal signals. In some cases statements or behaviour intended as feedback are nevertheless not complete and may make only oblique reference to the real message or give only part of it. This latter form still retains an implicit element.

A smile and a nod may be taken to imply encouragement or approval while a frown combined with a break in eye contact can be taken to imply disapproval. Equally someone who looks at their watch, and taps their feet may be giving someone a message about their impatience. In these cases feedback is implied. For feedback to be useful to a recipient, particularly in the context of interpersonal skills learning, a number of implicit aspects need to be uncovered:

1   It is the recipient who has to observe the non-verbal or covert messages and recognise that they contain some information.
2   He then has to establish correctly whether or not it was aimed at him rather than some other person or event.
3   He has to understand the meaning of the feedback.
4   He has to judge what specific aspect of his behaviour generated the feedback he receives.

Implicit feedback, therefore, makes it necessary for the recipient to work hard in order to learn something about himself. In day to day contact with others, the feedback people give and receive is more likely to be implicit than explicit. In IST the reverse should apply. By choosing to leave the implicit message concealed the trainer allows course members to sustain a sense of normality and probably, ease. In the early stages of a 'stranger-group' coming together, the fostering of a relaxed and friendly atmosphere may be important and leaving feedback implicit may help in this process (see Chapter 5). Equally, by giving implicit messages to course members a trainer can begin to regulate the interaction and relationships within the group and between himself and the group.

An important part of the trainer's function at the outset of a course may be to establish norms or guidelines for behaviour, generate the appropriate atmosphere and perhaps model or demonstrate the style of communication he wishes to encourage. This process is in fact a normal part of the relationship between trainer and group in the early stages. Leaving implicit feedback to be picked up by course members, encouraging some kinds of behaviour (asking questions, participating etc.) and discouraging others (interrupting, blocking etc.) can be effective in producing a good atmosphere without ever referring to the issues explicitly.

At its best feedback which is implicit can offer an opening for a course member to obtain some information about how he is affecting those around him without forcing him to 'face a fact'. Leaving some things unsaid reduces the chances of embarrassment and discomfort, and may produce significant learning.

The major disadvantage of leaving things unsaid is that it leaves the others guessing. The potential recipient could ask: 'Is he responding to me?' – 'What was it I did?' – 'What is it he is trying to say to me?'. While both giver and receiver leave these questions unasked and unanswered, understanding is likely to remain blurred.

Explicit

Feedback at its most explicit gives the recipient some clear information about his effect on others. So a smile and a nod might be accompanied by words like 'I am enjoying listening to you, I agree with what you are saying, please continue', while the frown with gaze averted might be supplemented by 'I am irritated by what you are saying and do not agree with you'. These examples are at a very simple level but can be applied to more complex exchanges.

The recipient in the case of explicit feedback has to make no guesses or assumptions about the effect on others of his behaviour. He simply has to hear it and pay attention to it. He does not have to guess at whom the feedback is aimed or what meaning to attach to it, or what part of his behaviour is attracting the response.

A problem with choosing to make all feedback explicit is that social interaction becomes rather laborious with frequent interruptions and diversions in order to ensure that complete information is out in the open.

A further difficulty for the trainer is that social convention and good manners normally require people to hide their feelings and 'being polite' often means withholding explicit feedback. Doing the opposite, that is encouraging openness in giving feedback is often the source of embarrassment and discomfort for giver and receiver alike so that participants in IST are very reluctant or resistant to setting side lifelong rules and conventions. For this reason, the introduction of explicit feedback can be eased by the introduction of a clear procedure. Basic guidelines are set out in Table 6.2.

In terms of the choices available to the course designer and course leader, it is evident that establishing the procedure of exchanging explicit feedback is more suitable to the 'feelings' approach where the time constraints of structure are less apparent and where the course objectives have been set out more in terms of awareness than in terms of skill development.

A final point in terms of this question of implicit–explicit feedback is that the two labels are for extreme ends of a continuum. Degrees of openness can be established in a group and adjusted to suit the group's needs and the training objectives. Indeed, as discussed in Chapters 2 and 5 on the design of training and the development of groups, the degree of openness and trust is likely to change as the

Table 6.2 Guidelines for giving and receiving feedback

Giver	Receiver
Check that the feedback you intend to give is wanted by the receiver.	Accept the feedback you are receiving as information.
Address the person directly.	Make your own choice about what you intend to do with the information (accept, reject, wholly or partly)
Be specific on what aspect of the individual you are giving feedback.	
Be clear about your own reaction to the other person – avoid blaming.	
Offer your feedback as information without attached conditions.	Avoid arguing, denying, justifying.
Offer as much as you think will be useful. Avoid giving a long list.	Ask for clarification only if you do not fully understand the feedback.

group progresses and the type of feedback can be adapted to suit the current needs.

Quantitative

Quantitative feedback involves classifying the results of the observation of a period of social interaction. The observations are grouped into types of behaviour exhibited by some or all of those involved and then each type is weighted by frequency of occurrence.

Most forms of interaction analysis[1] (see Appendix 1) involve making some recording of the number of occasions on which an individual or group display certain types of behaviour, during some form of activity or meeting. The recording is then presented to the participants in the form of numerical scores against one or other categories of behaviour. At its simplest a sociogram (see p. 172) provides participants with some information about how often they spoke during an exercise and to whom. Although simple to produce the data generated can demonstrate graphically important aspects of how a group operates in terms of leadership, membership and problem solving.

With a different perspective, interaction process analysis[2] records the kinds of behaviour exhibited in terms of 12 basic categories, enabling the participants in an exercise to see how the task, the group process and their individual contribution may be related. Here again the feedback given is normally in terms of the number of occasions a person, for example, 'made a suggestion' or 'asked for an opinion' during a particular period. Among the benefits of this form of quantitative feedback is that it allows the individual to form some view about the relationship between behaviour and its consequences in terms of task achievement or relationships.

One consequence of using this type of feedback is to reduce the level of risk for both giver and receiver, and therefore, lessen the discomfort which may be experienced:

1   Quantitative feedback carries less personal impact because data is based on behaviour not personality.
2   The information seems to be systematic and objective.
3   Each participant receives some feedback.

This mode of training seems particularly appropriate where the emphasis is on skills such as group leadership or group membership, group problem solving or basic interviewing. These frameworks and the feedback they generate can provide an important opening for a trainee which may lead to further and more personal development.

Qualitative

While quantitative feedback entails looking at a period of interaction over time and providing broad investigations of it, qualitative feedback entails looking in detail at a particular aspect of a person or his behaviour and providing an analysis of it in depth. Qualitative feedback does not aim to provide a view of the whole of someone's behaviour, but rather one feature is examined closely.

For example, by examining the quality of an individual's style of questioning and giving him one's reaction in detail, the individual can quickly come to learn when he appears, for example, at times curious, disbelieving or perhaps over protective. He can learn in each case how minor variations in his behaviour can create important changes in perceptions and reactions and also that group members will perceive and react to him differently. Using this learning the trainee can begin to make choices about what style is most appropriate at any particular time. This form of feedback requires that the course member participates fully in the activity and it may mean that he is the focus of attention for some time.

Often participants are encouraged to experiment with different ways of behaving to learn about how this affects others in the group. A process of this kind requires strong commitment from the participants to learn about themselves and a high degree of trust, openness and co-operation within the group. Above all, for learning by this method to be successful, the trainer requires a high degree of competence and self-awareness.

Descriptive

Giving descriptive feedback simply entails the giver first describing what he observes and perhaps what effect this behaviour has on himself. For example, 'Your voice is very low, your head is buried and I feel rather sad when I look at you'.

Feedback of this kind relies solely on the speaker's observation of the other and experience of himself and offers the recipient some information about how he appears to the outside world. Usually this is all that is needed for the receiver to learn about how he affects others. The giver may be keen to know what is happening inside the other person and so he could ask 'How do you feel?', or 'What is going on?' Sometimes the person receiving feedback will welcome the opportunity to express his feelings or convey some thoughts.

The use of descriptive feedback entails learning a new way of talking to others and it is not easy. Our experience is that the value in learning this process offers the greatest learning opportunities where rich feedback is an important part of the course. In courses where learning is more in terms of skill rather than awareness, and 'thinking' rather than 'feeling', the effort required to generate purely descriptive feedback is not worthwhile and could be counterproductive, thus increasing the threat. Obviously it is worthwhile experimenting with varying the degree to which descriptive feedback is encouraged depending on the purpose of the course, the expectations of participants and their previous experience of IST.

Evaluative

At one level 'You're not listening to me!' can offer an individual some information which allows him to pay attention to his own internal process and learn from it. At another level, and perhaps more frequently, it disguises the underlying norm, rule or value, 'You ought to be listening to me!' In this case, a distinction is being made between feedback which is offered so that the recipient is given an opportunity to learn and feedback which is given in order to impose a rule or value about the way people *should* behave.

Where a trainer recognises that much of the feedback being exchanged originates with values or rules, he can confront this process by asking the giver of feedback to make his value explicit (see table 6.3). The trainer can suggest to the giver that he states how people ought to behave, while making clear to the receiver that he is not compelled to accept someone else's rules for behaviour. In this way, the underlying values are brought to the surface and can be discussed more rationally.

Table 6.3   Examples of how values can be implied in feedback

Feedback	Value – People should:
'You are being defensive'	'. . . not be defensive'
'You are holding back'	'. . . express themselves openly'
'You are interrupting me'	'. . . let me finish what I want to say'
'You are talking very quickly'	'. . . take their time'
'You are telling me what to do'	'. . . leave others to decide for themselves'
Etc. etc.	

Once participants have understood that behind their feedback there can be some implied judgement or rule, then both giver and receiver can make their own decisions about its value. This allows the course to develop in the direction of choices for behaviour and the consequences of those choices, rather than in the direction of good and bad practices of social behaviour.

Past

Many exercises which are designed so that course members can learn from their own experience are based on this cycle:

Introductory theory
Practical activity
Analysis of the activity using feedback
Summarising (see Chapter 1.)

Frequently these exercises are designed so that some course members act as observers and give their analysis and feedback at the conclusion of the event.

This sequence can prove of great benefit to both participants and observers. Participants begin to see that events and behaviour to which they had attached meaning were seen completely differently by others. Individuals may begin to learn how their 'best intentions' were misunderstood or indeed well understood despite their behaviour. Observers can see the complexity of social interaction and begin to master some of the skills needed to understand what happens when people meet.

A disadvantage of this type of structured experience is that the link between the event and the feedback is weakened by the lapse of time. Participants can attempt to recall the events described by observers or other participants, but there is no way in which those same events can be re-experienced. Observers may discover that their observation differs markedly from the experience of participants but the reason for the difference has lost its importance or immediacy. One choice that the trainer has in these circumstances is to ensure that he has some form of recording of the original events. By using a tape-recorder or closed-circuit television, observation skills can be checked against a standardised definition of a type or category of behaviour. This procedure can be time consuming and may require expensive equipment and skilled operators, and therefore, is not always possible.

In any case the participant who is being observed has lost his opportunity to change his behaviour and experiment *at the time*.

Each exercise or training event becomes a discrete and fixed happening with learning restricted to thinking about the event in the past, and exploring in hypothetical terms 'what would have happened if . . .'. This form of learning can be productive, but may not always carry the degree of impact that is associated with 'here and now' feedback.

Present

Exchanging feedback in the present, that is expressing how one is being affected right now, enables the receiver to gain a deeper understanding and awareness of himself and his relationships. Making use of present oriented feedback and by experimenting with his behaviour, the trainee can experience readily the causes and effects which characterise the nature of his relationship with others.[3]

The detailed understanding gained from feedback in the present is unlikely to be achieved in any other way. However, along with the richness, the level of risk increases. Expressing any reaction to a person openly and fully at the moment of meeting entails a risk of upsetting him significantly. For example, one might truthfully say to someone 'While you are talking I am getting bored by your tone of voice and I am thinking about the items I need to put on my shopping list'. Although this is potentially rich feedback, the reaction of the receiver may be anger, disappointment, frustration or some other response, and unless the relationship has a sound base he may withdraw, feeling hurt and angry.

It is important to recognise, therefore, that exchanging feedback in the present requires sensitivity and a clear understanding between the parties concerned. The trainer needs to decide to what extent 'here and now' feedback can be tolerated in a group and what effect it may have. In general, taking risks of this kind is not necessary for courses designed to develop knowledge or techniques. However, for courses designed to enable participants to achieve personal insight, sensitivity or awareness it is an important learning vehicle.

Group

Many learning exercises and activities designed for management training are conducted in a fishbowl format. For the purposes of the exercise, the training group is divided into participants who sit in the middle of the room (and undertake a task) and observers who sit around the outside of the room and record their perceptions of what happens.

In designing the exercise, the trainer has the choice of how to direct the observers. Obviously these choices include the type of structured observation framework to be used (if any) and the key behaviour or aspects to look out for. Another consideration is whether to ask the observers each to watch one individual or whether to ask them to watch the whole group. Since the observations generate the feedback this decision will influence how much individual and personal feedback is given.

There are many circumstances in exercises or 'here and now' style learning where group based feedback seems more appropriate:

1 During the early phase of the group. At the beginning of a training programme, before the participants have developed some understanding of each other, both observers and participants are likely to be hesitant about giving and receiving personal feedback. By encouraging the group to concentrate on conceptual learning (such as the recognition of types of behaviour and their effects on the group) rather than personal learning the trainer helps to keep the risk level down.

2 Where the main approach is intended to be in terms of 'thinking'. Providing information about individual behaviour and its effect is likely to divert attention away from the gaining of knowledge about behaviour patterns in general. What tends to happen is that individuals become concerned with managing their immediate feelings and relationships – thus interrupting the conceptual learning.

3 Where the main objective of the exercise is group development or team building: the entire group's performance is what counts in these circumstances and the emphasis is likely to be on collective responsibility rather than individual behaviour. By concentrating on the events at a group level the team is less likely to engage in blaming or praising any one particular individual.

4 Where the training group's development of itself or its relationship with the trainer are issues. Learning about group development, authority relationships, dependency can often be stimulated by interventions aimed at the group as a whole. Examples of this type of intervention are:
'The group seems to be avoiding the possibility of conflict'
'What do you (the group) think I should be doing?'
'There seems to be a ritual for gaining membership in this group'

By crystallising some of the group's processes and putting them into words the trainer may help the group firstly to understand what is happening and secondly to decide what if anything they want to do about it (see Chapter 5).

Individual

Receiving individual and personal feedback is the best possible way of gaining understanding and insight into one's own interpersonal skills. Watching a few minutes of a closed circuit television recording with comments from trainers and colleagues about what the individual is doing or saying carries a substantial impact and can lead to significant skill development.

All this is true provided that the individual is absorbing what is said as information. Some trainees, however, can hear the feedback as a personal attack or confirming dreadful expectations of making a total mess of the desired performance. Just because the feedback is confined to a single individual it may encourage that person to be defensive or encourage the group to hold back or blame. The risk of the individual being hurt is much higher when feedback is directed at one person and, therefore, there is a joint responsibility between the trainer and the group to ensure that the trainee receives only feedback that can be used for learning.

Feedback media

The modes of giving feedback and degree of impact are closely related to the means used for conveying the information. Therefore the choices available to the course leader regarding course design demand that he consider, not only the type of feedback but also the means of giving it.

Three frequently used kinds of feedback media are:

1 Behaviour classification systems recorded in writing and presented in written form, or orally or both.
2 Recorded material using sound and/or visual recording which is played back with comments from course leaders and participants.
3 Direct verbal and non-verbal feedback during face-to-face contact about mutual experiencing of participants in the present.

Behaviour classification system

Using these systems such as Bales' 'interaction process analysis'[2] or Rackham's 'behaviour analysis'[4] as the vehicle for giving feedback, is a well tried method in IST.

In terms of the dimensions of feedback outlined above it tends to be:

High Risk or Information	Low Risk or Information
Explicit	Quantitative
	Past
	Evaluative?

The real value of using this form of feedback is that it makes explicit what in normal social contact remains implicit. By using a system of behaviour classification behaviour becomes a proper subject for attention and discussion. Since the content of the feedback tends to be quantitative, possibly evaluative and is given some time after the events to which it refers, this lessens the degree of risk and discomfort likely to be generated. It also reduces the richness of the feedback for the recipients.

Making reasonably successful recordings of social interaction in terms of categories requires considerable expertise and continuing practice, rather like shorthand script. The trainer must therefore decide whether to use expert observers who have received previous training, or inexpert course members who have just been introduced to the system and the concept, or perhaps just to do the recording himself. Each of these options involves benefits and drawbacks: on the one hand, experts are likely to be 'outsiders' to a group and may reduce the level of trust and openness in the group; on the other hand the data produced will carry considerable validity.

Having inexperienced course members making recordings ensures the active participation of the entire group and enables observers to acquire something of a new and useful skill. The disadvantage could be that the data is badly recorded and poorly fed back and omits or misinterprets what may have been key behavioural events.

The option of using inexperienced course members to provide some interaction analysis will have some effect on the acceptability of the data and consequently on the relationship among group members and between the group members and the trainer. By doing the work himself, the course leader may ensure that he provides feedback which is reasonably accurate and raises important learning points, but he also reduces the level of participation for course members and is likely to become exhausted.

Another important and rather vexed question in using interaction analysis techniques is concerned with the importance of internal psychological processes. There is a well-trodden path of controversy between those who believe behaviour is the only significant dimension in understanding and learning social skills and those who believe that the underlying internal processes need to be brought into awareness before social skills can be developed.

Ultimately individual trainers have to make their own choices. Clearly interaction analysis techniques have been designed to provide a picture of behaviour that is observable rather than examining internal processes. It is not possible, therefore, to use interaction analysis to explore deeper individual psychological issues although the feedback derived may raise deep rooted personal problems.

Audio-visual recording

Tape-recorders and closed circuit television systems have become widely used by trainers and teachers in many forms of training; in interpersonal skills training the media can be used as a method for teaching skills such as basic interviewing techniques, conducting discussions, negotiations or counselling.

In making a decision about how to use CCTV and how to handle the feedback the trainer has a number of factors to consider. In terms of the four dimensions of types of feedback recordings of this kind tend to be:

High Risk or Information	Low Risk or Information
Descriptive	Past?
Explicit	
Qualitative	

The information available is potentially very rich and for that reason and others, participants often experience a high sense of risk. The purpose to which the recording is put depends much on the course design and objectives as well as on the trainer's skill and sensitivity to social processes. The most consistent response from course members who volunteer or are nominated to undertake some form of role play or encounter which is recorded on CCTV is nervousness, anxiety and tension. In using CCTV participants frequently express hopes that they will provide a 'good performance'. They fear that they might 'make fools of themselves' and be ridiculed by other course members, and may seem concerned that their worst features will be the overriding focus of attention.

In most cases the course member is his own worst critic and will find reassurance and encouragement from course members and leaders. In rare cases, the participant is too fearful to take the risk without persuasion. The leader must then decide whether to use his power to encourage the individual or to leave him alone.

During playback, again, a course member may be highly critical of himself or may receive critical evaluative feedback from the group and trainer. Where a supportive and open atmosphere has been created, the temporary discomfort or embarrassment need not become an obstacle to learning and insight. It is crucial for the trainer to recognise the degree of discomfort experienced by participants and to ensure that the feedback does not become more for the benefit of the givers than the receiver.

The trainer can vary considerably the amount of detail he draws from a review of recorded material (this flexibility is valuable and decisions about it can be made during the actual process of feedback. (See also Chapter 7.) A five minute interview can be replayed in order to highlight important techniques for interviewing, without at any time drawing attention to the specific behaviour of the individual concerned. The same piece of tape can be reviewed in detail, drawing attention to fine nuances of body language and raising issues potentially of deep concern for those included. There are many options between these two extremes and the choice will depend on the aim of the training and the nature and expectation of course members, as well as the amount of time available to review a piece of tape. At whatever the level of detail a tape is analysed, the process tends to be time-consuming so that a course design should include ample opportunity to review and discuss recorded material. This time is often seen by course members as the most valuable and is often referred to as being the highlight of their training course and the session from which they learned most.

Direct feedback

Direct feedback about here and now experience will be:

High Risk or Information	Low Risk or Information
Qualitative	—
Present	—
Explicit	
Descriptive	

It is, therefore, the most risky and most potentially uncomfortable form of feedback. At the same time it offers the recipient a unique opportunity 'to see himself as others see him' and to learn precisely how what he does affects those around him. This style of exchanging feedback is characteristic of IST based on human psychology. More specifically in sensitivity training and its descendants over the last twenty years direct feedback is one of the major learning vehicles and techniques borrowed from these areas are becomming increasingly used by management trainers.

Referring to the 'thinking', 'doing', 'feeling' distinctions, direct feedback strongly emphasises the feelings responses and reduces the importance of thinking and doing as ways of learning interpersonal skills. For this reason direct feedback alone is not adequate for lasting learning and some opportunity for *thinking* about the feedback and *doing* experiments to test the validity of new understanding or insight is of great value (see Chapter 7).

The process of exchange between group members of their 'here and now' experiences of each other will frequently bring to light some aspect of an individual which he sees as a 'problem' or which he wants to change. This process of raising problems, which are sometimes deep rooted and sensitive, present the trainer with a delicate dilemma. If the course design is intended for participants to achieve some personal insight and awareness, and he has the skills, it seems normal that the leader will invite the course member to pursue his concern as far as he wishes, encouraging the group to give support and feedback and possibly providing creative solutions or alternatives.

If the course is designed entirely to teach particular skills, say in appraisal or selection interviewing, then the alternative choice of putting aside the personal issue in favour of continuing with the programme's primary aims may seem more appropriate.

Much training, however, requires a balance between personal learning and the development of new skills and knowledge. For example, some feedback exercises designed to develop a course member's sensitivity and skill in counselling will inevitably lead him to gain some insight to his own psychological and emotional process. This is normally a pleasant and satisfying kind of experience but occasionally an individual will be concerned at what he may believe to be a personal fault which comes to light. Here the course leader has a shared responsibility for making a choice between following up and hopefully resolving the personal difficulty experienced by the individual or moving the group's attention back to the development of skills or knowledge at the risk of continuing and growing distress on the part of the individual (see also Chapter 3).

Many factors can influence this choice, including expectation of successfully resolving the issue, the time available, the needs of other course members and the likely effect on the group of either decision. The course leader needs some skill and experience in making choices of this kind as the outcome can seriously influence the impact of the course and his relationship with the group.

The use of feedback in IST is not an open invitation for everyone to be completely frank with everyone else about how they are reacting to them. Feedback which does not give the recipient the opportunity to learn about interpersonal skills, relationships or himself is of little value in the context of training. Nor is the exchange of feedback enough, in itself, to ensure that personal learning or training takes place. What feedback does offer is one of the most potent means by which to increase an individual's or group's social skill in terms of understanding what happens and how it happens.

Conclusion

The main purpose of this chapter has been to specify the wide range of choice that the social skills trainer has in the use he makes of the process of exchanging feedback. Clearly the decision the trainer takes will vary greatly according to his own inclinations and skills, the background of the course members, the objectives of the training and the needs and interests of the client organisation(s). It is important that these decisions should be made in a conscious way, with some awareness of the advantages and disadvantages of each option.

References

(1) D.A. Dyer and W.J. Giles, 'Interaction Analysis', Chapter 3 in *Improving Interpersonal Relations – some approaches to social skill training*, Ed. C.L. Cooper, Gower, Aldershot, 1981.

(2) R.F. Bales, *Personality and Interpersonal Behaviour*, Holt Rinehart Winston, 1970.

(3) F. S. Perls, R. F. Hefferline and P. Goodman, *Gestalt Therapy – Excitement and Growth in the Human Personality*, Penguin Books Ltd, Harmondsworth, 1951.

(4) N. Rackham, P. Honey and M. Colbert, *Developing Interactive Skills*, Wellens, 1971.

7 Evaluating IST*

The main element of evaluation in IST is the gathering of information which is used for making judgements and decisions concerning the effectiveness of the training. The information is likely to be gathered from, and concerned with, all those involved in the training including the trainees, the trainer, the sponsors and the nominating agent.

The alternative to evaluating training is a reliance on faith and unsubstantiated consensus as guidelines to the value of a training intervention. In some cases this faith and consensus may guarantee the continuation or repetition of a particular event, but clearly cannot form a sound basis for making decisions about the future alternatives and possibilities.

Most organisational decisions are based on cost-effectiveness and require evidence of the achievement of objectives. Evaluation is, therefore, likely to be seen as important, especially in terms of outcomes from the design compared with those anticipated when the training was instigated. In addition, the decision makers are likely to want to know not only how effective the training was, but also what specific factors contributed to the outcome.

Much discussion concerning evaluation centres around its difficulties in the sphere of IST. Indeed, this was suggested in the introduction (see pp. xiii–xiv) when comparing IST with technical skills training. Unfortunately discussion of the difficulties can often

---

* This chapter is based on ideas contributed by Ben Bennett MA.

lead to the abandonment of attempts to implement systematic evaluation or even, in some cases, the abandonment of the training itself!

Evaluation to prove or disprove training

The stated reasons for abandoning evaluation or training can be many and various. Underlying causes include the following:

1 The major purpose of the evaluation is to *prove* that the training has been worthwhile, so that on subsequent occasions there will be no need to evaluate it.
2 The evaluation and the training need to be *separate* activities in order that *objective* evidence of success or failure can be provided.
3 The behaviour of trainees and other variables need to be *predictable* and *controllable*, which requires that:
4 Their behaviour and other variables need to be *definable* and *measurable*.
5 What happens during training and when it is being evaluated needs to be highly structured and *inflexible*.
6 The trainees need to be *passive* recipients of the training rather than active determiners of it.

This may be a somewhat exaggerated view and yet trainers do oppose detailed evaluation because they perceive it as presenting these kinds of difficulties. The perception is likely to be influenced by the demand that results should be 'scientifically valid'. This means that the data should have been gathered following principles of the physical sciences where hypotheses are tested under strictly controlled conditions, perhaps in a laboratory.[1] Being able to impose absolute control over the conditions of the training is clearly impossible so that straightforward causal models cannot be developed. What makes the physical science type of approach still less appropriate is the fact that unlike a gas or a liquid, people respond differently when being tested or when their behaviour is observed.

Nevertheless, at least in technical skills training some of the conditions required by a 'scientific' model can be met:

1 The use of a technical skill is largely observable and can be broken down into clearly defined behaviours, leading to:
2 The setting of precise learning objectives and the measurement of learning outcomes in performance terms, leading to:
3 Subsequent judgements about the value of training using comparative measurements of job or task performance and possibly cost-savings.

These possibilities are less available in the context of IST. It can be very frustrating to know the value of a learning experience and yet not be able to express it in a way which would make sense to a person who has not participated. Similarly, whatever the reality, it may be extremely difficult to demonstrate in causal terms that training leads to better performance.

Suppose, for example, that the interviewing course described in 'A framework for IST' (Chapter 1, pp. 8–9) was a preliminary design in response to analysed training and other needs (the nature of the group, the skills and preferences of the trainers, the culture of the organisation etc.). This course would involve elements of 'thinking', 'doing' and 'feeling', demanding flexibility of the trainers and trainees as it moved across the spectrum of approaches.

Understandably the participants might resist attempts at having their learning evaluated if it meant that the training methods had to be changed in order to suit the needs of systematic evaluation. On the other hand, those responsible for evaluation would resist being involved if they knew in advance that their results would be unreliable or useless because of the flexibility of the training methods.

The intention here is not to deny the value of technical skills training methods which are closely linked to those discussed in the 'doing' approach and interaction analysis in particular (see Appendix 1). However, if the choices of potential IST methods and course design are constrained by the requirements of evaluation, then the trainer is likely to feel hampered and may even obstruct or avoid any attempts to evaluate his work.

A trainer who is concerned with providing sound and consistent interpersonal skills training will resist attempts to reduce his flexibility or restrict the programme design. At the same time, both the trainer and others will want to assess the value of the training. It is necessary then to adopt a different set of principles.

The next part of this chapter is not intended to be an exhaustive list of tools and techniques for evaluating IST – details are provided in two useful publications[2,3] listed in the references. Exploring the model and its consequences is intended as much to stimulate thought and experiment as to provide unequivocal answers. Its primary purpose is to provide a set of ideas with which to consider the utility of the tools and techniques from other sources.

Evaluation to improve training

The principles of evaluation to improve IST are outlined below. They are expressed in such a way as to contrast with those required to prove or disprove IST.

1   The major purpose of the evaluation is to *improve* the training rather than prove or disprove it, therefore:
2   The evaluation and the training need to be closely *integrated*, rather than separated.
3   The evaluation and the training should be kept as *flexible* as is necessary for each to take account of the needs of the other, including unforeseen circumstances. Inflexibility introduced to control trainees' behaviour and other variables should be avoided.
4   The trainees need to be acknowledged as potentially *active* determiners of events rather than the passive recipients of training.

Although the purposes of evaluation can differ significantly this latter approach is more likely to provide realistic and useable results. The decisions about whether or not the training is needed are normally taken during the analysis of training needs. Adopting these alternative principles for evaluating the outcome then overcomes a major source of difficulty. (For further discussion about the alternative approaches see Burgoyne and Cooper.[4])

In doing so, it becomes possible to conduct the training and the evaluation in such a way that each meets the needs of the other. The apparently conflicting demands of effective training and effective evaluation can be accommodated by a combination of the above principles and a model of learning through discovery and change.

Evaluation as a process of learning through discovery and change

It must first be recognised and accepted that the effectiveness of each element, evaluation and IST, is mutually dependent and that both these elements are in turn dependent on making the most of learning by discovery and change. Trainers and trainees need to be partners in this process, each learning from the other and sharing common objectives. Perhaps this complex process can best be understood in terms of the four discrete stages of Kolb's learning cycle.[5] The design and content of the interviewing course referred to earlier provides a ready example of an IST programme for the discussion that follows.

Stage One: trying out new or established ways of thinking, feeling and behaving.
Stage Two: direct involvement in the here and now experience of

oneself in relation to (a) the activity in which one is engaged and (b) what is happening in one's immediate environment, and (c) to others.

Stage Three: using information about that experience, gained from within oneself and from others, to stand back and reflect upon it.

Stage Four: using familiar and new ways of thinking about the information and reflections in making sense of the experience and thereby confirming the utility and appropriateness of established ways of involving oneself, or indicating new possibilities and options for involvement in the future.

Let us examine this process from the points of view of a trainee and a trainer participating in the series of role-play interviews and reviews of them, based on difficult interviews that the trainees have personally experienced. The event will be described and interpreted using the learning model, firstly from the trainee's standpoint then followed by that of the trainer.

The trainee

The trainee taking up the role of interviewer, based on what was for him a difficult appraisal interview, for example, will participate in *Stage One* and *Stage Two* of the cycle of learning. He can experience himself trying out the approach and methods he used at the time he undertook the difficult interview; or he can experience himself trying out what are to him new ways of thinking, feeling and behaving. The new ways may have been learned on the programme or prior to coming on it, as a result perhaps of his reflections on a previous interview at work.

As long as the trainee becomes involved in the role-play activity, he has the opportunity to participate in *Stage Three* and *Stage Four* of the learning cycle. The main learning is likely to result from feedback gathered from other trainees and the trainer. He can reflect on the feedback in relation to the role play and make sense of it. In doing so, he may draw on familiar or new ways of thinking about his involvement in the interview. Any new approach is likely to have been stimulated by the trainer in the form of theories, ideas or frameworks about face to face communication. Often the type of framework used and the way in which the ideas are put across will be congruent (for example, interaction analysis for a 'doing' style approach or Gestalt for a 'feelings' based approach).

As the trainee makes sense of his experience during *Stage Four* he may confirm that his approach to the original appraisal interview was appropriate. On the other hand, he may decide that on the next occasion he will behave differently. Whether his conclusion is one of confirmation or the need to change, his making sense of the role play and his own involvement in it may include greater self-knowledge, greater understanding of communication and of interpersonal processes. Opportunities to put what he has learned into practice might (ideally) be planned into the training event and could arise later when conducting interviews at work. Such opportunities offer themselves as new experiences from which further development can arise in terms of gaining feedback, reflecting and understanding.

The trainer

In the process of helping the trainee to make greater sense of himself and others, the trainer is learning about the effectiveness of the course design in providing for the training needs.

For example, what is experienced by the trainee as the complete four step cycle of learning may constitute *Stage One* and *Stage Two* of the trainer's cycle of learning. Again, there are a number of ways in which these stages can be undergone.

The trainer can experience the event in terms of trying out a novel or a familiar design and method. The design and method could be new in the sense that they have evolved out of reflections on earlier experiences during the same programme. Alternatively, they may have been planned as a consequence of experience during a similar programme in the past.

The trainer's learning in the third and fourth stages of the cycle is likely to be based, firstly on feedback about the amount and nature of the involvement of trainees and secondly, on reflections on the experience of managing the learning process. The trainer can make sense of his experience using familiar and/or new ways of thinking about IST. A new perspective may be contributed by colleagues during regular meetings convened for the purpose of co-ordination and review which may be held outside the teaching sessions. A familiar model may be one that is normally used in the context of learning interviewing skills (e.g. transactional analysis) but which on these occasions is applied to the relationship between the trainer and his training group.

The trainer, as he makes sense of his experience, can make choices about his future behaviour. He may confirm the effectiveness of his work or decide on the need for and type of changes that can be implemented. Whatever the result, he has the opportunity to develop his self-knowledge with the implications for all his relationships not just those which occur in his training role.

The chance to put new decisions into practice may be taken as the current training event continues or held over until the next similar event. The optimum learning takes place where the trainer uses these future occasions as offers of new experiences which once again engage him in the cycle of learning.

In this way the trainer and the trainees engage in evaluation of training as the event takes place. More importantly, the trainer can use the learning to improve the effectiveness of the training. As suggested, he has opportunities to make changes in his own behaviour and the course design, if appropriate and necessary, to meet the learning needs of trainees more effectively. He can, therefore, train, evaluate and improve the training as it happens.

He could also treat the complete training programme as *Stage One* and *Stage Two* of the cycle. His participation in *Stage Three* would then include gathering information from the trainees and others once the programme has been completed. With the benefit of greater distance through a longer time scale, he can then stand back and review the training event, its effects and his contribution to it.

Stage Four of the cycle for the trainer could involve considerable discussion with nominators and fellow-trainers and others in order to set the training in the context of the working environment. This would be particularly important where the working environment contains influences that obstruct the trainees in continuing or implementing their learning.

In addition, new approaches to the training may be gained from the trainer's attendance at seminars and other self-development activities. He can also use the experience of the training and its evaluation as an opportunity to participate in a personal process of learning. Once the trainer has learned how to learn, his development of himself, his relationships and his skills and knowledge as a trainer are likely to become an integral part of his work.

Finally, optimum use can be made of participation in this learning cycle to improve training if the trainer and others have previously undertaken an analysis of training needs. This includes a number of activities and processes which are described in detail in Chapter 2. Using the resulting plan the trainer can evaluate his effectiveness and complete Stages Three and Four of the cycle. In many cases a clear expression of intentions based on analysed needs will provide important criteria on which to base judgements about mounting, modifying or managing the required training. Without them the process of reflecting back can become vague or confused.

So far this chapter has aimed to show how evaluation as a basis for improving training can be a learning process that the provider shares with his client. The next part discusses the case for widening the group responsible for evaluation to include, for example, the participants and nominators.

Widening membership of the group that has responsibility for evaluating IST

The limitations to effective evaluation can stem from the adoption of an inappropriate model or the constraints of particular training methods. A further set of problems can occur as a result of the wide range of uses to which IST can be put. For example, a series of IST events may be implemented to achieve specific task objectives such as improved decision making, or introducing new work methods; alternatively, the training may be aimed at achieving commercial objectives such as cost-savings on recruitment or as a result of tighter contract negotiations; or the training may have a social objective such as increased team commitment or improved morale.

In the example of appraisal interviewing, used earlier in this chapter, learning about the effectiveness of the training was based on the assumptions that:

1 The trainer had direct involvement in the analysis of training needs and the subsequent course design.
2 The training was carried out in the form of an event or programme which was repeated so that the results of evaluation could be transferred in the form of improvements in subsequent events.
3 The trainees, nominators and others concerned with the training were available after the event to review its effect.

Without these conditions the trainer may be so detached from the results of his work that he may feel little responsibility for the outcome. The sense of involvement and responsibility will obviously vary from individual to individual, but the circumstances that form a background against which the trainer works will also have a considerable impact.

For example, at one end of the scale is the in-company trainer who is employed specifically to provide a particular series of training events as a part of an organisation development programme. At the other end of the scale is the individual consultant who presents a one-off training event which is attended by no more than a single manager from any one organisation.

Although the orientation of the providers may be very different, the problems of evaluation are likely to be similar. Ultimately what is achievable is a matter of degree. In one context the choice may be between one type of approach or another for the organisation; in the other context it may be a question of one external resource or another for an individual.

In this process of decision making it is often the nominating manager rather than the trainer who has a key role to play. To the extent that he is making realistic decisions as a nominator he is also evaluating IST. In order to do this he, in common with the trainer and the trainee, has the four stage learning cycle on which to draw.

The purpose of the training function may then be to provide information about available training and new ways of thinking about IST in relation to subordinates and their jobs. Further, the training department has as one of its responsibilities the coaching of nominating managers in the skills of evaluation in order to improve company training decisions and choices.

It is in this way that the membership of the group responsible for evaluation can be widened to cope with the range of ways in which IST is used. More importantly the membership can be extended to include the manager who is undergoing the training. The training can be designed in such a way as to encourage his learning how to learn as a part of his interpersonal skills development. In so doing he is developing his skills as an evaluator, in that he can evaluate himself and his interpersonal skills. More particularly, he is able to evaluate the training in terms of the opportunities it provides for developing those skills. By recognising the nominator and participant as integral parts of training evaluation, the choices as to the nature, timing and location of the training can be increased. Such a shift may in itself require and result in a learning process.[6]

This approach to evaluation then gives rise to a method of management development (which will include IST) which is a form of self-development (see Chapter 8). Any decision to undertake off-the-job training will, under this method, require that the participant has, prior to attending the programme, identified his training need and assessed the course for its utility and suitability. During the programme he will need to have involved himself in it as a trainee. After the programme he will have to evaluate its impact in terms of the original (and any new) objectives and assess its effectiveness at work.

The use and management of feedback in evaluation

Earlier in this chapter the trainer's involvement in evaluation was discussed – in particular the trainer should assess his experience and involvement. In order to do this he must be able to obtain sufficient relevant information about the effects of the training. This requirement generates an interest in the use and management of feedback not only as a part of the trainee's development, but also in the trainer's learning and ability to evaluate.

Feedback as a means of helping the trainee in IST was examined earlier (see Chapter 6). In the context of the trainer's learning for the purpose of evaluation it is any communication received by the trainer that offers information about how the training (and therefore the trainer himself) affects the participants and sponsors.

In managing feedback for the purposes of the trainee's learning, the trainer needs to choose types which are consistent with a suitable risk level, the amount of structure and the approach to learning (see Chapter 1). With regard to managing the feedback for the purpose of evaluation the choice will depend upon two key questions which are raised in the following sections.

Have the trainees changed as a result of training?

The choices, frequency and timing of feedback can be related to the amounts and kinds of changes that are expected of the trainees. For example, if the training is intended to develop specific behavioural skills (e.g. less talking, more listening), are the trainees learning with these behaviours as an integral part of their repertoire? This would imply that they had completed all four stages of the learning cycle in relation to the skills and are ready to try these new ways of doing things at work.

Other questions that might be asked of the training are:

1   Do the trainees in fact try out these new ways of behaving at work?
2   Do they continue to develop and refine their skills having returned to their jobs?
3   What factors, other than the impact of the training, help or hinder the application of new skills and their continued development?

In the case of training aimed at developing new ways of experiencing self and others the questions could be:

1   Do the trainees in fact feel differently about themselves and others?
2   What is the likely impact of the learning on their relationships?
3   Are the trainees able to conceptualise their learning?
4   Are the trainees able to translate their learning in terms of new choices for behaviour and are these changes perceived by others?

In the case of the training aimed at developing new ways of reflecting upon and thinking about relationships, the questions could be:

1   Do the trainees have the ability to demonstrate their understanding of new models or concepts?
2   Are the trainees able to recognise situations where these concepts or models can be applied?

3   Do the trainees feel able to use the training at work?

Questions of the kind outlined above are likely to reveal whether or not trainees have changed as a result of their experience. A second question concerned with evaluation now needs to be asked.

How have the trainees reacted to opportunities for involvement in training?

The typical issues tackled under this heading are the trainees' reactions to the content and structure of the events in terms of enjoyment, the pace of the event, integration etc. Indeed many of the factors to be taken into account in the design and development of IST can provide anchors for questions to be asked of trainees. These then elicit immediate responses and provide a component of the evaluation feedback.

Since in most kinds of IST and particularly the 'doing/feeling' approaches, direct involvement is a prerequisite for the opportunities for change, then in many cases the effectiveness of the training is proportional to the willingness to become involved. The trainer can, therefore, quickly assess the trainee's reactions and the effectiveness of some aspects of his work by the extent to which participants take the opportunity to participate.

Types and choices of feedback in evaluation

The dimensions of feedback applied earlier, in the context of trainee learning, can also be applied and managed in the context of evaluation:

Implicit	Explicit
Quantitative	Qualitative
Descriptive	Evaluative
Present	Past
Individual	Group

The choices that are made and the decisions taken about the frequency and timing of their use will depend upon a number of interrelated factors. For example:

1   The questions that are being asked of the trainees.
2   The membership of the group that has responsibility for undertaking the evaluation.
3   The way in which the IST methods are being used (in-company training, external training with stranger groups, as a part of processes of self-development etc.).

4   The purpose of the evaluation (to improve the training as it happens or future training of the same kind, or to improve decisions about the use of established in-company or external programmes).

5   The resources available to those carrying out the evaluation (their skills, expertise and interests, the time available between events or programmes to enable plans for improvements to be formed and implemented etc.).

With these considerations in mind, perhaps the most fundamental choice, which affects all others, is that between *implicit* and *explicit* feedback.

In his role, the trainer will be learning about the effects of the training as it happens and responding by making choices about his future conduct and the content of the programme. If he does so the feedback for evaluation will be *implicit*. The problems associated with implicit feedback are that the receiver, in this case the trainer, is left to do most of the work. For example the trainer has to notice that there is some feedback being given, then to decide which aspects of the participants' behaviour can be taken as feedback at all. Then he will need to ascertain whether the feedback is aimed at himself, the training or some other aspect of the situation. Further, he has to interpret the signal and finally respond appropriately. All this is hard enough, but can be made even tougher if the social rules do not encourage him to reveal either that the feedback has been received or that it has been responded to.

Key influences on the receiving and interpretation of implicit feedback will be the feelings that the trainer has about himself, the group and the content of the training. A trainer who feels unsure and doubtful may well selectively perceive feedback which seems to reinforce that feeling and conversely an over-confident trainer may selectively ignore feedback which might undermine his self-confidence.

Explicit feedback avoids these pitfalls and provides much data on which to base an evaluation. However, as the feedback becomes explicit so the process of training and that of evaluation become separate and are less likely to provide the integrated learning and development which might otherwise occur. Another difficulty is the time that it takes to gather and process the explicit feedback which might otherwise be used for training or back at work. In this sense the training and evaluation may be seen as getting in each other's way.

The decision concerning *quantitative* or *qualitative* feedback may well depend on the members involved in the training and whether or not the training event will be repeated.

Quantitative evidence is very suitable in evaluating behaviour change for example, on a series of training events where behaviour analysis has been used. On this type of programme the quantitative results can perform many functions because feedback is provided for participants as well as trainers. The use of quantitative evaluation is likely to be less appropriate when applied during feelings based training as the process of data collection is likely to contrast with the learning methods.

The issue of whether feedback should be *descriptive* or *evaluative* does not seem to make sense at first glance. Obviously feedback that is aimed at evaluating training will be evaluative. Yet on closer examination there are important choices for the trainer to make. Once the distinction is made between the process of gathering information on the one hand and reflecting on it to make sense of it, on the other, the trainer has the choice about the type of information he wants.

Where the trainer asks the participants primarily to make judgements about pace, integration methods etc., he is less likely to obtain details about the participants' actual experience. What he will get is a synthesis of the experiences compared with expectations, which lead the trainee to evaluate his experience in terms of 'good' and 'bad'. These judgements will have been influenced by many events (previous experiences of IST, relationships within the training group, expectations based on previous course members' reports, state of health etc.) not all of which are relevant to the purposes of the evaluation.

The trainer can, alternatively, invite participants to give feedback in the form of a description of their experience (including such areas as periods of interest or boredom, involvement or withdrawal, learning, experimenting, feeling happy, sad, angry etc.) and the events which give rise to them. The trainer and nominators as well as participants can then use their own perspectives to help make judgements based on clearer information.

In effect, by asking trainees to provide just an evaluation, the trainer loses the opportunity to make his own judgements about whether to and how to improve the training. The information and the evaluation become jumbled in the evaluative feedback.

The question of whether the feedback should be obtained in a *past* or *present* mode need not be approached as an issue of 'either–or'.

Effective evaluation as has been said earlier is a continuing process involving trainer, participants and nominator. Taking feedback about the participants' experiences of the training as it occurs is a part of the work of a trainer. In so far as the trainer is a model for participants, the ability to accept and use the feedback may need to be demonstrated. This type of feedback can be encouraged by asking participants how they feel and what they want during exercises or during periods set aside for reflection and review.

Further information can be gathered at the end of a training event. Often this exercise of reflecting on their experience also helps to complete the four stages of the learning cycle and, therefore, need not be presented as separate from the training. Nevertheless, the resulting feedback will be in a 'past' mode.

The need to follow up on IST is evident. New skills require reinforcement and refinement if they are to become part of the established repertoire of a manager. One of the most effective ways of reminding a participant of his learning is to invite him to re-evaluate the effects of training. This process can take place in the form of an interview, a questionnaire or (if resources permit) a follow-up training session in which the group review their learning and continue their development. The feedback gained from these three stages will therefore be a mixture of past and present, each serving a dual purpose of training and evaluation.

The final dimension concerning feedback for evaluation is the one which has the group at one end and the individual at the other. Again the choice need not be an 'either–or', as receiving feedback from the group does not exclude receiving individual views.

Among the factors to consider in making this choice are:

1   The level of trust in the group.
2   The stage of the group's development.
3   The orientation of the training towards group or individual learning.
4   The chances of suppressing important feedback.
5   The amount of structure in the programme.

The problem associated with taking individual feedback is that it may not readily reduce into a usable form. Twelve participants can reflect twelve different experiences. The result may be too much detailed data and not enough generalisation. The benefit is, of course, that the detail may provide key pointers to improvements.

Taking whole group feedback may distort the entire meaning of the feedback or equally may produce such broad generalisations that the feedback becomes meaningless.

Perhaps the best method for generating usable information is to invite sub-groups of three to six members each to produce a report with an explicit invitation to dissenters to have their views heard. This method can encompass most types of training event, leaving only unstructured or highly individually focused events to be handled differently.

Conclusion

The purpose of this chapter has been to explore a range of choices available when evaluating IST. The close relationship between training and evaluation has been emphasised, with recognition that both are based on a process of learning. The implication is that evaluation is undertaken in order to improve training rather than to decide upon whether or not to continue with it. Thus evaluation implies a willingness to change methods, designs and behaviour. The close links between evaluation and training also imply that much of what constitutes evaluation is simply a part of good training practice.

The argument has been put for the widening of the group responsible for evaluation so that it includes the managers undertaking training, the nominators and the sponsors.

The question of how the data for evaluation is assembled was reviewed looking in particular at the types of feedback available. The ability to choose and manage the type of feedback received is likely to affect significantly the trainer's and sponsor's capacities to make judgements about the effectiveness of the training and to plan any desirable changes.

References

(1) D.T. Campbell and J.C. Stanley, *Experimental and Quasi-Experimental Designs for Research*, Rand McNally, Chicago, 1963.
(2) A.C. Hamblin, *Evaluation and Control of Training*, McGraw Hill, 1974.
(3) P.B. Warr, M.W. Bird and N. Rackham, *Evaluation of Management Training*, Gower, Aldershot, 1970.
(4) J.G. Burgoyne and C.L. Cooper, 'Evaluation methodology', *Journal of Occupational Psychology*, 1975, vol. 48, pp. 53–62.
(5) D.A. Kolb and M.S. Plovnick, 'The experiential learning theory of career development; In: *Organisational Careers: Some New Perspectives*, J. Van Maanen (Ed.), John Wiley & Sons, 1977.
(6) J.G. Burgoyne and R. Stuart, 'The nature, use and acquisition of managerial skills and other attributes', *Personnel Review* vol. 6, no. 4, 1976, pp. 19–29.

8 IST in perspective

This concluding chapter is concerned with looking both backwards and forwards. The backward look will consist of describing three of the most important underlying influences on IST: behaviourism, psychoanalysis and humanism. This description will draw together many of the themes discussed earlier and will then provide a starting point for a consideration of the future.

The past

Behaviourism

Behaviourism, which is largely based on the work of J.B. Watson (1878–1958) and B.F. Skinner (born 1904), stresses the importance of behaviour as the main intervention point, whether it be in training or therapy. Consequently, internal processes, people's thoughts and feelings, are regarded as phenomena that can only be guessed at in a very inexact way: in helping people to change, it is much more effective to concentrate on behaviour first, on the assumption that internal changes will follow in time. Attention to behaviour is regarded as being more effective because the person's progress is observable, measurable and can be objectively assessed. In the world of therapy this could mean that somebody suffering from agoraphobia is now willing to stand in the doorway of their house, whereas previously they would have been too scared to. In management training it can mean a trainee, who was previously reticent and withdrawn, increases the number of contributions he makes at meetings by 50 per cent.

The impact of behaviourism in management and management training has been considerable, and in many ways very positive. Interaction analysis, more fully described in Appendix 1, has strong links with behaviourism and can help people identify in a very specific way their typical behaviours, the possible and probable consequences of those behaviours and their alternatives. Management by objectives,[1] with its philosophy based on target-setting, key results areas, measuring achievement and improvement plans, has strong elements of behaviourism. The idea of behavioural training objectives, that is specific and identifiable forms of behaviour to be achieved at the end of the training programme, has made a particularly valuable impact in technical training.[2]

Also, in recent years, behaviour modification, well established as an approach in therapy, has been applied in management relationships. This approach is described in more detail in the second half of this chapter.

In IST the most important positive influences of behaviourism have been:

1   A means of clarifying expectations leading to a basis of agreement in formal or informal contracts between the trainer and the trainee or the trainer and the client organisation. 'What will the trainees be able to *do* as a result of the training?' 'What sorts of things will you, the trainer, *do*?'

2   Its emphasis on identifiable and reachable goals and hence a means of measuring progress. An example would be an agreement between the trainer and the trainee, that the latter asks for feedback in private from one other course member, since he was unwilling to ask for it from everybody in the full group. If the goal turns out to be unacceptable or unattainable then there is a clear basis for renegotiation.

3   The idea of behavioural rehearsal, meaning the importance of trying something out and seeing whether it 'works'. Role plays, Gestalt experiments, and many other training techniques, fall into this category.

4   The idea of positive reinforcement, meaning the importance of active encouragement as a means of reinforcing change. This encouragement could be a smile, a word or even something more tangible like a prize. A key question for any trainer is, 'What am I doing to encourage the trainee to sustain the changes he/she has made?'

5   It can be incisive and quick in that it encourages somebody to *do* something and then look at the consequences, rather than divert

too much attention worrying about how or why that person may or may not be willing to do something different in the first place.

Our main reservation about behaviourism is in terms of *whose* criteria of performance are being used. There is a danger of the trainer deciding, quite possibly unilaterally, that he knows the right behaviours for the trainee to engage in. This can put the trainer in a one-up, rather paternal role, the result of which could be a high degree of dependency in the group. The individuals in the group become concerned to satisfy the trainer and reach *his* standards of performance, rather than think about their own sense of satisfaction and what 'works' for them. In a lot of technical training the trainer will have right answers ('If you hold the machine in that way you'll hurt yourself'), but in IST it is not so clearly and easily defined.

Behaviourism means splitting off specific behaviours from the rest of the person, that is other behaviours as well as internal processes. For some people a behavioural experiment is not enough as the basis for change. What they require is a greater awareness of self: 'What sort of person am I?' 'How do I want to be in the world?' 'Why do I feel scared at the thought of being in a position of authority?'. It is here that psychoanalysis and humanism have an important role to play.

Psychoanalysis

Psychoanalysis,[3] originating in the work of Sigmund Freud (1856–1939) has, during the century, became probably *the* most important form of psychotherapy. It has had such a widespread influence that it has had a dramatic impact on IST. We wish to stress that we do not advocate that each trainer should have, as part of his training programme, three years of psychoanalysis!

Within the context of IST Freud's work has directly influenced a number of particular training approaches (e.g. 'T' group, Tavistock, transactional analysis, see Appendix 1). In addition, it has been a pervasive force in stimulating the study and exploration of the following areas:

1 The relationship between intra-psychic processes (what goes on inside people) and behaviour. Freud developed a theory of the sorts of things that could go on inside people – e.g. trauma, sexual drives, aggression – and said that they had a direct influence on, though did not specifically cause, behaviour. Therefore, for people to change they must have a better understanding of their internal processes.

2 Self-observation and introspection. A valuable source of self-knowledge is self-observation; that is, learning to look at one's

thoughts, feelings, motivations, hopes, fears and behaviours. In IST a question from the trainer such as 'What are you saying to yourself now?', has a direct link back to techniques used by Freud.

3 The way in which the past can influence the present. Values, attitudes, beliefs acquired in childhood are likely to have a direct impact in the present. Therefore, people can relate to others in the 'here and now' as if they were figures from the past, e.g. seeing and treating an older woman as a mother figure. Closely associated with this is the idea of *patterns* of behaviour which are 'learnt' in childhood and perpetuated into the present. Freud, who was especially concerned about sexual drives, might have expressed it in terms of punishment in childhood for masturbation leading to the repression of sexual excitement in adulthood. A parallel, more closely related to management training, would be somebody being scared in childhood of their irascible father and subsequently in later life having problems in handling authority figures.

4 The power of the 'here and now' as a basis for exploring relationships. In particular, the importance of looking at the relationship between the leader (therapist) and members of the group (client) since that is a crucial way of learning about the frequent human process of attributing to current relationships qualities which have their origins in the past and have no basis in present reality. For example, Freud called it 'transference' when he found that a client might start relating to him as if he were the father which the client had had in childhood. A number of management training approaches explicitly explore the relationship between the trainer and the group (e.g. 'T' group and Tavistock) or implicitly recognise the necessity of being sensitive to its dynamics.

5 Openness and resistance to openness. Freud believed that people could learn about themselves by reporting without censorship any thoughts or feelings they had (free association) and by being aware of how they used defences (such as displacement where feelings are shifted to another person or situation) to resist being open. A number of IST approaches (e.g. encounter) stress the importance and value of openness and others (e.g. Gestalt and transactional analysis) and provide methods for exploring resistances to openness, though without using Freud's terminology.

Our reservations about the value of the contribution of psychoanalysis to management training are fairly minor. If the trainer takes a strongly psychoanalytical orientation, as with the Tavistock approach, and some variants of the 'T' group, then he can become a distant figure who shares very little of himself, appearing not to be a 'real' person because his main roles consist of commenting in an 'objective' way on what he sees happening and providing an interpretation of those events. Also psychoanalysis emphasises understanding rather than experimentation and is based on the assumption that a better understanding of internal processes will somehow automatically lead to better relationships, however they may be defined. The value of experimentation has already been discussed.

Humanistic psychology

Humanistic psychology, originating in the work of people such as Abraham Maslow (1908–70), Kurt Lewin (1890–1947), and Carl Rogers (b. 1902), draws on elements of behaviourism and psychoanalysis, and at the same time has a very distinct set of principles:

1 It is concerned with the total man, stating that it is misguided to divide man into various packages of thoughts, feelings and behaviour. All aspects of an individual are interrelated, just as that individual cannot be understood in isolation from his environment.
2 Focus on the 'here and now' as a valuable way of learning.
3 The subjective is important in terms of feelings, and from the fact that each man must be his own judge and not 'swallow whole' other people's values. He must 'chew' them and 'spit out' whatever does not make sense for him.
4 Experimentation, not 'talking about', is the more effective way to learn.
5 There are no right answers. Each person, who is by definition unique, must find his own path to self-fulfilment.
6 Feelings are an important dimension in relationships and generally should be expressed rather than repressed.
7 People have great potential for growth, generally much more than they realise.

The positive value of these principles has been expressed elsewhere in the text. However, they do not provide a totally coherent framework. Our reservations about humanistic psychology concern particular ways in which it *may* be applied.

Firstly, there may be conflict between the idea of experimentation and the importance of the person 'feeling OK' about the experiment in the first place. If the trainer pushes too hard about 'having a go' then he may encourage dependency (which is anathema in humanism) and ignores the trainee's uneasiness about, or lack of commitment to, the experiment. Conversely, if the trainer spends a long time examining the trainee's uneasiness he may drift into 'talking about'. Even after the experiment, particularly if it is a fairly 'dramatic' one, such as expressing genuine warmth for the first time in thirty years, the trainee may still feel uncomfortable. As with any acquisition of new skills usually an awkward period follows where it feels contrived or mechanical.

Secondly, the expression of feelings may be counter to the organisation's culture and there is the possibility of the trainee swallowing it whole as a 'should'. 'I must always express exactly what I feel regardless of time or place.'

Thirdly, the idea of each man being his own judge and, in colloquial terms, 'doing his own thing', can lead to selfishness and a lack of concern for others. With some exaggeration this could be expressed as, 'I don't care what you think. It's what I feel that's important and if you don't like it that's your problem'. A counterbalance to this last point is that a number of the humanistically based approaches do put a high value on caring, warmth and supportiveness (e.g. encounter groups).

The future

In looking at the future, the economic fortunes of the UK and the Western World are clearly an important factor; but, it is not necessarily true that the greater the recession the less money that will be spent on IST. Managers in times of financial constraints become more discriminating in how they spend their money and normally want training that is clearly related not only to their job but to their particular organisational culture. There may well be a growth of in-company training including organisational development work and team building.

The most powerful external influence on British IST has been the United States, where behaviourist, psychoanalytic and humanistic approaches have been practised and developed. If the European Community grows, not simply in terms of increasing its membership, then Europe may become more evidently an initiator of new ideas and techniques. Just one small sign of a 'European identity' is the founding of the European Association for Transactional Analysis which is beginning to establish its independence of its US 'parent' organisation, the International Transactional Analysis Association. Centres for the training of IS trainers have been created in the UK, Holland, Germany and Italy.

Rapid technological growth may affect IST in a variety of ways.

One is distance learning.[4] Its most important impact is, and in the immediate future will probably continue to be, in the 'thinking' approach with television, programmed learning tests, guided reading, audio and video cassettes. Here the immediate face-to-face aspects, the key to many IST methods, are lacking. In the longer term it will be possible easily to provide video link-up between a variety of people in different locations and to move towards the 'doing' approach. An example would be a role-play interview which is observed and analysed by a number of people all at different locations.

Another consequence of technological growth is the probable increase in leisure time which could follow, providing an opportunity for more people to examine their beliefs, attitudes and relationships in more depth. Equally the converse could happen where face-to-face communication at work becomes less important and pleasure and hobbies take precedence over personal development. Technological growth is likely to demand of the manager increased skill and sensitivity in managing change. One fundamental decision he will need to make is the extent to which he attempts to keep himself technically up-to-date, or allows and trusts his staff to acquire a growing area of technical expertise in which he does not share. Certain jobs and skills will rapidly become obsolete and managers may well need help, for example through counselling, to cope with voluntary or enforced career changes. Periods of unemployment will occur more frequently. From all this a 'new breed' of manager is likely to emerge who is highly adaptable, can cope with ambiguity and whose effectiveness depends on assertiveness and a willingness to manage the organisational system rather than be managed by it. IST for this type of manager is already being widely offered (e.g. assertiveness training).[5]

Behaviour modification

As was mentioned earlier, behaviour modification is a quite recent approach to management training[6] and has very evident links with behaviourism. Behaviour modification is concerned with the precise identification of a problem behaviour (e.g. coming in late), the trigger or cue for that behaviour (e.g. a sudden and heavy influx of invoices requiring processing) and the pay-off from the behaviour (e.g. a lot of attention, albeit hostile). The aim then is to alter the cue (e.g. arrange that invoices arrive in a regular flow – this may mean the manager 'hoarding' some invoices), having identified the 'desired' behaviour (which in this instance is obviously punctuality) and the pay-off is changed to a reward of going home early if the agreed quota of vouchers is processed ahead of time. Here, in sharp contrast to the humanistic approach, underlying attitudes and feelings are ignored *either* on the basis that these are difficult and perhaps dangerous complications to attempt to analyse, *or* on the principle that it is the behaviour which is the problem and that simply correcting the behaviour will solve the problem.

Management self-development

One of the clear legacies of humanism is an emphasis on people taking responsibility for their own learning. Indeed, Maslow's concept of self-actualisation is a theme guiding the idea of management self-development.[7]

In recent years increasing attention has been paid to management self-development and, in fact, it has a wide range of applications extending far beyond IST. Essentially self-development means the manager taking the initiative in identifying his learning needs and then matching these with learning opportunities. These could consist of training courses but, equally, they could be essentially based on the job, e.g. job rotation, periods of secondment, coaching, guided reading, and receiving feedback from colleagues, bosses or subordinates. In all these an underlying assumption is that the manager has learnt how to learn. Frequently the starting point is a self-assessment form which, for example, could help the manager identify his management style or styles and then decide whether or how he might change.

Some of the advantages of self-development are firstly, that much of the learning can be clearly job-related because it is frequently acquired on the job; secondly, it is *probably* less expensive than development based on courses. As a consequence much IST may, in the future, take place through self-development. An increase in interpersonal skills may not only be the aim of a number of self-development programmes, but also the means since managers will need to acquire skills in giving and receiving feedback and establishing clarity over the relationship between individual and organisational objectives. This leads to one of the potential difficulties of self-development programmes in that they require an organisation to be flexible enough not only to cope with individual objectives but also to provide the time and effort which will be required to identify those objectives. It could be argued that an organisation needs to be largely effective in the first place in order to introduce self-development.

Counselling training

Counselling training[8] is likely to become increasingly important.

There are a number of reasons for this.

Firstly, as already stated, self-development programmes require a large element of counselling. This is different from coaching, which is concerned with teaching somebody how to do a job.

Secondly, despite the vagaries of economic fortune, a trend has been established in many organisations whereby people are not willing simply to accept the role allocated to them. They want to work in an environment and structure which is sensitive to their needs. Counselling, whether carried out by full-time or part-time counsellors, will be one significant way of bridging the gap between varying expectations. There may also be some particular needs, the most graphic illustration being the 'mid-life crisis', when people make a fundamental re-appraisal of their life values.

Thirdly, if training in the 'feelings' area continues to increase, then a possible result is that more managers will be making re-assessments of their relationships in general, not just at work. Organisations *may* decide that they should offer support, and counselling would be one way of doing this.

Couples training courses

The organisation's concern about employee relationships in general could lead to couples training courses. If increasing numbers of managers go on training programmes which encourage them to look at their relationships in general then clearly domestic life could be subject to some re-examination. It is likely that if a manager decides to be more open about his feelings with his boss then he will translate this into his home life, for example with his wife. If one member of a couple makes changes then clearly these can have a dramatic impact, positive or negative, on the other. It could be that there will be an acceptance of the need for spouses to attend follow-up training courses with their husband or wife, so as to understand better what has been happening or may happen.

Neuro-linguistic programming

As was indicated at the beginning of this chapter advances made in the realm of therapy have often made an important contribution to management training. This is now starting to happen with neuro-linguistic programming (NLP).[9] NLP was developed by Richard Bandler and John Grinder during the 1970s. It is still largely a 'therapy' tool, but is now starting to be applied in organisations. Bandler and Grinder's ideas come from their observations of those who were generally regarded as effective therapists (e.g. Fritz Perls, and Milton Erickson) and discovering what techniques they used.

Their observations led them to develop a number of key concepts:

Representational systems. There are four ways in which people organise their experience, based on the four senses of seeing, hearing, feeling and smell/taste. For example, in remembering an event in childhood, one person might recall the sound of his mother's voice while another might visualise his mother. Indicators of people's representational systems come from the words they use ('I *hear* what you say', 'I *see* what you mean', 'It *smells* fishy to me', 'I can't quite *grasp* (feeling) your point') and from unconscious eye movements which generally form a pattern according to how information is assessed or retrieved. (For example, somebody using recollected visual images to recall events usually moves his eyes upwards and to the left). The consequences of this would be that (using this example) a therapist or counsellor could firstly 'key' into a client's representational system by watching their eye movements and saying to somebody with a visual system 'How do you see things now?' and *not* 'How are you feeling?'. Secondly, the counsellor can establish a common level of communication and then encourage the person to achieve a different perspective of their problem by getting them to use a different system, 'You have given a clear picture of the problem and I would now like to know how you feel about it all'.

Pacing. This means mirroring the verbal and non-verbal behaviour of the client, not only using the same representational system but gradually copying the other's breathing patterns and body movements. This helps to establish rapport and enables the counsellor to 'get inside' the client and then, by changing his own non-verbal communication, he can often lead the client to change his, perhaps breathing more deeply and making himself more grounded and better able to problem-solve.

Anchoring. This involves getting the client to remember a particular experience (usually good) e.g. 'Can you remember a time when you were particularly creative?'. Once the client has a clear recollection of the occasion then the therapist might then touch a part of the client's body, e.g. upper arm. Subsequent touching of this spot, with the same pressure, can then become a trigger, to be used either by the client or therapist to generate good feelings, in this case creativity. The client can thus be led to the point of problem definition, and then touched on the upper arm as a stimulus to identify some creative solutions. Anchoring can also be done using specific voice tones or gestures.

Generalisation/deletion/distortion. This refers to another way in

which people organise their experience, either positively or negatively. Generalisation can be the basis for learning, 'All fire is
dangerous and should be treated carefully!'. Equally it can be a block
to learning, 'All women make bad managers'. Deletion means
excluding certain stimuli; this is necessary for concentration on
particular activities, e.g. ignoring the jet plane overhead in order to
score a winning tennis point. Deletion works negatively when relevant information is ignored. 'I won't be able to cope if I get promoted'.
Here, detail about not coping is being deleted. Distortion can be
positive as the basis for creative ideas and fantasies, 'What would it
look like if . . .?'. It is negative if information is used and distorted to
support destructive beliefs about self. 'My husband doesn't like my
new dress, therefore he doesn't love me, in fact, nobody loves me.'

Bandler and Grinder recognised several ways of confronting the
negative aspects of generalisation, deletion and distortion and encouraging the person to be more specific ('In what particular ways
would you be unable to cope if you were promoted?'), to think
through the consequences of change ('What would happen if you
. . .?'); or to reassess the reality of his generalisation, ('You have
never met a woman who was a good manager?').

NLP is in a state of rapid growth and presents the prospects of
some exciting new developments both in the world of therapy and, in
time, management training.

Recently Steve Lankton has developed these concepts further. He
refers to his system as psychological level communication (a more
descriptive label than neurolinguistic programming), and concentrates on what he calls 'self image thinking' to assist people to make
significant behavioural changes.

From the premise that 'images guide behaviour', Lankton has
developed techniques that assist people to eradicate archaic (usually
childhood) and negative images from their memory, and replace
them with more positive images which, in turn, lead to positive
behaviour. Lankton's techniques are particularly acceptable in
organisational settings, where generally the culture is against the use
of therapeutic and clinical jargon.

Outward bound training

A final thought on future developments is the relationship between
physical activity and management training. 'Outward bound training'[10] is already well established as a basis for looking at group
leadership and membership skills, often in conditions of physical
adversity. A newer approach, with clear links to humanism, is the
'inner game'.[11] Here strong parallels are drawn between sport and
management. For example, a manager or tennis player can reduce his

effectiveness by paying too much attention to the 'noise' in his head –
'You won't make it', 'You'll make a mess of it', 'Lose this and you've
lost everything'. Management training based on the inner game uses
sport, backed up by business games, case studies, role plays and
feedback, as a way of achieving what is called 'relaxed concentration', free from self-defeating doubt and anxiety.

Conclusion

There is likely to be a continuing need for managers to look at
themselves and their management of relationships. IST can, in a wide
variety of ways, contribute to this scrutiny and help improve the
quality of organisational life and task performance. The signs are
that exciting times lie ahead. IST, and all those who share and
participate in it, will need to grow in order to meet the increasing
demands which are likely to be placed on it. Growth can best be
achieved in IST through the acceptance of the validity of a variety of
approaches. As soon as the value of one approach is seen as being
dependent on proving the worthlessness of another, then credibility
will be lost as battle lines are formed and energy which could be
directed to meeting training needs and demands is expended in
achieving pyrrhic victories. The variety of approaches that have been
developed have more similarities than differences. It is to be hoped
that as knowledge and practice become more sophisticated the splits
between the different 'schools' will be integrated and IST will offer a
broad and powerful range of methods which can be adapted to the
needs of the trainees.

References

(1) J. Humble, *Management by Objectives in Action*, McGraw-Hill,
     Maidenhead, 1970.
(2) R.F. Mager, *Preparing Instructional Objectives*, Fearon, 1975
(3) For a brief description see J. Kovel, *A Complete Guide to Therapy*,
     Penguin, Harmondsworth, 1976. Chapter 3.
(4) For a fuller discussion of distance learning see copies of the journal
     Teaching at a Distance, published by the Open University, Milton
     Keynes.
(5) C. Kelley, *Assertion Training – a Facilitators Guide*, University
     Associates, La Jolla, California, 1979.
(6) P. Honey, *Solving People-Problems*, McGraw-Hill, Maidenhead,
     1980.
(7) A. Mumford, *Making Experience Pay*, McGraw-Hill, Maidenhead,
     1980.
(8) A.G. Watts (Ed.), *Counselling at Work*, Bedford Square Press, 1977.

(9)   R. Bandler and J. Grinder, *Frogs into Princes*, Real People Press, Moab, Utah, 1979.

(10) For further information on this type of training contact: The Leadership Trust, Symonds Yat West, Ross-on-Wye, Herefordshire HR9 6BL.

(11) For further information contact: The Inner Game, 200A West End Lane, London NW6 1SG.

Appendix 1 – an outline of current approaches

This appendix gives the reader further information on a variety of training methods, most of which have been referred to elsewhere in the text. We do not give an exhaustive analysis of each method, but an outline sufficient to allow the reader to decide whether he wants to pursue further the contact points and recommended reading. Generally there is description without evaluation.

The broad categories of 'thinking', 'doing' and 'feeling' have been retained because these reflect the major emphases of the methods contained within them. However, as all categorisations are generalisations it does not mean, for example, that none of the methods referred to in the 'doing' section ever allow the exploration of feelings.

There is a fourth and general section to the appendix describing methods which do not fit into the other categories.

Contents *page*

The thinking approach

The training methods referred to here are primarily concerned with presenting information, some (e.g. films and books) on the basis of one-way communication. From this base a number of training designs can follow, such as discussions and role-plays. There can, therefore, be a gradual movement into the 'doing' approach.

Books

Some of the management and management training journals which include book reviews are:

> *Management Education and Development*. Journal of the Association of Teachers of Management.
> *Management Review and Digest*. British Institute of Management.
> *Personnel Management*. Institute of Personnel Management.
> *The Training Officer*. Marylebone Press Ltd.

Case-studies

> The Case Clearing House of Great Britain & Ireland,
> Cranfield Institute of Technology,
> Cranfield,
> Bedford MK 43 0AL.
> Tel. Bedford 750903

This organisation is a source of case-studies covering a wide range of topics including financial management, organisational behaviour, production and operations management and marketing management.
Reading:

> *Case-Studies in Management* M. Ivens and F. Broadway. Business Publications 1964.
> *Case-Studies in Human Relations, Productivity and Organisation* M. Ivens and F. Broadway. Business Publications 1966.
> *Case-Studies and Role-Plays – What, Why, When and How*. Personnel and Training Management Yearbook 1980. Kogan Page.

Distance learning

This means the trainee learning while being geographically at a distance from the trainer. Some typical methods used here are television, guided reading, programmed learning texts, video cassettes and audio tapes. (The latter have even been used for running encounter groups.) The growing sophistication of communications technology will probably make distance learning an increasingly attractive proposition. The Open University, a leader in providing distance learning packages, has plans for running IST courses for managers, and already has, for example, some written and television materials on transactional analysis.

Also, there is a possibility that an 'Open Tech.' may be launched which, while being primarily concerned with technical training, could lead to the production of material for interpersonal skills training for supervisors. As yet it is too early to say what will happen here.

Contact:

> The Open University,
> PO Box 188,
> Sherwood House,
> Sherwood Drive,
> Bletchley,
> Milton Keynes MK3 6HL.
> Tel. 0908–71231

Films

1. The British Institute of Management has a film information service. This service does *not* involve lending or selling films but can provide information on:

> (a) films which are available under certain headings e.g. industrial relations, management of change etc.
>
> (b) sources for these films.

For further information contact:

> Film Information Service,
> British Institute of Management,
> Management House,
> Parker Street,
> London WC2B 5PT.
> Tel. 01-405-3456

2. A number of the management training journals describe and review training films, including those relating to IST, e.g. *Industrial and Commercial Training*, published by Wellens Publishing and *Journal of European and Industrial Training*, published by MCB Publications.

3. *Personnel and Training Management Yearbook and Directory* published annually by Kogan Page. This book has a list of addresses for obtaining film catalogues. In addition, it provides information on courses, official bodies, information sources as well as dealing with current personnel issues. (In 1982 this was re-named *The Personnel and Training Databook.*)

The doing approach

This approach usually means that there are plenty of opportunities to practise specific skills (e.g. leadership) in activities which may or may not be clearly job-related. Also the programmes will generally be tightly structured to provide a basis for the gradual and sometimes measurable acquisition of skills. The tight structure is intended to ensure 'psychological safety'. Often there is a theoretical model which provides the rationale for the training.

Those involved in this type of training, whether as trainer or user, need to be particularly aware of the extent to which the programme is flexible enough to accommodate individual needs. It is likely that the main theme will be about specific behaviours rather than the exploration of feelings behind those behaviours (e.g. 'What should I *do* in order to be a more effective leader?', not, 'How come I'm always putting myself down as a leader and end up feeling inadequate?').

Action-centred leadership (ACL)

Action-centred leadership was originally devised by John Adair and is concerned with the specific actions which a leader needs to take in order to be effective. Adair has stressed the need for the leader to manage the three different, yet interrelated functions. These are represented by the overlapping circles shown in Figure A1.1.

Fig. A1.1

1 *Achieving the task*, which is concerned with work allocation, planning and the evaluation of results.

2   *Building the team*, which pulls people together and includes motivating, encouraging, training and giving a sense of direction.
3   *Developing individuals*, which means taking account of, and making use of, individual abilities.

If the leader emphasises one of the functions too much, such as giving exclusive attention to the task, then the other two will suffer, in this case communication breaking down and the team fragmenting.

The training itself, normally lasting 2–3 days, is based on a number of activities (e.g. 'tower-building' or putting jig-saws together), where there is an appointed leader whose *specific* actions are noted, and subsequently analysed by observers under the headings given above. Often two groups are run in parallel so that the nature and consequences of different leadership actions can be seen.

Usually a film, '12 o'clock High', is shown as a vehicle for analysing the three functions and for observing and reporting on the leadership actions carried out by the characters. There is also some theory and discussion on motivation and systematic problem-solving, together with case-study material. The participants are encouraged, as the course proceeds, to note down action points about leadership which are particularly relevant to them in their jobs. In the final session, delegates are asked to produce an action plan to be implemented on their return to work.

Reading:

The Manager as a Leader Edwin Smith. Industrial Society, 1980.
Training for Leadership John Adair. Gower, 1978.
'Action-centred Leadership' John Adair. Gower, 1979.

Contact:

Industrial Society,
Peter Runge House,
3 Carlton House Terrace,
London SW1Y 5DG.
Tel. 01–839–4300

Coverdale training

The methods usually known as Coverdale training have grown from work initiated by Ralph Coverdale (1918–75) during his time with The Steel Company of Wales in the 1950s and the Esso Petroleum Company in the early 1960s. Developments have continued subsequently in the operations of The Coverdale Organisation, both before and after Coverdale's death. From the start he worked in collaboration with Bernard Babington Smith, formerly Senior Lecturer in Experimental Psychology at Oxford University.

Coverdale originally set out to devise an approach to management training which responded to needs seen as acute by senior company officials; in particular the need to encourage managers to accept their responsibility for managing men. An underlying obstacle to this acceptance seemed to be that men tended to be promoted for their technical, not interpersonal, skills.

In looking at the management training currently being used, Coverdale found that in general it was concerned with providing knowledge about management techniques. This was often not seen as relevant to the particular circumstances at work, and even where it was, managers rarely had the skill to use the new knowledge constructively. The use of the case study method did not seem to provide an answer, as although case studies involve thought and judgement, they do not call for action and the taking of responsibility for that action. This Coverdale saw as of profound importance for managers, whose job involves getting things actually done and living with the consequences of their actions, not just saying what they would do if they ever were in the situation described in a case history. Small group work did, however, seem to him to have much value and potential relevance as a result of:

1   His own experience in market research using group interviews.
2   The published results of small group work up to that date (1957) especially that of Lewin.
3   His own experience of T-Groups run by the Tavistock Institute.

On the other hand he had some reservations about their use for managers, and held strong views about the Freudian-based interpretations he met in connection with T-Group work.

From 1947, when he had gone up to Oxford to read psychology and to work for a higher degree, Coverdale had known Bernard Babington Smith. In 1959 he approached the latter to ask him for help in developing a new method of management training. Thus two streams of thought and experience were joined in the initial development of Coverdale training. Coverdale's background, which included training in a Jesuit seminary and army service as well as industrial experience led him to believe that any new approach to management training should stress training rather than esoteric analysis. Babington Smith's views complemented this since he had developed strong views supporting discovery learning. He also shared Coverdale's reservations about Freudian theory believing that its emphasis on unconscious processes and the need for expert analysis would be of limited value in management training. In the early days of his work with Coverdale, Babington Smith's chief contributions were:

1   The principle of the three records. This meant paying attention in any situation to:
    (a) what people could tell about themselves
    (b) what others reported about them
    (c) some impersonal record of performance.
    This approach underlies the emphasis placed in Coverdale training on establishing common understanding, the clarification of aims and the importance of observation.
2   The distinction between 'open' and 'closed' situations. Here the point is that in a closed situation a solution to a problem is sought but in an open one action leading to progress is what is required. Coverdale seized on this and made it a cornerstone of the work 'since managers are dealing with open situations all the time'.

The first courses developed by Coverdale and Babington Smith were composed of sessions of group work, demonstrations and lectures. The group sessions, with their emphasis on process issues, were of most interest to participants. However, through their lack of structure, confusion and a build-up of tension arose. As a result Coverdale came to believe that much of the training should involve set 'tasks' because he felt:

1   action produces a different psychological climate and brings a release of tension;
2   it is essential in getting things done, the job of any manager;
3   the emotions aroused are those associated with getting something done.

Initially it was expected that inviting groups to choose and design their own tasks would ensure commitment. Groups however found doing this so difficult and time-consuming that the choice and design of tasks became a matter for the staff. Through carrying out a number of tasks, groups were encouraged and helped to develop into self-regulating groups, form teams for any objective, and observe how they did so.

While many interesting and potentially useful discoveries were made by participants on the early courses, they encountered problems in transferring their learning to work. This confirmed that discovery alone was insufficient and led to the development of a generally applicable framework, which constituted a *systematic approach to getting things done*. This envisaged successive cycles of preparation, action and review in relation to aims, continually incorporating fresh information supplied by observation, thus ensuring progress and enabling learning from actual experience to take place. It was seen as particularly appropriate for managers in business since it did not presuppose that there was a 'problem' for which the correct 'solution' was to be found. As Babington Smith pointed out, much of education dealt in terms of 'closed' problems where the answer may be deduced from the data available, whereas in the 'real' world managers found themselves in situations where they did not know whether solutions existed but nevertheless it was clear that something had to be done. In parallel Coverdale drew the distinction between acquiring knowledge, where it is assumed that known answers exist and the students can learn 'about' them, and learning 'how to' in an 'open' situation with no real answers, only ways of making progress.

The latter relies on learning through and from experience. As courses were run in line with these conclusions, participants discovered for themselves a range of topics which appeared important. These topics, which gradually became built into the design of subsequent courses and are therefore generally referred to as 'themes' underlying Coverdale training, include:

Observation
Aims
Systematic approach
Process planning (planning for improved co-operation)
Listening and support
Skills recognition and use
Authority

The Coverdale basic course has now developed to a point where it is generally seen as comprising two parts, each a week in length. The first part (Part I) concentrates on providing an opportunity for participants to experience a deliberate attempt at team formation and to highlight for themselves useful lessons arising from their own observations of that experience. Thus the groups are not structured in the sense of having a chairman or leader appointed nor are they encouraged to start by appointing one merely *because* they are used to functioning that way elsewhere. What they are encouraged to do is to discover, through working together, the resources and skills available in the group and develop a structure in terms of these. With each group on a course is a member of staff, described as a 'coach', whose job is to help the group towards becoming an effective team and to explore and discover for themselves in doing so.

His concern is not to tell them what to do, nor to interpret what is happening for them; it is to encourage the group to think about and test ways of working for themselves, to draw their own conclusions based on their own observations, and to test and modify these in the light of further experience.

The second part of the basic course (Part II) was designed to meet the need of practising managers who observed that, while the experience of team formation was valuable, nevertheless the actual work situation was such that people worked in different groupings, coming together to get a job done and then breaking up. Part II is intended therefore to enable participants to explore further the areas discovered as important in Part I but in a variety of different groups and situations, including some more closely related to those at work. Parts I and II are 'task-centred', with tasks of various types being provided for groups to carry out e.g. being given an hour to 'report on health hazards in the vicinity'. Participants are explicitly invited to look outwards at what they can contribute to the team and how they can help others as well as themselves, in the belief that understanding and achieving this brings personal development at the same time. Since the courses are primarily concerned with 'how' to do things and developing ways of working together and not with improving technical skills or knowledge, the Coverdale Organisation believes it is desirable for tasks generally not to be closely related to participants' normal work. The question of the transfer of learning is left until the final stages of these courses or subsequent workshops and on-site activities.

Thus the body of methods now embraced by the term 'Coverdale training' includes not only off-the-job training courses but on-site follow-through activities and workshops. Associated consultancy activities include the development, steering and monitoring of large-scale unit and organisation development programmes.

Reading:

Training in Small Groups B. Babington Smith and B.A. Farrell (Eds). Pergamon Press 1979.
Coverdale on Management Max Taylor. Heinemann, London 1979.
'Coverdale training' S. Roche. Manpower and Applied Psychology, Spring 1967.

Contact:
The Coverdale Organisation,
3 Logan Place,
London W8 6QN.
Tel. 01–370–6237

Interaction analysis (IA)

IA is the quantitative analysis of interaction between people, and requires the use of an observation framework which has on it a number of behaviour categories. The outline of a typical course design, using IA to develop interviewing skills, would be as follows:

1 Theory and full group discussion on interviewing skills.
2 Introduction of an IA observation framework together with some practice in using it, so that course members become familiar with the behaviour categories.
3 A role-play interview, probably recorded on closed-circuit television, together with observers using IA to analyse the interaction of the interviewer and interviewee.
4 Review of the role-play interview with a particular emphasis on observers feeding back the results of their analysis; this to be followed by a discussion of the implications of these results.
5 Summarising theory about interviewing, possibly leading into another role-play interview.

A particular framework will be looked at and its possible uses described. One of the most versatile and popular IA frameworks was devised by Robert Bales. His framework has a number of variations, one simplified adaptation looks like this:

Type of behaviour	Interviewer Scores	Interviewee Scores
Social-emotional positive		
Task-tells		
Task-asks		
Social-emotional negative		
TOTAL SCORE		

Fig. A1.2

The basic distinction which Bales draws is between behaviour concerned with the task (e.g. giving and receiving information related to achievement of the task) and behaviour concerned with the communication of feelings (in Bales' terms positive feelings – 'I like you', 'Welcome!', or negative feelings — 'I'm getting fed up with you'). In the context of appraisal training examples of the categorisation would be as follows:

Social-emotional positive:
  Offering a chair,
  'I'm glad to see you',
  Smile,
  'You've been working really well',
  'I'm glad to have the chance to talk to you'.

Task tells:

  'I'm concerned about the quality of your work on the Williams Project',
  'I want to tell you about a number of changes which are going to take place',
  'One of my subordinates has been coming in consistently late for six months'.
  (All of these in an even tone of voice.)

Task asks:

  'How do you think you have been doing lately?',
  'Have you got any questions?',
  'What do you think of my performance?'
  (Even tone of voice.)

Social-emotional negative:

  Not offering a chair,
  'What the hell have you been up to!',
  'I've come to tell you what you can do with your job!'

As can be seen, tone of voice is important and, for example, a request for information expressed in an angry way would be classified as social-emotional negative. It is important to remember that each item of behaviour can only be scored once. Over the period of a role play interview, therefore, an observer might have a score sheet as shown in Figure A1.3, overleaf.

Some of the implications to be drawn from this would be that the interviewer was being highly directive, (Task tells 21 Task asks 3) rather negative (Social-emotional negative 13, Social-emotional positive 3) and that the interviewee had little opportunity to give her views on her performance. (Interviewer 40 Interviewee 17). It is likely that in a subsequent role play the interviewer would be encouraged by the trainer to alter his behaviour, especially increasing 'social-emotional positive' and 'task asks'.

From this example of the use of a Bales' framework some aspects

Type of Behaviour	Interviewer (Bill)	Interviewee (Freda)
Social-emotional positive	|||	|||
Task-tells	̶H̶H̶ ̶H̶H̶ ̶H̶H̶ ̶H̶H̶		||||
Task-asks	|||	̶H̶H̶ ||
Social-emotional negative	̶H̶H̶ ̶H̶H̶ |||	|||
TOTAL SCORE	40	17

Fig. A1.3

of the general philosophy of IA, which is rooted in behaviourism, become evident:

1 With practice, behaviour can be categorised easily and simply.
2 All the 'important' behaviours can be encompassed within a single framework.
3 People can change their behaviour and consequently encourage others to change.
4 The outcomes from interactions depend on behaviour.
5 IA is a way of giving objective and specific feedback.
6 Behaviour change is generated by giving objective and valid data on behaviour to the actor.

The validity of these points will be considered later.

IA in its pure form is quantitative i.e. involves scoring. However the frameworks can be significantly modified so that scoring is not required – they will then give a 'general flavour' of the interaction. An example of how this can be done is given below. Edgar Schein's original observation framework consisted of nineteen types of behaviour which could occur in groups. Clearly the use of such a framework required a lot of practice, and would not be appropriate on a lot of IST courses where time was limited. A modified version of Schein's framework has been developed by a colleague, Ben Bennett, for this reason:

– – – – –

Group behaviour: observation and interpretation framework. When a group member behaves, his behaviour can be interpreted as being *primarily* directed towards one of the following: achieving the group's task (task oriented behaviour), building or maintaining a cohesive group (group oriented behaviour), or expressing personal needs and interests (self oriented behaviour).

1   TASK oriented behaviour:
Behaviour directed towards achieving the group's task. For example:

  (a) making suggestions, defining problems;
  (b) seeking or giving information;
  (c) clarifying, interpreting or summarising ideas;
  (d) seeking or taking decisions . . . etc.

2   GROUP oriented behaviour:
Behaviour directed towards building or maintaining a cohesive group. For example:

  (a) reconciling differences between group members;
  (b) reducing tension through humour;
  (c) keeping communication channels open;
  (d) modifying personal views in the interests of group cohesion . . . etc.

3   SELF oriented behaviour:
Behaviour expressing personal needs and interests. For example:

  (a) dominating others, being aggressive or blocking;
  (b) seeking help or recognition through self-deprecation, personal confusion or not listening;
  (c) pairing up or forming sub-groups for support or protection;
  (d) withdrawing . . . etc.

Observation Roles:

1   Note and describe illustrations of behaviour in each of the three categories. What effects did the behaviours have on others?
2   What in your judgement was the *relative* amount of each of the three kinds of behaviour in the group as a whole?

Here the observers (perhaps watching their colleagues take part in a mock meeting) are not being asked to identify all the specific behaviours which are taking place, but simply to get a general sense of what is happening, together with some examples. The disadvantage of this approach is that it is not comprehensive and 'scientific', but the major advantage is that it is easy to use. When considering the use of IA frameworks the trainer is faced with a fundamental decision about how far he is simply concerned that information for discussion be generated, and how far he wants a detailed and 'objective' analysis of the total interaction. Allied to this decision, the trainer should also think about the specific purposes of his training and decide which of the various frameworks is most appropriate.

Areas of application. IA has a wide range of applications in management training, particularly where understanding communication is important.

1   Interviewing:

A typical approach to interviewing training using interaction analysis is outlined above. Under this heading would come almost any face to face conversation that has a purpose, usually related to work. Examples of interviews include:

Selection
Disciplinary
Coaching
Problem solving
Information gathering/giving
Appraisal
Counselling

Each type of interview requires a different approach and style and this will be reflected in the balance of the communication pattern.

2   Group problem solving:

The ability of a group to work together effectively and to solve problems depends on the ability of group members to contribute

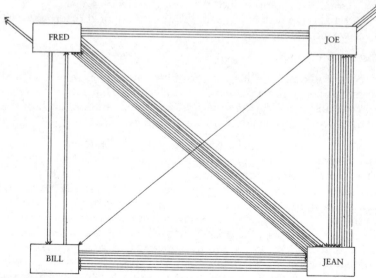

Fig. A1.4 A sociogram

constructively and to accept the contributions of others. It was with this in mind that Bales and Schein developed their frameworks.

For learning about groups, trainers could use the sociogram which scores a number of contributions made by each group member and to whom as shown in Figure A1.4.

This diagram show dramatically the flow of communication and the focus on each member. Each line represents a single communication from a member to another or to the group as a whole and the arrows give the direction. Lines going outwards from individuals indicate comments directed to the group as a whole (e.g. Fred made two comments to the group.) The sociogram can be used simultaneously with Schein's broad divisions between task, group and self oriented behaviours (see above).

Observing group behaviour in this way, using one observer to produce concurrently a sociogram and others to produce data based on Schein provides the participants with a valuable mixture of feedback. The sociogram provides straightforward numerical data unaffected by the content of the interaction. Schein-based recordings give the opportunity for qualitative feedback, based on the details of particular exchanges in the group discussion. Together a clearer, all-round picture of the contributions to the group's performance can be achieved.

These techniques lead readily to exploring group membership and leadership skills and team development. The training can be conducted as a part of a specific programme or can be incorporated into normal working meetings. In the latter case it would be called 'process consultation'.

3   Negotiation:

A number of frameworks have been successfully applied in this context. Among these is Neil Rackham who, using eleven behaviour categories, has devised a controlled pace negotiations exercise. Using a different perspective, Damien Dyar has designed a more purpose-built series for his training design.

Both approaches are based on the assumption that successful and constructive negotiating depends on the participants emphasising particular patterns of communication and reducing others. Rackham's controlled pace exercise involves separating the negotiating teams and having them exchange a series of communications in a type of role-play context. The teams are required to communicate alternately, categorising the communication at each stage. The negotiating process is deliberately slowed down and the pattern of exchanges is related during a review of the activity, to the success or failure of the outcome.

Advantages and disadvantages.

Advantages:

A real value of using this form of feedback is that it makes explicit what in the normal process of communication remains implicit. By using a system of behaviour classification, behaviour becomes a proper subject for discussion and learning in this area becomes possible.

In applying these carefully designed systems for observing, the information provided is generated systematically. This means that each participant receives an equal amount of attention whether or not they were particularly active in the event being analysed. Another consequence is that much of the evaluative or judgemental bias typical of discussions about communication can be replaced by reference to agreed evidence and data. Also the training is usually safer because the feedback is based on behaviour rather than the person, and everybody has the opportunity to give and get feedback.

More specifically, the particular advantages of the different frameworks are:

Bales' framework

    (a) Gives a model of a group development so that phases of the group can be recognised.

    (b) Provides a clear distinction between the *content* of what is being said and *process* of how communication is taking place (although the value of the distinction is reduced because Bales says that a comment must *either* be task or social-emotional, never both).

    (c) Recognises the importance of non-verbal behaviour.

    (d) Can be adapted to 1:1 encounters as well as group behaviour.

    (e) Can be readily simplified so that inexperienced course members can learn to use it.

Schein's framework

    (a) Can be used to identify leadership responsibilities and assess the effectiveness of a leader.

    (b) Brings to light the group's orientation in terms of emphasis on the needs of the task, group or individuals.

Rackham's framework

    (a) Particularly useful for looking at negotiating behaviour between groups.

    (b) Has high face validity and can fairly easily be used by the inexperienced.

    (c) The eleven category framework makes useful distinctions between broad categories of behaviour i.e. clarifying, creating, conflicting.

Disadvantages:

Taking an overall view of interaction analysis systems, there are a number of weaker points. Because the data which is provided is given some time after the events to which they refer, the impact is significantly lessened. Participants have to recall the events described and may find that their perceptions differ markedly from the observer's analysis. Whatever the outcome, each training event can become a fixed happening with learning restricted to 'What would have happened if . . .'

Making accurate recordings of interaction in terms of behaviour categories requires considerable expertise and continuing practice. Having inexperienced course members recording observations creates the possibility of faulty analysis and important omissions or mistakes. Using experts can be expensive and intrusive particularly when used 'on-line'.

Generally the frameworks do not cover the sequence of communication, silences or 'air time', although these problems can sometimes be overcome by making additional notes. Also no weighting is given to any particular comment, even though it may have been particularly significant.

A final drawback of this approach as a whole is that it ignores some of the realm of underlying feelings and intention. Rackham's framework does not make any distinction between content and process. Using interaction analysis, subtle expressions of support or hostility tend to be ignored in favour of a kind of skimming of the surface of behaviour.

Reading:

Improving Skills in Working With People D. Dyar and J. Giles. Training Information Paper No. 7, HMSO 1974.
Personality and Interpersonal Behaviour R.F. Bales. Holt, Reinhart and Winston, 1970.
Behaviour Analysis in Training N. Rackham. McGraw-Hill, 1977.
Process Consultation E. Schein. Addison Wesley, 1969.

Contact:

Terry Morgan and Maggie Rickman,
54 Adela Avenue,
New Malden,
Surrey.
Tel. 01–949–3900 (Behaviour analysis)

P. Honey,
Ardingly House,
10 Linden Avenue,

Maidenhead, Berks.
Tel. 0628–33946 (Developing interactive skills)

Roffey Park Management College,
Horsham,
West Sussex.
Tel. 029–383–344 (Overview of IA)

Managerial grid – Robert Blake and Jane Mouton

Generally when this type of training is referred to it means either of two related but different activities: either a public five-day seminar with participants from different organisations or an OD intervention consisting of six phases (starting with a Grid seminar) over several years. The Grid seminar is always the starting point. This is designed to be trainee-centred and is intended to help managers look at their management style and its implications for relationships and task achievement, also helping them plan individual changes, if any, in the context of their own organisation culture.

The Grid identifies five basic management styles with a strong emphasis on the management of conflict. The Grid has two axes, both scaled 1–9, the vertical one reflecting 'concern for people' and the horizontal one 'concern for production'. So a 9,1 style manager has high concern for production and a low concern for people: he aims to suppress conflict. The 1,9 manager has a high concern for people and a low concern for production and in his desire to keep people happy he smooths over conflict. The 1,1 manager shows little concern for people or production and makes every effort to ignore conflict by claiming that it is not his responsibility. The 5,5 manager balances the necessity to produce work and maintain morale and will look for compromise in resolving conflict aiming for workable solutions. The 9,9 manager with a high concern for people and production will confront conflict by identifying underlying causes, resolving differences and seeking creative solutions.

The seminar requires considerable preliminary work – reading *The New Managerial Grid* – completion of instruments to test the understanding of theory, examining one's own value system and perception of style and an analysis of organisational culture. The seminar teams work on decision-making exercises that are scored, enabling these teams to measure success and develop improvements, and there are inter-group exercises and experiences of being in a new team, all giving participants an opportunity to observe each others' behaviour. This culminates in personal style feedback being given to individuals by their team with suggestions for improvement.

The six-phase Grid OD programme involves the application of

Grid ideas and principles to self-determining OD units. After Grid seminar participation in 'stranger' teams, actual work groups go through structured experiences in team development examining their effectiveness and ways of improving it. This is followed by a similar process between departments needing to jointly improve their co-operation. The major improvement phase for a unit is for the top team to work on an 'ideal strategic model' which, once finalised, can be monitored by them with teams in the hierarchy (hopefully already more effective through team and inter-group development) carrying out action plans to achieve the model. Grid OD has to have the involvement and commitment of the top management group and they, together with other management teams, attempt to achieve greatly improved performance once obsolete practices, precedents and traditions have been eliminated from the culture.

Reading:

'Evaluation of Grid Training – Phase I' P. Smith and T. Honour. *Journal of Management Studies* Vol. 6. 1969. pp. 318–30
The New Managerial Grid R. Blake and J. Mouton, Gulf, 1978.
Group Training Techniques M.L. and P.J. Berger (Eds). Gower, 1972.

Contact:

Alan Marsh (Management & Development) Ltd,
110/111 The Strand,
London WC2.
Tel. 01–836–8918.

Managing effective relationships (MER)

MER, developed by Helen Clinard, is based on the assumption that managers, and indeed everybody, can increase their interpersonal skills and achieve more satisfying and effective relationships by consciously managing their behavioural responses to other people. It offers a systematic way to consider the courses of action that are available for responding to interpersonal situations. In all this, the key focus is on understanding the kinds of responses to specific and observable behaviours which are most likely to get the results one would want. For example, in giving constructive feedback, one option for a manager would be to identify objectively the specific behaviour of the other person which is causing the problem, disclose the tangible effect which that behaviour has on him and his primary feeling about that problem (not his feelings toward the person causing the problem).

Example:

> 'Your coming in late this morning made it difficult to know how to apportion the work for the day. I felt concerned about asking Mike to leave his work again to cover your job'.

This contrasts with generalised and evaluative confrontation, such as, 'I'm fed up with your coming into work late all the time. Your problem is that you are bone lazy and I'm really annoyed at you'.

The basic framework in the approach is a model, the MER lens, which suggests that the observable behaviours of another person with whom I have a relationship could be sorted into six basic categories:

1 Behaviours of the other person which I like (APPRECIATED).
2 Behaviours which indicate that the other person is bothered (OTHER'S PROBLEM).
3 Behaviours about which I feel neutral (NO PROBLEM).
4 Behaviours which indicate that the other person and I have a conflict of needs (OUR PROBLEM).
5 Behaviours which I do not like because they have a tangible effect on me (MY PROBLEM).
6 Behaviours which go against my values or which I think are not in the best interest of the other person (VALUE CONFLICTS).

The purpose for categorising these behaviours is to enable people to choose the most appropriate skills with which to respond to the behaviours.

The basic categories can be summarised as shown in Figure A1.5.

Some words of explanation about some of the particular skills referred to are as follows:

1 Tracking positives: looking for and responding to the desirable behaviours of others which you like or wish to encourage.
2 Facilitative listening: attentive listening behaviours including paraphrasing the content of the message and reflecting the feelings of the talker.
3 Solicited consulting skills: skills of counselling or helping a person with his/her problem when he/she wants your help.
4 Constructive confrontation: letting a person know how his/her behaviour is causing you a problem in a way that is most likely to cause the other person to want to change without feeling defensive, resistant or resentful.
5 Unsolicited consulting skills: skills in approaching a person about a behaviour that is in conflict with your values (or which you think is not in the other person's own best interest). These skills are designed to maximise that person's receptiveness to what you have to say and to minimise the chances of a defensive, resistant or resentful response.

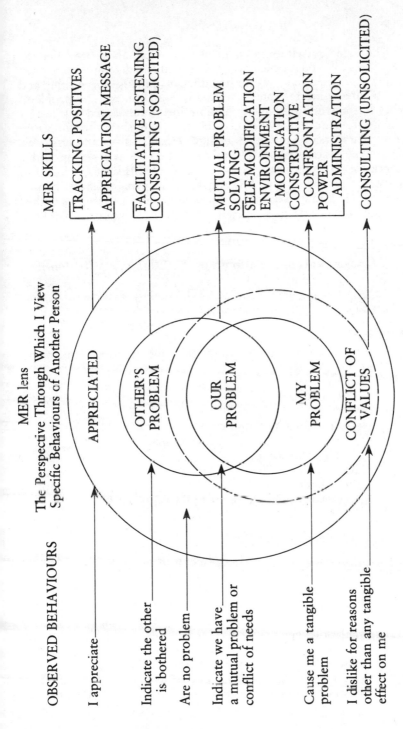

Fig. A1.5

The training itself initially consists of presentations in which the detailed skills and procedures are outlined and demonstrated. Then course members have the opportunity to practise these skills and procedures using role plays, normally based on real-life problems they face at work or home. Sometimes people are asked to role play the person they are having the problems with, since this will probably give increased insight into that person's values and attitudes. During these activities some course members act as observers with a check-list of specific behaviours, related to the MER lens, to look for. Observers practice special skills suggested for giving feedback. Participants are encouraged to identify and build on their strengths as they develop confidence and competence in the various interpersonal skills.

Reading:

'Managing effective relationships' H. Clinard, *BACIE Journal*. March 1978; April 1981.
'Interpersonal communication skills training' H. Clinard. *Training and Development Journal*, August 1979.

Contact:

British Association for Commercial and Industrial Education,
16 Park Crescent,
London W1N 4AP.
Tel. 01–636–5351.

Helen H. Clinard,
Effectiveness Training and Consulting,
3290 Highcliff Road,
Pfafftown, NC. 27040,
United States.
Tel. (US) 919–924–2258; (US) 919–724–7835.

Team integrating systems (TIS)

This was developed by Dr R.M. Belbin of the Industrial Training Research Unit during the last ten years or so and is based on research into the personality factors that make a team succeed or fail. The research was initially carried out by observing the participants of management games at the Administrative Staff College, Henley.

The main point emerging from Dr Belbin's work is that a certain mix of roles is required to make a team effective – producing creative ideas, showing concern about deadlines, challenging assumptions, gathering information, formulating schedules and so on – and that, on the basis of personality people generally have a favourite role.

Getting the right mix of complementing roles is vital in a team's success. Consequently, putting together a group of highly intelligent and creative people probably means that an effective team will *not* emerge because, for example, nobody in the group is willing to carry out routine organising work.

The ITRU offers seminars which are designed to give participants an appreciation of TIS together with an understanding of their own favourite team roles. This is achieved through the use of psychometric tests and inter-group exercises, using Monopoly, where the seminar leaders put the participants into teams and predict, on the basis of test evidence, which team will win.

Reading:

> *Management Teams: Why they Succeed or Fail* R.M. Belbin. Heinemann, 1981.

Contact:

> Industrial Training Research Unit Ltd,
> Lloyds Bank Chambers,
> Hobson Street,
> Cambridge,
> CB1 1NL.
> Tel. 0223–51576

3-D theory and training – Bill Reddin

3-D training owes its name to the fact that it has three related orientations.

Firstly, it strongly emphasises the need for the manager to be specifically aware of the output required of him and for which he is accountable. This is done by stressing what are described as 'effectiveness areas', i.e. what the manager is expected to produce, having jointly clarified his role in terms of knowing what he can demand of others and what they can demand of him.

The second and third orientations are to do with management style and the extent and way in which the manager has a *task orientation* (e.g. initiating, organising, directing) and a *relationships orientation* (e.g. listening, trusting, encouraging). Reddin diagrammatically represents these orientations on a matrix: the horizontal axis indicating task orientation, the vertical axis indicating relationships orientation and both on a scale of 0 (low) to 4 (high). This management style concept has a superficial similarity with Blake and Mouton's Grid, but in fact differs from it in that Reddin does not identify a 'best style' but stresses the need for appropriate behaviour and effectiveness. For example, somebody who is low on task and relationships orientation would, *in the appropriate circumstances*, be effective and described in 3-D theory as bureaucratic, i.e. good at methods, systems and procedures and having a keen eye for detail. The appropriateness of the circumstances can depend on five factors: the manager's boss, his subordinates, his colleagues, the climate of the organisation and the technology of the manager's job e.g. as an accounting manager or a project team leader. 3-D training, consequently, aims to increase the following managerial skills:

1   Style awareness, i.e. the manager being aware of, and objective about, his behaviours and the impact they have on others.
2   Style flexibility, i.e. the ability to alter style, obviously knowing what the options are, according to changing circumstances.
3   Situation sensitivity; in order to be flexible there is a need to be sensitive to what other people or the situation requires.
4   Situation management, i.e. the ability to change the situation, for example in terms of the technology or the demands of others, whether colleagues, subordinates or boss.

In all this, the major stress is on the particular behaviours the manager could/should be demonstrating; internal process is not dealt with.

The initial vehicle for 3-D training is the Managerial Effectiveness Seminar (MES) and it may be run in company or as an 'open' programme with representatives from different organisations. Where it is run in company it can lead to other interventions (described briefly below) which can be combined in various ways to lead to organisational development.

The MES is highly structured and after a relatively short period of apprenticeship even those without formal training experience can administer and lead it. A considerable amount of preliminary work (about 40 hours) is required of those who are going to attend the seminar. This work consists of reading, including programmed learning texts, and questionnaires to help the manager understand the basic theory and reflect on his own management style. The seminar itself is heavily based on small groups (5–8 people) which form teams for the whole of the six days and are faced with tasks in which they are required to make consensus decisions.

Examples of the training activities are:

1   Regular reviews by the team of its own style and effectiveness.
2   The use of film and case-study material as a basis for learning the theory.
3   Detailed analysis by the team of each member's job in order to identify 'effectiveness areas'.
4   Feedback by the team to each of its members on his managerial

styles and skills as demonstrated during the week and practical suggestions for changes he should make to become more effective at work.

The trainer or leader does not make process interventions and the format, with its tightly defined procedures and tasks is intended to make the whole activity 'psychologically safe', e.g. there is no open-ended exploration of feelings as there is in some of the feelings-based approaches.

Follow-ups to the MES are basically in company consultancy and are designed to cover such needs as:

1   Clarification of roles and authority.
2   Team-building.
3   The identification and resolution of inter-group conflict.
4   The establishment of organisational objectives and strategy.
5   The review and revision of organisational structure.
6   The generation of planned change.

All these activities are based on the particular needs and concerns as expressed by, and identified in, the client organisation.

Reading:

Managerial Effectiveness W.J. Reddin, McGraw-Hill, 1970.
Effective Management by Objectives W.J. Reddin, McGraw-Hill, 1971.

Contact:

Busvine Associates Ltd,
9 Pembroke Road,
Sevenoaks,
Kent,
TN13 1XR.
Tel. 0732–53125

The feelings-based approach

A number of the methods described in this section have been strongly influenced by what is known as the 'growth movement', also known as the Third Force; the First Force being experimental psychology (a strong influence in IA) and the Second Force being psychoanalysis. The theoretical basis of the 'growth movement' is humanistic psychology. Its broad principles are:

1   People have an infinite potential for growth. One of the key

    figures in stressing this was Abraham Maslow (1908–1970) whose theories of motivation have been well documented.

2 People can change and develop, acquiring new skills and attitudes as a means of self-fulfilment. The nature of this self-fulfilment varies because each person is unique and has to find his/her own way.

3 A key way in which people can acquire these new skills and attitudes is by focusing on the 'here and now', including the 'how' of their feelings rather than the 'why'. This is based on the assumption that exploring the 'why' can lead to intellectualising and thus distancing from the immediate experience. There is a lot of difference between, 'Why do you feel bad?' and 'How are you making your self feel bad?'.

4 The way to learn is through experiencing and experimenting, not 'talking about'.

5 There are no right answers. In the final analysis everybody has to be his/her own judge and decide what is best for himself/herself. In making these judgements feelings are very important, after all there is no objective truth only subjective values.

6 People are basically good and competent and know, inside or outside their awareness, what they need. Those who are uncertain about their needs can be helped, not so much by an expert but by another human being who respects and does not judge them.

7 People must be taken as a whole: everything each person does, thinks, feels or imagines is a potentially important source of information about him/her. Therefore it does not make sense to make a mind/body split and say that either can be considered in isolation – they can only be understood within the context of each other and their environment. This is a reaction against experimental psychology which frequently seeks to describe and understand people by analysing them in a totally alien environment, e.g. a laboratory.

    A consequence of these principles is that the training emphasises the person rather than the person as a manager. Put another way, participants are likely to be encouraged to think about themselves as people, prior to considering the implications for themselves as managers. The course may or may not deal with the role of the manager and the organisational context. The participant may be left to make the connections for himself.

    Often there will be no theoretical model which is presented to the participants as a rationale or framework for the training. (An obvious exception to this is training based on transactional analysis.) Also there is characteristically a lack of (traditional) structure in that exercises or tasks are not provided.

An important strength of this approach is the opportunity it provides for a fundamental reappraisal of self.

Within the growth movement there are differing attitudes to the idea of responsibility for self. Some approaches (e.g. the 'T' group with its strong democratic origins) stress the responsibility of the individual to the group; others (e.g. Gestalt), say that the individual is, and can only be, responsible for himself/herself.

Reading:

Ordinary Ecstacy J. Rowan. Routledge and Kegan Paul, 1976.
The Politics of the Family R.D. Laing. Pelican, 1976.
Motivation and Personality A.H. Maslow. Harper and Row, 1970.

Contact:

The Association for Humanistic Psychology,
66, Southwark Bridge Road,
London SE1 0AS.
Tel. 01–928–8254.

Self and Society the AHP Journal is available from the above address.

Bioenergetics

Bioenergetics grew from the work of Wilhelm Reich (1897–1957) who trained as a psychologist and then developed his own therapy based on stressing the importance of the body as a source of information about a person's emotional well-being. Reich's ideas were modified by one of his pupils, Alexander Lowen, and this led to bioenergetic therapy.

The cornerstone of bioenergetics is the belief that the body can hold onto feelings and that they then affect muscle tension, posture and breathing patterns. The feelings which are being held onto normally relate back to early childhood experience and were somehow forbidden at that time. For example, a little boy's mother may have died and he was told that he should not cry because it was not 'manly'. Therefore, using his muscles he locked his grief into his body, probably the upper chest, and might spend the next twenty years diverting energy to maintain that block; that energy could have been used more 'productively', such as in expressing happiness or excitement.

The role of the bioenergetic therapist is to help the client locate these blockages and then through massage or exercises (sometimes supplemented by Gestalt or psychoanalytical techniques) to achieve emotional release. This finishing of 'unfinished business' will be accompanied by muscle relaxation in the particular area where the blockage occurred.

The example of emotional blockage given above is perhaps a rather dramatic one and clearly it can develop in many ways and over an extended period of time. Certainly up until recently there was often a lot of pressure on women in British culture not to express anger ('You won't get a man', 'It's not ladylike') and this could lead to anger feelings being locked into the body, probably the jaw. The implication of this for a female manager in her working and personal relationships could be that she would deny herself option of expressing her anger clearly and directly; she might substitute another feeling instead (e.g. guilt) or else release her anger in spasms of vindictiveness, these possibly occurring long after the original event which stimulated her anger. This would have consequences for her work collegues – 'Why is she so bitchy today?' or 'I don't think she liked what she did but she won't tell me straight'.

There is a strong link between bioenergetics and bodyscript work in transactional analysis.

Reading:

> *Bioenergetics* A. Lowen. Penguin, 1975.
> *Betrayal of the Body* A. Lowen. Collier, 1974.
> *Bodyscript Blockbusting* E. Childs-Gowell and P. Kinnaman. Transactional Publications, 1978.

Contacts:

> Gerda Boyesen Centre,
> Acacia House,
> Centre Avenue,
> The Vale,
> Acton, London W3.
> Tel. 01–749–4952.

> Tom and Carole Faulkner,
> 7 Sarre Road,
> London NW2 3SN.
> Tel. 01–794–7867

Encounter groups

This is in many ways a generic term since it can cover a wide variety of activities and approaches and additionally is sometimes used to describe any sort of group which is vaguely based on humanistic psychology.

'T' groups provided an important basis for the development of encounter groups, although they subsequently came to have important differences (see below). The other key factor was the work of Carl Rogers who, in 1946/47 at the University of Chicago, began training counsellors by using experiential group methods with a strong emphasis on personal awareness. Later, Will Schutz became a leading and innovative figure in the encounter movement when he began using structured exercises as a way of accelerating the identification of personal and interpersonal issues within the group. (E.g. In order to highlight the question of trust one person in the group is asked to allow himself to fall backwards into the arms of somebody else.) He also devised questionnaires, one of the best known being FIRO-B (see *Instrumentation in Human Relations Training* J.W. Pfeiffer and R. Heslin, University Associates, 1973), to focus on concerns about affection, inclusion and control.

The broad aims for this type of training (and indeed the facilitator or leader could well start with little more than these) would be: (a) being open to senses and feelings; (b) searching for a definite identity (a clear sense of oneself); (c) recognition and achievement of potential; (d) compassion and warmth towards others, by being accepting and not judgemental.

The encounter movement has grown, becoming increasingly eclectic and differing from the 'T' group because of the greater amount of control in the hands of the leader – who is frequently the provider of exercises. Encounter groups generally devote more attention to individual, rather than total group, process. The activities could include massage and other forms of non-verbal exercises; Gestalt; psychodrama; fantasy and dream work as well as other techniques designed to encourage openness and trust.

In recent years a highly confronting and controversial variation of the encounter group has been run by Chuck Dederich, the Synanon Group, as a way of trying to help drug addicts.

Reading:

Encounter Groups C. Rogers. Penguin, 1970.
Joy W. Schutz. Penguin, 1967.
Confrontation: Encounters in Self and Interpersonal Awareness L. Blank, G. Goltsegen and M. Goltsegen (Eds). Macmillan, 1971.

Contact:

>   The Open Centre,
>   188 Old Street,
>   London EC1.
>   Tel. 01–278–6783

The Gestalt approach

The word 'Gestalt' comes from the German and has no exact English equivalent. An approximate translation is 'whole picture' or 'complete image' and refers to the result of integrating a series of detailed perceptions into a complete experience or meaningful image which is more than the sum of its parts. Examples of this would be the way in which a collection of notes played in sequence resolves into a melody: a few lines, drawn on paper, become a face.

The 'Gestalt' phenomenon was studied by German psychologists in the nineteenth century. They explored the ways in which humans and other animals integrate their perceptions and make sense of the world.[1] During the late 1940s and 50s a group of psychotherapists in America began to combine these ideas with existing knowledge of psychoanalysis and their understanding of phenomenology. One result was a new approach to psychotherapy[2] in which the processes of Gestalt formations and destructions were applied to the whole range of human experience. The idea that the fulfilment of all human needs required first the formation and subsequently the destruction of a well-formed Gestalt led to the development of new understanding and subsequently implied methods of therapy.

The Esalen Institute in California, established in the early 50s by Frederick Perls and others, became a centre for Gestalt therapy and other new approaches to personal growth.

Since that time Gestalt therapy has become widely known and used by therapists and many books are available on the subject.[3] There are a number of centres at which Gestalt training can be received with major European centres in Germany, Holland, Italy, England and Scotland. Gestalt methods are now frequently and often successfully applied in management training programmes.

Applications. Since its broader development in the late 1940s and 50s, the Gestalt method has been used extensively as a tool in psychotherapy. In this sphere it continues to be recognised as having a powerful and effective contribution to make. More recently the approach has been applied in organisations as a tool in organisation development and in process consultancy.[4,5]

With its emphasis on contact, creativity, adaptation and awareness, the Gestalt method lends itself to opening up blocked channels of communication within organisations. In particular it has applications in areas such as:

Team-building
Authority relationships
Sensitivity training
Developing skills in self-expression, listening, non-verbal communication, creativity and assertiveness
Conflict management
Counselling
Trainer development

Gestalt formation and destruction. The basic idea of the Gestalt approach is that in maintaining a balanced state of well-being, human needs arise and are satisfied in a pattern of Gestalt formations and destructions. Needs are present in a hierarchy so priorities resulting from the relationship between the individual and the environment are fulfilled to drop away, then to be replaced by other needs. (See Figure A1.6.)

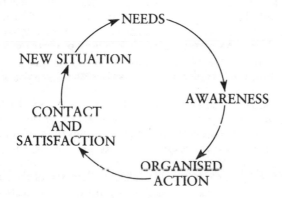

Fig. A1.6

The Gestalt approach. All those but the mentally or physically sick and the poor and oppressed can, if they wish, orient and organise themselves sufficiently to satisfy their needs concerned with physical functioning. Other needs are more elusive, like the needs to give and receive approval, love, recognition, interest, communication etc. In these circumstances a person is perhaps unable to perceive his need clearly or does not know how to get satisfaction.

Assumptions. Several pivotal assumptions about the nature of man form the base of the Gestalt approach.[e]

1 Man is a whole who is (rather than has) a body, emotions, thoughts, sensations and perceptions, all of which function inter-relatedly.
2 Man is part of his environment and cannot be understood outside of it.
3 Man is proactive rather than reactive. He determines his own responses to external stimuli.
4 Man is capable of being aware of his sensations, thoughts, emotions and perceptions.
5 Man, through self-awareness, is capable of choice and is thus responsible for covert and overt behaviour.
6 Man possesses the wherewithal and resources to live effectively and to restore himself through his own assets.
7 Man can experience himself only in the present. The past and the future can be experienced only in the now, through remembering and anticipating.
8 Man is neither intrinsically good nor bad.

Learning methods. The normal setting for Gestalt-based training is a small group of, say, 6–12 participants under the direction of a trained leader. The group forms a social environment within which individuals become aware of themselves and others. The work arises out of the blocks that people place in the way of their need satisfaction as they arise from moment to moment.

The learning event is likely to be based more or less explicitly on a set of ground rules.

Firstly – be aware of your experience here and now. Much of the initial learning of the programme is addressed to the development of awareness, since it is awareness which provides the raw material for self-development and the identification of needs. Breathing, smells, tensions, avoiding contact, excitement, interest, memories, images, irritation, rejection, each provide valuable data about the individual and his wants. In the initial stages of a training course the trainee will be asked to notice where his attention takes him and as patterns emerge to notice how he stops himself.

A second ground rule concerns responsibility and patterns of speech. Many people have been taught to say 'one', 'we', 'people' or 'you', when they mean 'I', and 'can't' when they mean 'won't'. The 'you' is changed to 'I' as the individual is actually talking about the prospect of his own actions and the 'can't' is changed to 'won't' since the suggestion (for example, telling each member of the group something about himself which he finds attractive), clearly is feasible and the issue is the person's willingness rather than ability.

Each individual is encouraged to speak for himself and to check with each member of the group about their experience rather than assume and generalise (e.g. 'I'm feeling frustrated at the moment; do you feel the same way?'). A corollary of this is the ground-rule: 'turn questions into statements'. Questions can serve to avoid the individual's having to take the risk of expressing his own views and concerns against a background of uncertainty and manipulate the other into doing just that.

The value that the Gestalt approach places on action, exploration and experiment results in a special view concerning thinking about or talking about on the one hand, and acting or making contact on the other. In a Gestalt training event the mental process is rejected in favour of outward action.

Let us take an example of someone who wants attention – the simple recognition of existence. In order to get it the person may need to begin the process of making contact, perhaps with eyes, perhaps by saying 'Hello!', perhaps by making a noise of some kind or more directly by saying 'I want your attention!'.

Instead of taking action, the individual engages in mental activity. He holds a conversation with himself, on the one hand imagining what he might do, and on the other hand censuring, criticising, squashing down the need or imagining rejection and experiencing the concomitant bad feelings. The two conflicting forces within him absorb all his energy, contact and satisfaction are blocked.

Obviously, the intellectualising process of thinking and talking about are essential means of solving problems, managing machines, understanding and predicting events etc. They serve as functions for staying alive and saving a lot of unnecessary trouble and effort. In relationships and in the need for personal contact, however, the Gestalt view is that thinking gets in the way. One of the purposes of Gestalt training is to enable the individual to take the risk of engaging in action instead of thought.

This emphasis of Gestalt on learning by discovering, by direct experience, makes it exciting and sometimes confronting and painful.

As with most other forms of IST, a main learning method is through the exchange of feedback. In a Gestalt training event the feedback is likely to be direct from person to person, using 'I' and 'you', descriptive in the sense that the giver simply describes his own experience not attempting to interpret what the 'other' was doing. The receiver of the feedback is not encouraged to respond to feedback, to argue, explain, defend or in any way discourage the giver.

The ground-rules, together with accommodation and a timetable, are the main structural elements of a training event. There are few other constraints, with work proceeding as needs arise and individuals come forward to meet these needs and find themselves unable to complete the Gestalt. The leader works with the individual to explore 'the blocks' or interruptions. The process is one of discovering unfinished business and building the self-support necessary to let go of a block, integrate a split, making contact and closing the cycle.

Common features of the Gestalt approach are:

Top dog:Underdog dialogues, or two-chair work, in which an individual explores his internal splits by acting out a dialogue moving between two chairs, usually one part expressing a 'should' and the other a 'want'. With this process the individual clarifies and identifies the blocks and interruptions in the cycle of need satisfaction, exploring them and moving toward some new insight or creative adaptation which is likely to result in integration and completion.

The use of dreams, imagery and fantasy as a guide to Gestalt formation. Dreams exist as internal activity and yet are concerned with the person in his environment. Fantasy and dreams in Gestalt work are re-experienced and enacted in the present. A person who describes their dream as the experience of flying in an aeroplane is told 'Be the aeroplane – describe yourself as an aeroplane'. The results of such explorations are exciting, dramatic and effective. Some accounts of dream-work can be found in Frederick Perls' *Gestalt Therapy Verbatim*.

The results of training. The simple purpose of Gestalt training is to develop awareness of what is happening inside and outside and increase the ability to deal with what *is* rather than what ought to be or might be. The task is not easy. The results can be disturbing and uncomfortable and the training requires the guidance of an experienced Gestaltist.

As a training tool the Gestalt method is likely to be most effective for those individuals or organisations who see themselves as stuck with old patterns of behaviour which bring about unwanted consequences.

To be a trainee and to learn does not require any understanding of the theory of Gestalt. On the contrary, as intellectualising is discouraged, theory and abstraction are abandoned in favour of experience.

At worst a trainee will become more entrenched in self-limiting patterns of behaviour and will continue to see others as the 'cause of his problems' or continue to blame himself for the difficulties that the environment presents.

At best the trainee may discover how he limits himself: he will realise how he has been imagining things about others and reacting to unreal perceptions: he will understand how he has shied away from openness and directness with himself and others; he will be able to see the differences between himself and others; he will have a wider repertoire of behaviour, be more flexible, less manipulative, more willing to assert himself or engage in conflicts; he will be more creative and enthusiastic by looking for and finding ways of being satisfied rather than waiting for things to go wrong and saying 'I told you so'. In short, a successful trainee will take responsibility for his own life and continue to discover ways of satisfying his needs by creative adaptation.

References

(1) W. Kohler, *Gestalt Psychology*, Liveright, 1929.
(2) F. Perls, *Gestalt Therapy. Excitement and Growth in the Human Personality*, Penguin Books, Harmondsworth, 1973.
(3) E. and M. Polster, *Gestalt Therapy Integrated*, Vintage Books, 1973
(4) S. Herman and M. Korenich, *Authentic Management: A Gestalt Orientation to Organisations and their Development*, Addison Wesley, 1977.
(5) N. Clark and J. Fraser, *The Gestalt Approach an Introduction for Managers and Trainers*, Roffey Park Institute, 1982.
(6) W. Passons, *Gestalt Approached in Counselling*, Holt, Rinehart and Winston, 1975.

Contact: the authors at:
Roffey Park Management College,
Forest Road,
Horsham,
West Sussex.
RH12 4TD.

Neuro-linguistic programming (NLP)

For description see pp. 153–4.

Reading:

Frogs into Princes R. Bandler and J. Grinder. Real People Press, 1979.
They Lived Happily Ever After, L. Cameron-Bandler. Meta Publications, 1978.
Practical Magic, S. Lankton. Meta Publications, 1980.

Contact:

Ron Clements Associates,
29 Paxton Gardens,
Woking,
Surrey.
GU21 5IS
Tel. 09323–43301

Psychodrama

This approach to helping people explore and improve their relationships was created by Jacob Moreno (1892–1974) in Vienna in the
1920s. It grew rapidly when he moved to the US in 1925.

The basis of psychodrama is role-play, which is initiated by the
client (or protagonist) who then, with the help of the trainer (direc-
tor) and other group members sets the scene and enacts certain
problems concerning the past ('I feel my mother deserted me when
she died'), present ('I want to find a way of getting on better with my
boss') or future ('I'm taking up a new job next month and I'm not
sure I'll be able to cope'). The problems may vary in dramatic
intensity, but it is important that they are of real concern to the client.
This points to one of the major differences between 'standard' role
plays in management training and role playing as it is used in
psychodrama. Frequently in the former, role plays are imposed (e.g.
'You pretend to be Mr Smith the senior manager . . .') also, these
types of role play are not designed to encourage catharsis or personal
emotional discharge, whereas this would be quite a common occurrence in psychodrama. (Hence the inclusion of psychodrama as part of
the 'feelings' approach.) Despite these differences there are
similarities between psychodrama and management training role
plays in that they both provide opportunities for insight ('I did not
realise I gave that impression'), developing choices ('I realise now I
could have handled it differently') and the checking out of fantasies
('I didn't realise I had the skills to handle that sort of person; I have
always avoided them in the past for fear that I would make a fool of
myself'). There are a number of specific psychodrama techniques
some of which have been, and others which could be, used in
management training, among them are:

1   Role reversal (e.g. the protagonist plays the part of the boss with
    whom he is having difficulties).
2   Two-chair technique where the client can enact from each chair
    various aspects of internal conflict. (This was subsequently 'bor-
    rowed' by the Gestalt school.)
3   The mirror. Here somebody else in the group (an auxiliary ego),
    acts out the role of the protagonist, thus enabling him to stand
    back from himself and perhaps gain insight into how he appears
    to others.
4   The double. Here another person 'becomes' the protagonist,
    with him or her helping to express what is felt but not said. The
    double is like another self and can be enormously supportive.
    Sometimes the doubles takes over the lead; for example, expres-
    sing certain feelings which his intuition says that the protagonist
    is unwilling to express.

Reading:

Psychodrama: The Theory and Therapy, I. Greenberg (Ed.).
Souvenir Press, 1975.

Contact:

Secretary,
Holwell Centre,
East Down,
Barnstaple,
Devon.
Tel. 027–182–267

Psychosynthesis

The basis of psychosynthesis was formulated by Roberto Assagioli in
1910. It has developed extensively since then, helped by the fact that
within a well established framework it comprises a rich variety of
techniques including many from other approaches (e.g. Gestalt).

It has two broad aims, *personal* and *transpersonal* psychosynthesis. The former involves an emotional well being based on a clear
awareness of oneself, one's potential and the realisation that by
taking responsibility for oneself life can become richer and fuller.
One of the ways in which personal psychosynthesis can be achieved
is through catharsis; this is the discharge of feelings which may have
been accumulating for many years, for some people since childhood.
Transpersonal psychosynthesis with its strong spiritual aspect has an
emphasis on altruism, humanitarianism and co-operation but it also
includes moments of creative insight and inspiration.

As indicated psychosynthesis accepts the use of a wide variety of
techniques including meditation, symbolic art work, group dynamics, body movement, relaxation, music and catharsis.

Reading:

Psychosynthesis R. Assagioli. Turnstone Books, 1980.

Contact:

The Secretary,
Psychosynthesis and Education,
38 West Hill Court,
Millfield Lane,
London N6.
Tel. 01–340–1612

The 'T' (training) group

The idea of the 'T' group came from Kurt Lewin (1890–1947), who fled Nazi persecution and went to the US with strongly held beliefs on democracy and the need to combat prejudice and racism. He became involved in training using group discussion and role play to help teachers and social workers learn about leadership and explore ways of combating social and religious prejudice. In the evenings the teaching staff would hold meetings to discuss the progress of the course and analyse the behaviour of the participants. Soon the participants heard about this and asked to attend the sessions. They were allowed to do so, and these joint review periods became important to all concerned. It was here (in 1946) that the basic formula of the 'T' group was established – sharing feedback in the 'here and now'.

Despite Lewin's death in 1947 the impetus for this new form of training had been generated and a series of programmes based on it were run at the National Training Laboratories, Bethel, Maine.

Basic philosophy. The 'T' group eventually led to a number of variations (Tavistock, encounter and instrumented laboratories, e.g. managerial grid and Coverdale), but its broad basic philosophy has been:

1 People can learn from their experiences (particularly of themselves) and should not be regarded as empty vessels waiting for an expert to pour knowledge into them.
2 Everybody can learn from everybody else (particularly through feedback).
3 Feelings are important.
4 Here and now focus.
5 Structured activities, such as those commonly occurring in the 'doing' approach, are an unnecessary distraction away from the group learning about itself. The group's sole task is to examine its own process.
6 Even when apparently 'nothing' is happening in a group, there is a lot to learn, e.g. by exploring the forces which are causing 'nothing' to happen.

Aims of 'T' group training

1 An increase in awareness of oneself and others i.e. to be more sensitive to one's own feelings and reactions and to be better able to assess the feelings and reactions of others. The underlying assumption here is that frequently people reduce their effectiveness in their relationships by, *consciously or unconsciously*, blocking out of their awareness sensitivity either to their own

internal process or to the behaviour and attitudes of others. For example somebody who is scared when meeting strangers compensates for this by being consciously aggressive or the person unconsciously ignores the fact that, beneath a polite exterior, two of his colleagues are engaged in scoring points off one another.

2   An increase in the ability to assess the total group process i.e. being able to see the group as a whole and consider whether it consists of sub-groups, is dependent, lacking in trust etc. This is sometimes done by encouraging the group to see how it relates to other groups.

3   The third aim following on from the other two is that the trainee's greater awareness should be accompanied by a greater awareness in handling this new knowledge – whether to intervene or not, how to comment and give feedback, how to receive feedback, how to cope with his own feelings and the feelings of others.

The "T" group has been used extensively to train managers because it highlights many of the problems which can occur so easily in organisations – stereotyping, lack of trust, win–lose orientation, problems in handling authority figures (e.g. over-compliance or rebellion) an excess of judgemental feedback.

Role of the trainer

1   Give non-judgemental feedback at individual and/or group level.
2   Encourage others to give and receive non-judgemental feedback.
3   Being non-directive in order to give the group 'space' (and to provide a focus for exploring the issue of 'authority').
4   Keep group focused on 'here and now' relationships.
5   Encourage experimentation, sometimes using structured exercises (e.g. 'blind mill' where one person closes his eyes and is led round by another. This is to explore trust).
6   Encourage people to re-examine their assumptions.
7   Encourage the expression of feelings.
8   Encourage people to be specific.
9   Sometimes to provide short theory sessions on individual or group process.
10 Generally the trainer is not self-revealing. He expresses concerns about the group, but not about himself. This can mean that the trainer puts himself in the difficult position of encouraging others to do something he is unwilling to do.

Effectiveness. Research into the effectiveness of the 'T' group (and 'unstructured' training generally) has proved somewhat inconclusive. Amongst the variables being researched are:

1 Organisational support (in particular the impact of in-company 'T' groups).
2 Learning styles (e.g. learning through concepts rather than direct experience).
3 Personality profiles.
4 Trainer's style, e.g. aggressive, low profile supportive etc.
5 Types of learning – compliance, identification and internalisation.
6 Characteristics of the group, e.g. previous experiences in training, social/educational background etc.

So far the crucial question regarding the long-term effects of the 'T' group remains unanswered.

Reading:

> *Hurt or Helped?* C. Cooper and D. Bowles. Training Information Paper 10. HMSO, London, 1977.
> *Group Training Techniques,* M.L. and P.J. Berger. Gower, 1972.
> **Group Processes and Personal Change**, P.B. Smith. Harper and Row, 1980.

Contact:

> Group Relations Training Association
> Walter Truman Cox
> 1 Gentian Close
> Birmingham B31 1NN

Tavistock training

This particular approach began in 1957 when a conference was jointly organised by Leicester University and the Tavistock Institute of Human Relations. Over the years the nature of the conference has changed significantly and a number of variants have emerged. Described here are the main philosophies and activities which characterise the approach. We also want to make it clear that the Institute offers other types of training apart from that mentioned here. From the beginning, continuing through its evolution, three major influences have been at work; the 'T' group, the work of Wilfred Bion and open systems theory (boundary management).

The 'T' group has been important because of its stress on examining relationships in the 'here and now' (the 'T' group is more fully described on p. 196–8); secondly, and possibly more importantly, there has been the contribution of Wilfred Bion who trained as a psychologist and developed theories about the psychoanalysis of groups, *not* the individual. Thus, the Tavistock approach is in some ways a mixture of opposites since the 'T' group emphasised the individual learning about himself in relationship to the group but not, as in Bion's theory, as a manifestation of *group* process.

The assumption underlying Bion's work, and the Tavistock training method which emerged from it, is that when individuals come together then the group creates a life of its own and develops its own particular systems and identity. Hence when the conference works in groups of about ten people for the study of small group behaviour, the trainer (consultant) who is attached to each one only comments on the *group* process. The primary task of such a group is to study its behaviour as it occurs.

The consultant is especially likely to give feedback bearing in mind the 'basic assumptions' which underlie the group activity. These basic assumptions comprise, according to Bion, the collective fears, defences, desires and feelings of the group and could manifest themselves in such ways as dependency, fight or flight and pairing. In this way the group insulates itself from, and defends itself against, reality (e.g. the reality which gives the lie to dependency is that the group must rely on its own resources and cannot wait for a leader magically to appear and solve all its problems). The consultant is offering hypotheses on what is happening and why. He may give descriptive feedback and perhaps use it to challenge the group e.g. by saying 'I notice that the three women in the group are sitting together', when the group has been saying that gender is not an issue for them.

The consultant tends to distance himself emotionally from the group and says little about himself in the belief that if he did so he could be seduced into the group's assumptions and way of looking at the world. This is one of the reasons why the consultant never spends more time with the group than has been programmed.

Tight time limits are also a manifestation of the third major influence in the Tavistock approach – boundaries and boundary management:

1   It is possible to think of people as forms of open systems. At the individual level a person, in order to survive, has to have interchanges with his/her environment. These interchanges take place at a biological level (e.g. taking in oxygen and giving out carbon dioxide) and at a psychological/social level (e.g. giving and getting warmth, affection etc.). For the individual an important day-to-day perhaps minute-to-minute, task is the management of his boundary with his environment, e.g. 'Will this food harm

me?', 'How should I conduct myself with this person?' A lot of energy is devoted to dealing with problems of boundary management.

2   A group can also be seen as engaged in boundary management. A lot of a group's energy is directed towards maintaining its external and internal boundaries. A price is exacted for membership. 'In order to join us you must conform in the following ways . . .' 'In order to stay part of this group you must . . .' If an individual is seen to be stretching the group boundary in some way then he will probably be put under pressure to conform or leave. The smaller the group the greater the potential power of the individual.

3   In a small group the boundaries are usually patrolled quite easily: lines of communication are short, there is probably a lot of face-to-face contact and there is frequently a sense of common identity. It is here that the leader may well have an important role to play in managing the external and internal boundaries.

4   Large groups or organisations can also be regarded as open systems involved with boundary management. Often organisations are obsessed with boundary management because the problems associated with it are so great: long lines of communication, lack of common identity, sub-groups and sub-cultures. Therefore, organisations usually have elaborate control mechanisms, both formal and informal, a hierarchy, appraisal/report schemes, computerised personnel records, job descriptions, regulations, dress, status symbols etc. etc.

5   Sometimes the boundary becomes too rigid and there is a danger of the following results: employees are brain washed into conformity, leave the organisation, or form pressure groups. A rigidly structured organisation is likely to be slow in responding to environmental/market requirements and changes. Concern with internal boundaries and communication can divert attention away from customer relations.

At the conference a considerable amount of time is spent exploring a number of boundaries at the individual, group, intergroup and organisational levels and the way they are managed, for example through roles and leadership. The conference contains the atmosphere and dynamics, behavioural and psychological, of an organisation, albeit temporary.

The inter-group event at the conference is designed to help the total group (about 60 people) explore the phenomena of inter-group relations. This is done by letting the group organise itself, having been told which resources (i.e. rooms, consultants) are available. The large group event again involves bringing the whole membership together including up to four consultants but without the specific brief of examining inter-group relations. The aim is to experience being part of a large group and to pay attention to all the assumptions, emotions and roles which may emerge.

As can be imagined from the description so far, 'authority' is a key issue at these conferences and this is deliberately the case. One of the underlying purposes of the method is that participants should learn about how they respond to faceless authority and how they can easily submit themselves to the collective unconscious authority of the group. This is one of the ways in which an apparently rational person can give way to primitive feelings (e.g. football hooliganism). In organisations, too, group decision-making can be severely impaired by the underlying group process (e.g. the marketing department is concerned to defeat the production department even though it means a Pyrrhic victory).

At the conferences there are application groups to help participants relate their learning back to work.

Reading:

Exploring Individual and Organisational Boundaries W.G. Lawrence (Ed.). Wiley, 1979.
The Psychoanalysis of Organisations Robert de Board. Tavistock Publications, 1978.

Contact:

> Group Relations Training Programme,
> The Tavistock Institute of Human Relations,
> Tavistock Centre,
> 120 Belsize Lane,
> London NW3 5BA.
> Tel. 01–435–7111

Transactional analysis (TA)

TA is a rich and versatile tool which can be applied in the areas of 'thinking' (theory presentation) 'doing' (observation frameworks) and 'feeling' (personal awareness). However it has a strong humanistic emphasis, hence its inclusion in this section.

It is a theory of personality, behaviour and communication, thereby linking internal process and external behaviour. Eric Berne (1910–70), the originator of TA, had traditional training as a psychoanalyst and then found it in many ways inadequate, particularly when, attached to the army, he was faced with assessing the suitability for discharge of 25,000 soldiers in four months. There was obviously not enough time for each man to have the normal 45-minute psychoanalytic session. Berne also began moving away from psychoanalysis by paying increasing attention to particular clusters of behaviours as well as the internal processes of his patients. In doing this he concluded that three basic patterns emerged and that these, when accompanied by complementing thoughts and feelings, constituted what he called 'ego states'.

In observing his patients and others, he found that they could behave and express values which were essentially the same (or which they believed to be the same) as their parents' or those of other authority figures which they had experienced in their childhood. This is the parent ego state and functions in basically two ways – the critical parent tends to be judgemental and controlling, using words like 'ought', 'always' and 'disgraceful'; but the nurturing parent is caring, can be smothering, and is concerned to support, look after and dispense tender and parental loving care.

People could also act in a cool, calm and rather detached way, analysing and estimating probabilities. This is the adult ego state, sometimes referred to as the computer part of the personality. It is important for problem solving, using words like 'What?', 'How?', 'When'? 'Where?' 'Why?', and for re-evaluating personal values and beliefs.

Finally, it seemed to Berne, people carried with them certain feelings and behaviours acquired or experienced in childhood. This is the child ego state and can function either in a free child way, being curious, egocentric, impulsive and fun-loving *or*, in an adapted child way, the latter consisting of ways learnt for getting along with and getting attention from authority figures: rebellion, politeness, depression, guilt and compliance.

The standard way for representing the ego states is:

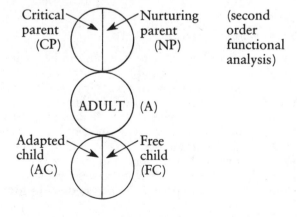

Fig A1.7

It is important to realise that none of the ego states is by definition 'good' or 'bad', but that each can function positively or negatively as the examples in Table A1.1 show.

The child ego state is often regarded as having a third function in the 'little professor', which is a source of intuition and creative insight giving rise to expressions like 'I've got a gut feeling that . . .'.

This, then, is the major behavioural dimension to TA. The personality aspect derives from the assumption that although people could (should) distribute their energy freely amongst the ego states, frequently this does not happen and somebody may spend a lot of time in an inappropriate ego state: e.g. when faced with a problem he does

Table A1.1   Functions of ego states

	Positive	Negative
CP	Warning of danger – 'Don't touch that electric fire!'. Disciplinary – 'I'm not prepared to put up with this sort of behaviour for much longer'.	Dominating and constricting – 'You're stupid, you never get anything right!'.
NP	Caring and supportive – 'Don't worry, I'll support you in any decision you make'.	Smothering – 'Don't worry, I'll sort it all out for you'.
A	Problem-solving – 'What are the alternatives?'. 'What exactly happened?'.	Cold and distant – 'I understand that you are upset about your wife leaving you. It would appear that there are three courses of action open to you . . .'.
AC	Polite/courteous 'I'm sorry'. 'Please may I . . .?'.	Over-compliant. Sycophantic. Rebellious in order to gain attention.
FC	Loving, sexy, warm, open, intimate, close.	Egocentric. Selfish.

not use his adult but goes into whining despair (AC). It is also possible to argue that certain jobs encourage a particular energy distribution amongst the ego states, and that problems can occur when changes take place: a nurse will probably be strong in nurturing parent and may find it difficult to exercise discipline (i.e. use critical parent) when she is promoted and given responsibility for staff. Or somebody may be given a new job requiring a lot of creativity and initiative (FC and A), and then experiences problems when precedents have been formulated, routines established and there is then a greater demand for conformity (AC). Indeed, once the procedures and patterns have been established new ideas can end up being regarded as, at best, a nuisance.

Often people can be seen to have favourite ego states which they use in times of stress. For example, in times of organisational change one person may start telling others off, another will want to look after them, another will want to analyse the consequences and another will be caught up in the hopelessness of it all.

The communication facet of TA concerns the ways in which people use their ego states to 'transact' with each other. There are three basic types of transaction:

1   Complementary, where the person gets a response from the ego state he aims at, returned to the ego state which he used to initiate the transaction:

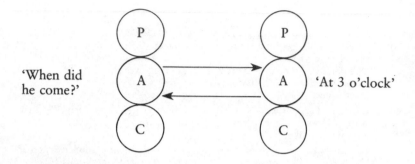

2   Crossed, where there is an 'unexpected' and/or 'unwanted' response:

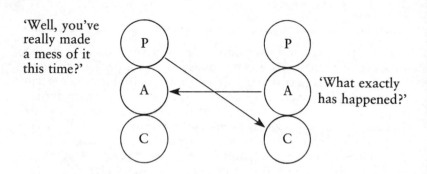

3   Ulterior, where there are two levels to the communication, social on the surface and psychological underneath. The latter equates to external process.

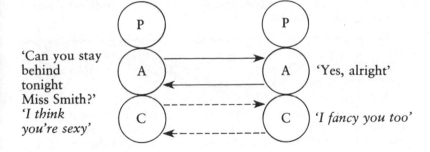

'Can you stay behind tonight Miss Smith?' '*I think you're sexy*'

'Yes, alright' '*I fancy you too*'

The analysis of transactions can be used to help people develop choices in their communication, e.g. whether and how to cross transactions; sensitivity to hidden messages. They can also provide a means for examining distinctions between self-perception and the perceptions of others. A person may have a sense of himself as being in adult and yet be seen by others as in critical parent.

Internal process can also be examined through the 'internal' dialogue, i.e. looking at the ways in which the ego states within an individual can interact and sometimes conflict. A frequent conflict is between the 'oughts' of the parent and the 'wants' of the child. 'You really ought to work harder . . .'. 'I know, but I don't want to.'

Ego states are the cornerstone of TA, which is why considerable space has been devoted to them. However, there are a number of other facets to TA and these can be used to help people learn, amongst other things, how they may be:

1   Living their lives positively or negatively according to a self-fulfilling prophesy. 'My role in life is to look after others because they cannot do it for themselves.' (Life positions.) 'I can't enjoy myself until I've retired.' (Scripts.)

2   Wasting time trying to score points in relationships. E.g. The person who is *always* trying to find the faults in others. The person who is *always* saying that life is unfair. (Games.)

3   Not looking after themselves. Positive feedback is diminished. 'He says I did a good job but it wasn't really.' Negative feedback is exaggerated through internal processes. 'Somebody did not like the talk I gave. I really am a terrible person!' (Strokes.)

4   Putting others down. (Strokes.)

5   Unconsciously using feelings to try to manipulate relationships. The person who, for example, acts depressed in order to get attention. (Rackets.)

6   Avoiding responsibility for problem-solving. 'I just can't do anything about this problem.' (Discounting.)

7   Compulsively – not expressing feelings, wanting to be perfect all

the time, rushing about, trying and failing, wanting to please everybody. (Drivers.)

The advantages of TA are its versatility and the fact that it spans the 'thinking', 'doing', 'feeling' spectrum. Consequently, it can be used as the basis of a straight theory in-put, an interaction analysis observation framework, or a tool for looking at 'here and now' relationships in 'unstructured' training. It is one of the few theories which directly relate personality to behaviour and communication. Finally, it can be used at the microcosmic level for looking at individuals and at the macrocosmic level for looking at the personality and culture of organisations (e.g. organisational scripts). Some organisations can seem highly 'parental' in their values, others cool and analytical and others highly energetic and full of Child.

Some potential drawbacks of TA are firstly that some of the language is North American and may not be readily accepted by other audiences.

Also TA as yet is not supported by a solid research base, but few, if any, of the humanistic methods are. Finally, TA, because of its breadth and depth can go deeply very quickly, stimulating people to think about their home relationships and perhaps thinking back on their childhood.

Reading:

Transactional Analysis: A Basic Introduction for the Manager D. Barker and K. Phillips. Roffey Park College, 1980
Am I OK? P. Phillips and F. Cordell. Argus Communications, 1975.
T.A. and Training D. Barker. Gower, 1980

Contact:

Institute of Transactional Analysis,
BM Box 4104,
London WC1N 3XX
Tel. 01–404–5011

Ron Clements Associates,
29 Paxton Gardens,
Woking,
Surrey,
GU21 5TS
Tel. 09323–43301

Mike Reddy,
90 Church Road,
Woburn Sands,
Bucks. MK17 8TR
Tel. 0908–582477

Roffey Park Management College,
Forest Road,
Horsham,
West Sussex, RH12 4TD.
Tel. 029–383–344.

General section

This part of the Appendix gives details of a number of approaches which have an IST component to them and do not fit clearly into the other major categories used above. It is not claimed that they have any other common factors.

Action learning

Action learning was developed by Reg Revans as a result of ideas he developed in the early 1950s. In 1977 the Action Learning Trust was set up to support and encourage its growth.

The specific format of action learning programmes can vary widely, but they have the following general characteristics:

1 By definition the emphasis is on action; practical or 'project' work is directed towards the achievement of solutions to a *real* problem.
2 Regular (frequently a day each fortnight) group meetings in which the participants from a variety of different projects come together, probably supported by an adviser, in order to:
    (a) exchange and test out ideas
    (b) review progress
    (c) provide mutual support
    (d) have formal learning sessions
    (e) clarify and work through feelings.

There are four types of format:

1 A familiar problem in familiar surroundings. This means a group of managers from the same organisation engaged on work-related problems. The project groups do work which would have been required of them anyway, but it is carried out within the framework of an action learning programme.
2 An unfamiliar problem in familiar surroundings. This means working in an in-company team set up to look at problems outside its jurisdiction. An example could be a group with a strong personnel background working on a production problem.
3 A familiar problem in unfamiliar surroundings. This means the

employee from one organisation going on full or part-time
secondment to help another organisation with a problem which
is within his specialism.

4   An unfamiliar problem in unfamiliar surroundings. Here a senior
executive, normally at board level, goes on full-time secondment
into another company to help that company work on a problem
which is not within his specialism or particular experience.

All the formats are designed to generate new perspectives on real
problems. Clearly when people's action learning programmes are
based on unfamiliar problems and for unfamiliar surroundings, then
the dangers of tunnel vision based on traditional prejudices are
reduced. Also, where there is secondment, the participant is probably less susceptible to in-company pressures and politics, (e.g. his
career is not at stake).

Action learning programmes can be unstructured, being little
more than self-help groups; alternatively they may have a tightly
defined set of activities. In either extreme the unpredictable can
emerge where, for example, the problem as originally stated later
turns out to be a symptom.

Reading:

'An action learning trust.' R. Revans.
Journal of European Industrial Training Vol. 1, No. 1, 1977.
'Action Learning for Supervisors' D. Boddy. *Journal of European
Industrial Training* Vol. 4, No. 3, 1980.

Contact:

Action Learning Trust,
21 Ludlow Avenue,
Luton,
Beds,
LU1 3RW.
Tel. 0582–30965

Business games

These can vary widely in their form and content. Some fit clearly into
the 'thinking' area and are designed to convey information, but with
the participant engaging in practical work. For example, action
mazes are paper passing activities which present the participant with
a series of consecutive decisions and he then has to deal with the
consequences of those decisions. When applied to industrial relations training the learning aim could be purely factual (e.g. learning

about disciplinary procedures in relationship to company policy and employment legislation) or deal with attitudes (e.g. the consequences of win/lose orientations).

Other types of business games can be extended role-plays, (sometimes lasting several days), with various items of information being fed in. There may or may not be a right answer or winner.

One of the dangers with games is that they can become so complex that people spend too much time trying to understand the rules, rather than carrying out the task. Some games are designed to be like the work environment and can be highly realistic.

For further information:

Handbook of Management Games C. Elgood. Second edition, Gower, Aldershot, 1981.
Handbook of Games and Simulation Exercises G.I. Gibbs. E & F.N. Spon, 1974.

Eastern philosophies and IST

There can be no doubt that Eastern philosophies have contributed and continue to contribute to the understanding and development of IST.

As a broad generalisation the impact of Eastern philosophies stems from their emphasising the value of 'being' and of transcending the temporal and material world. In contrast much of Western culture is rooted in 'The Protestant Ethic' which concerns itself with 'doing' and the spiritual and material rewards for achievement.

There is a growing realisation that Western values alone can create limitations to the effectiveness of organisations. The ethic of achievement and material reward only offers partial solutions to organisations or individuals under stress. Redundancy, for example, can provide an opportunity for a fundamental reappraisal of values and attitudes to life.

In the search for new answers to organisational problems some of the Eastern philosophies seem to offer interesting possibilities. In particular the religions of Hinduism, Taoism and Buddhism, with their values in terms of transcending materialism to spirituality, offer effective techniques such as meditation and yoga.

These approaches have also directly contributed to the understanding of humanistic psychology and are reflected in approaches such as Gestalt and bioenergetics.

Some of the growing sources of reading in this area provide practical guidance on the application of Eastern philosophies in an organisation setting:

Reading:

Ordinary Ecstasy: Humanistic Psychology in Action J. Rowan.
Routledge & Kegan Paul, 1976.
Zen in the Art of Helping D. Brandon. Routledge & Kegan Paul,
1976.
Transcending the Power Game R.G. Sill. Wiley, 1980
*Authentic Management: A Gestalt Orientation to Organisations
and their Development* S. Herman and M. Korenich. Addison
Wesley, 1977.

Contact:

Open Centre,
188 Old Street,
London EC1.
Tel. 01–278–6783.

Chairman of the British Wheel of Yoga,
Joy Burlington,
80 Leckhampton Road,
Cheltenham,
Glos.

Innovative teamwork programme

Abraxas Management Research, in association with Synectics Inc.

The Innovative Teamwork Programme (ITP) was developed by
Synectics Inc. of Cambridge, Mass. The programme focuses on
methods and techniques that can help increase a team's effectiveness
in two ways:

1 By increasing the ability of team members to co-operate in
   problem-solving.
2 By increasing the 'innovation' quotient of a team's problem-
   solving efforts.

Its OD dimension lies in an underlying assumption that one of the
most effective ways to build a team is to have people go through the
experience of successfully solving problems together.

The ITP is a participative three-day training course for small
groups. The training is based on the familiar cycle of short 'theory'
input, practical exercise and review, but with the added dimension
that the tasks performed are 'real' problems which participants bring
with them. A key concept is the 'itemised response': in essence the
'client' (the individual with ownership of the problem or issue) must
look for the positive aspects of any proposal made. The itemised

response calls for the client to look first for the useful elements of a suggestion, and to convert its drawbacks into statements beginning 'how to', which invite further development to overcome the drawbacks.

The itemised response allows a number of benefits:

1 It keeps the group from throwing out any potentially useful ideas.
2 It helps create a climate in which other people will more willingly offer suggestions, knowing their ideas won't be promptly rejected.
3 By opening up suggestions to further development it makes room for team members to create ownership of a suggestion by helping to develop it.

By developing together, diversity of opinions within the team is shown to be an asset rather than a liability. Approximate, irrelevant and unrealistic thinking is deliberately encouraged in the search for new solutions to difficult problems.

A further element in ITP is the distinction between 'process' and 'content'. Responsibility for process control is clearly identified at the beginning of each session, either by allocating different aspects of the process to different members of the group, or by appointing a single 'process control' manager, who tends to concentrate on that function rather than contribute to the task. After the problem solving activity, the process of the session is reviewed by the trainer and the group, usually (on the course) with the aid of a videotape recording of the meeting, to identify which aspects were successful and what improvements would be sought in a subsequent session.

Reading:

Open to Change V. Nolan. MCB Publications, 1981.
'Training: a creative route to organisation development' Vincent Nolan. *London Business School Journal*, Autumn 1979.
'A re-appraisal of creativity techniques in industrial training' T. Rickards and B. Freedman. *Journal of European Industrial Training* Vol. 3, No. 1, 1979.

Contact:

Abraxas Management Research,
68 Churchway,
London NW1 1LT.
Tel. 01–388–7281.

Kepner-Tregoe training

Kepner–Tregoe training originated in the work begun in 1958 by

Benjamin Tregoe and Charles Kepner who, while employed by the Rand Corporation, began analysing the skills required of a 'good' decision maker. Subsequently, the Kepner–Tregoe organisation was established and has developed substantially over the years.

At present two basic types of training and consultancy are offered: the 'strategic dimension' and the 'operational dimension'. The former generally involves Kepner–Tregoe staff working with the senior managers of a company, the aim being to help that company consider where and how it is directing its efforts and to consider the need and/or desirability for change within the context of a broad strategic plan.

The 'operational dimension' has within it several elements. Firstly, there is training in what is described as problem analysis, decision analysis and potential problem analysis. This has the clearest direct link back to Kepner and Tregoe's original work in formulating a systematic approach to identifying and solving problems and making decisions. The training usually lasts five days and there is a strong emphasis on in-company material and 'live' problems, supplemented by case-study material. The course member has feedback from three sources: tape recordings which are made when the course group is engaged in working on a problem; the course group, which gives feedback both to individuals and groups on the use of the ideas being presented; the trainer who gives feedback with a particular emphasis on questioning skills. In all this the interpersonal dimension is considered only in so far as it specifically relates to effective problem-solving and decision-making procedures.

Interpersonal relations are explored more fully in the second element of the operational dimension – this is concerned with leadership styles and their consequences. This two-day programme is based on the research of V. Vroom and P. Yetton. Prior to coming on the course participants are given thirty short cases as a basis for thinking about their management style – 'What would you do if. . . .?' Answers to these cases are then analysed by a computer. A major part of the course consists of the participants comparing their responses firstly against a leadership model, then with each other, thirdly with data which has been developed for the organisation and finally, with other comparable groups from other organisations.

The final element of the operational dimension is called performance analysis which is a problem-solving approach for examining how an individual's performance is dependent on a number of variable factors which go well beyond the issue of his own ability or lack of it.

The majority of Kepner-Tregoe training is carried out in-company. Frequent use is made of personnel from within an organisation, not necessarily trainers, to lead the various course groups through the training.

Reading:

The New Rational Manager C. Kepner and B. Tregoe. Kepner & Tregoe, 1980.

Contact:

Kepner–Tregoe Limited,
1 Station Approach,
Maidenhead,
Berks SL6 1EW.
Tel. 0628–38083

Appendix 2 — confronting blocks to problem-solving

Confronting blocks to problem-solving

Block	Example	Possible confrontation
Generalising	This person uses generalisations as basis for believing that he/she cannot do anything differently. 'After all everybody has this problem.' 'One has to cope as best one can.'	'How specifically is this a problem for *you*?' 'Say "I" rather than "one".'
Talking about	This person talks about a whole range of things rather than face up to his/her particular problem. 'This friend of mine had the same problem and she had a terrible time . . .'	'What does this mean for you?' Focus on 'what' and 'how' rather than 'why'.
Having rigid expectations of others	This person has rigid expectations of others and frequently uses them as the basis for subsequently being angry or disappointed. 'In the light of all the sacrifices I've made I think I have a right to expect some gratitude from all my clients.'	'How have you come to have this expectation?' 'How long are you prepared to wait for your clients to express gratitude?' 'What are the consequences for you of having this expectation?' 'You sound as if you're setting yourself up to be disappointed.'
Blocking out internal awareness	This person blocks out awareness of internal processes. 'Of course it doesn't worry me in the slightest.'	'Not the *slightest* little bit?' 'What you're saying doesn't match your tone of voice.' 'What are you feeling?'
Blocking out external awareness	This person blocks out awareness of other people's behaviour and attitudes. 'Jean looks perfectly happy to me.' (Jean is on the verge of tears.)	'What do you see when you look at Jean?' 'What are you aware of?'
Self-interrupting	This person has difficulty in maintaining concentration and interrupts himself/herself by jumping from one point to another, agitation or	'I notice that you haven't answered my question.' 'What are you doing?' 'Exaggerate your foot-tapping. Is there a message

	withdrawal. The agitation may be retroflection, e.g. anger turned against self rather than others.	for yourself or somebody else?' 'Sit still and concentrate on what I'm saying.' Imagery work e.g. drawing.
Catastrophising	This person uses a catastrophic fantasy as an excuse for avoiding responsibility and not taking action. 'I couldn't possibly do that, she would never speak to me again!'	'Would it have to end up that way?' 'What is the worst thing which could happen to you?'
Imagining artificial constraints	This person imagines artificial constraints as a basis for believing that nothing can be done to solve the problem 'I can't do that.' 'My boss would never agree to it.'	'Say 'won't' rather than 'can't'. 'How do you know?' 'How could you persuade her?'
Projecting	This person attributes to others qualities which are really in himself/herself. 'The trouble with you is that you are so damned aggressive!'	'Try saying that about yourself.' 'Does what you have said apply to you at all?'
Minimising	This person minimises his/her feelings or the extent of their problems as the basis for believing they do not have to be faced up to. 'It's so unimportant: it is not really worth worrying about.'	'Is it really so unimportant? You've spent a long time talking about it.' 'Tell me of any feeling no matter how small, which you have when you think about this problem.'
Sticking to obsolete rules	This person uses old rules of behaviour even though they are not helpful in dealing with current problems and relationships. 'Of course I must always be polite to people.'	'That sounds like a rule for you.' 'What's the benefit for you of that rule?' 'Where did you learn that?' 'What does politeness mean for you?'
Entering a vicious circle of top dog/underdog conflict	This person is caught up in a conflict between personal 'oughts' and 'wants'. The 'oughts' may have been swallowed whole (introjects) in childhood on the basis that this was how life had to be.	'What do you want to do?' 'What do you think you ought to do?' 'Is there any way of reconciling your 'oughts' and 'wants'?' Two-chair work (see p. 192).

Index

219